To: Dorothy

from Lee

Aug.   2006

dubwise

Klive is out of town
+ not available to sign
this copy. He would have
written: "Thanks for your
support." !

dubwise

reasoning from the reggae underground

klive walker

INSOMNIAC PRESS

Library and Archives Canada Cataloguing in Publication

Walker, Klive, 1953-
 Dubwise : reasoning from the reggae underground / Klive Walker.

Includes bibliographical references.
ISBN 1-894663-96-9

1. Reggae music. I. Title.

ML3532.W182 2005   781.646   C2005-903565-X

The publisher gratefully acknowledges the support of the Canada Council, the Ontario Arts Council and the Department of Canadian Heritage through the Book Publishing Industry Development Program.

Printed and bound in Canada

Insomniac Press
192 Spadina Avenue, Suite 403
Toronto, Ontario, Canada, M5T 2C2
www.insomniacpress.com

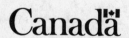

THE CANADA COUNCIL | LE CONSEIL DES ARTS
FOR THE ARTS | DU CANADA
SINCE 1957 | DEPUIS 1957

ONTARIO ARTS COUNCIL
CONSEIL DES ARTS DE L'ONTARIO

Table of Contents

Preface

by Herbie Miller

My many telephone conversations, e-mails, and occasional meetings with Klive Walker, the author of these essays, gave me reason to anticipate the clarity and objective reasoning this book you are now reading conveys. Above all, the two books about reggae written by Jamaicans notwithstanding, those sessions alerted me to a cultural thinker concerned with conveying to the world of reggae readers a perspective that has been missing. Although it is clear throughout, in the final chapter Walker explicitly announces that he is writing from an insider's point of view. The closeness of the author to the perennially unfolding rhymes and rhythms in which the beat of reggae vibrates, brings an authentic sensibility and fresh new insight to the writing on Jamaica's music history and cultural complex. This fresh vision reflects the approach of elder Caribbean thinkers like Wilson Harris, Kamau Brathwaite, Rex Nettleford, Brian Meeks and scholars of Afro-American culture like Sterling Stuckey, Robert Farris Thompson, and Sam Floyd, Jr., who all call for and participate in sensibilities that are not strictly governed by Western philosophical concepts and methods of investigation. Instead, they employ Afro-Caribbean and diasporic tools of analysis that are better suited to recognize, assess, critique, and report on the cultural dynamics of the African diaspora.

Dubwise considers overlooked aspects of Jamaican culture such as jazz, which was as popular on the island in the '40s, at least in Kingston and the coastal towns, as was ska two decades later. Walker points out that jazz was the agency for diversity that welded together communities separated by race, economics, nationality, and class before the liberal politics of the reggae-dominated '70s. These pages introduce the reggae enthusiast to the brilliance of musician Leslie Thompson, possibly the first Jamaican artist with an international reputation. Thompson performed with jazz's first stars in the '20s, both on the instrument he is best known for, the trumpet, and the trombone, on which he was just as skilled. Readers become acquainted with the ubiquitous Bertie King, the Panamanian-born Jamaican reed master who appeared on the British jazz scene after a prolific career in Jamaica to become that country's outstanding alto saxophonist and clarinetist during the WWII era.

Leslie "Jiver" Hutchinson comes in for equal treatment. The trumpeter from the Jamaica military band migrated to England after first visiting in 1933 to become a first-call trumpeter to many of London's best known big bands. Hutchinson was a charter member of Ken "Snake Hips" Johnson and his West Indians, Britain's first all-black orchestra during the WWII years and leader of his own band, the Leslie "Jiver" Hutchinson All Coloured Orchestra. Other important Jamaican jazz musicians such as Harold "Little G" McNair, Wilton "Bra" Gaynair, the elusive trumpeter Sonny Grey, the distinct Dizzy Reece, and the ingenuity of Joe Harriott are all covered by Walker with wisdom and clarity and without the sentimentality that often besets the views of writers less attuned to the more stealth-like Jamaican signifiers that they so often miss.

Walker's intimate familiarity with the subtle nuances and gestures within the island's culture, and how this is infused into the music, illuminates this work in ways only hinted at previously. Ska is treated not merely as a shantytown outgrowth but rather as the Jamaican equivalent to jazz. For the author, *ska* represents a synthesis of plantation influences and learned Western harmonic concepts creolized to announce something fresh, challenging, and lasting. Walker chronicles the activities of leading *ska* musicians and their relationship to jazz beyond the overstated references to Jamaicans learning jazz from American "fake books" and "big-band charts." Instead, he locates them in the melting pot of the emerging diasporic continuum that started with the slave trade. He understands their jazz aesthetic as no different from the uniqueness that distinguishes musicians from different regions within the United States, musicians whose jazz speaks a common language using different accents. *Dubwise* convincingly argues that unlike previous musicians, the generation that created ska consciously remained home to establish an indigenous popular music.

The record is set straight in many instances. For the first time, readers are told Roland Alphonso did not attend Alpha. This is the only instance where an in-depth discussion of Don Drummond's importance to reggae is developed. Here, the mystifying veil is removed and Drummond is analyzed through his real contributions and achievements and is placed along with Rasta drummer Oswald

"Count Ossie" Williams on the same artistic footing as Bob Marley.

Without attempting to diminish any of Marley's genius and his penchant for clever and meaningful lyrics, Walker makes clear the debt the celebrated Wailers, like so many Jamaicans, owe to the mother of Afro-Jamaican culture, Miss Lou, the Honorable Louise Bennett-Coverley. Walker's writing reveals that artists from the era that produced Bob Marley were as youths listening attentively to the radio broadcast of *Miss Lou's View* and possibly hearing Bennett in her role on the radio soap *Life in Hopeful Village*. They were fixed in front of the TV set watching Bennett's *Romper Room* program and eventually attending shows on which she was featured.

Careful and sensitive attention is paid to the overlooked role of female producer Sonia Pottinger and the role of Marcia Griffiths and Judy Mowatt not just as backup singers for the Wailers but as women's advocates, producers, and individual artists who contributed significantly to the music's growth and popularity.

Tracing the Caribbean diaspora further, the Canadian contribution to the reggae narrative is explored beyond any attempt to include that destination in previous narratives. If only for the chapters on jazz and ska, this is a book for all research libraries and enthusiasts of Jamaican jazz and world music. There is much to savour from these pages; they represent the missing chapters to those other books on reggae already on your shelves. Between these pages is a perception, indeed, a history that has been well worth the wait.

Introduction

Journey through the Reggae Underground

In some ways, this book is a reflection of my personal relationship with Jamaican music and a mirror of my journey through the Caribbean diaspora.

The first time I heard Bob Marley's music, I was a boy growing up in the U.K. in 1964. Marley's lead vocal spun off the black vinyl of the Wailers' first Jamaican hit "Simmer Down" at a South London blues dance. Ska and rhythm and blues fuelled the U.K. version of Jamaican blues dances concerned with soothing the blues of hardworking Jamaican immigrants like my parents. I was ten years old, not old enough to participate in an adult party. I went with my parents to the house where the dance was being held and they escorted me to the bedroom on the second floor where I would be joined by other boys and girls who were the children of my parents' friends. At the time, I did not know that the lead voice on that recording belonged to Bob Marley, but his tone and style of singing became a part of my music consciousness.

Another important Marley experience occurred in Jamaica in 1970 when I was sixteen. That year, the Wailers' Lee Perry–produced recording "Duppy Conqueror" was a hit in Jamaica. The Wailers were scheduled to appear on Jamaica Broadcasting Corporation's weekly television program that showcased the artists responsible for the island's most popular tunes. I had already discovered that "Simmer Down" was the Wailers' recording and by that time, for me, they had inched past the Heptones and Paragons as my preferred harmony trio. I sat in the living room of my parents' house, eagerly awaiting the on-camera entrance of Bob Marley, Peter Tosh, and Bunny Wailer. I was thinking that a wider audience would now discover the Wailers' distinctive singing style and producer Lee Perry's innovative locomotory rhythms.

On the small screen everything about the Wailers had a raw rebellious flavour—the way they looked, their attitude, and the song's lyrics. The ever-charismatic Bob wore flared pants, shirt outside his pants, his face framed by a big semi-unkempt Afro. His half-shut dreamy eyes betraying a disposition described at the time as "well-charged" or "well-red" from inhaling one draw too many. As the music faded, he fell to the ground face-first and was assisted to his feet by Bunny and Peter on either side of him, each gripping an upper arm.

During that period of the Wailers' career, I had seen Bob Marley in the Cross Roads area of Kingston. He looked like a struggling Jamaican artist as he walked across the road carrying a cardboard box of the Wailers' 45-rpm recordings as if he was on his way to do business with some record-store owner. As a result of witnessing the Bob who fell on his face and Bob the struggling artist peddling his own records, I don't completely indulge the mythology erected after his death that reinvented him as a prophet and shaman. I view him as a progressive Rastaman, social activist, skilled and gifted songwriter, and capable bandleader. That vision of Bob Marley is what informs the "Roots Souljah" essay.

On the first weekend of November 1991, as a Toronto resident, I created my own Marley experience through the execution of my idea to bring together a variety of reggae experts as part of a conference and festival tributing Bob Marley. The Jamaican-Canadian Association–sponsored festival named Catch A Fire–The Perpetual Flame: A Celebration of the Life and Influence of Bob Marley was held at Toronto's Harbourfront Centre. The program featured reggae films *The Harder They Come*, *Rockers*, and the *1979 Reggae Sunsplash*. The festival offered a concert showcasing the Caribbean-Canadian reggae of roots artist Errol Blackwood, dub poet Lillian Allen, and the Ahdri Zhina Dancers. Panel discussions, however, were the festival's main focus. We were successful in assembling analysts such as Jamaican reggae historian Garth White, Jamaican broadcaster Dermot Hussey and Toronto-based African-American music journalist Norman "Otis" Richmond. Other important panellists included Neville Garrick, a colleague of Bob Marley who toured with the Wailers as a lighting artist and technician, Roger Steffens, the Los Angeles–based actor and speaker who, at the time, possessed the largest archive of reggae recordings and memorabilia. I presented in two panels "Marley's International Status" and "Bob Marley: His Early Days as a Musician," in which I discussed, among other topics, my personal experiences growing up in Jamaica as a teenaged fan of Bob Marley's music. The festival's success—impossible without the crucial organizational skills of writer, poet, and community activist Paul Kwasi Kafele, who coordinated the festival with me—hinged, in part, on its showcase of experts whose viewpoints reflected different perspectives of Marley. Perspectives tempered not only by the personal relationships that panellists Hussey, G. White, and Garrick had with Marley but also by their intimate understanding of Jamaican culture. As a result, the conference strengthened my resolve to write a book about the music from an insider perspective.

The writing on Bob Marley rarely, if at all, references the impact on Marley's art from other icons of Jamaican culture. In the essay "Rain A Fall, Dutty Tuff," I discuss poet and folklorist Louise Bennett's influence on Bob Marley's work, while "Roots Souljah" includes a look at a variety of individuals influential to Marley, one of whom was hand-drummer Oswald "Count Ossie" Williams. When I visited the Count Ossie Cultural Centre in the fall of 1998, I did so because I was aware of Ossie's pivotal contributions to the development of ska and reggae. My experience at the centre deepened that understanding.

On a warm October Sunday evening I set out with my cousin Bunny McCook to visit the Count Ossie centre in Rockfort, East Kingston. I was hoping to interview Sam Clayton, the manager and philosopher of Count Ossie's still-active band, the Mystic Revelation of Rastafari (MRR). Bunny knew Clayton through his uncle Tommy McCook, the gifted tenor saxophonist who died five months earlier. I myself was familiar with Tommy as a frequent visitor to his Slipdock Road residence in the late '60s.

The Centre, a two-storey structure, looked similar to the other homes that surrounded it in this residential neighbourhood. The second floor was one large rehearsal space with a spotless, burgundy, hardwood floor. Every Sunday evening at the centre is a scheduled MRR band practice. This particular rehearsal doubled as a commemoration of the 22nd anniversary of Count Ossie's death. This special gathering brought together MRR drummers skilled in the art of what they called the "mighty slap" an open-handed rhythmic slap to the face of the funde, repeater, or bass drum.

When all the drummers and special guests had arrived, Sam Clayton addressed the gathering with remarks about the significance of Count Ossie and his legacy. While the musicians were preparing for their musical tribute to the Count, Clayton greeted my cousin as a *bredren* and spoke with me in a respectful and friendly manner but gave us an initial warning that an interview with him might not be possible that night.

Clayton went down to the library, housed on the building's lower level. On his return, he handed me the original booklet that accompanied the double vinyl-record package of MRR's 1971 classic *Grounation* album and a photo album documenting the band's history during the '60s while the Count was still alive.

At this point, the room contained at least twenty *bredren*, most of whom were creating therapeutic, ancestral drum *riddims*. As I began to read the *Grounation* liner notes and lyric sheet, the walls, the roof, and especially the floorboards seethed with the thunder of drums creating a trance-like atmosphere in the room. Billowing ganja smoke, floating out of *chillum* pipes and *spliff* joints, swirled, filled the room, and climbed toward the ceiling before dissipating. I made notes and took photographs of photographs to the provocative intoxicating syncopation of the "mighty slap." The band's singing and chanting merged with the words and images I processed, while my body moved to the drumbeat as if responding to a natural urge.

An interview with Sam Clayton did not seem likely that night. An alternate date was tentatively arranged. Bunny and I soon indicated our intention to leave. We sped out of Rockfort with the pungent smell of weed in our nostrils, even though neither of us smoked, and with the drumbeat still echoing in our ears. We spoke with sheer frustration about the fact that we would give anything to have been in Rockfort over thirty-five years before, in the same room with trombone genius Drummond, McCook, jazz tenor sax man Wilton "Bra" Gaynair, and the Count Ossie drummers. We considered the pure musical pleasure of witnessing first-hand the cream of Jamaica's jazz musicians jamming together. The contributions of Count Ossie as an iconic figure of Jamaican music are described in the essay "Blue Beat, Nyabinghi, Bebop."

Jazz trombonist Don Drummond was another significant Jamaican music icon influential to Bob Marley. In fact, I first engaged Drummond's distinct trombone sound in the same environment where I heard "Simmer Down," at the U.K. blues dances I attended with my parents. The dance was percolating on the main floor of a house and I felt the deep vibrations of the ominous ska bass wash over my body as I negotiated my way through a dark room filled with well-dressed adults—through the smell of curried goat, weed, and beer to the stairway taking me to the bedroom. The bedroom was well lit and the air was fresh, but the

Peter Tosh performs at the Ontario Place Forum, Toronto, July 1980.
Photograph by Isobel Harry.

music's pulse could be heard loud and clear. The troubled yet
beautiful Jamaican jazz notes flowing out of Drummond's trombone epitomized the sound of ska while the music's rhythm erupt-
ed in ominous bass lines and manic drumbeats. Drummond's
trombone notes rummaged around in my subconscious as they
accompanied the laughter, talk, and play of myself and the other
kids until we eventually fell asleep. Drummond and other stars of
the ska era, such as McCook, tenor sax man Roland Alphonso, guitarist Ernest Ranglin, and trumpeter Johnny Moore, were all talented jazz musicians. A fact that led me to the realization that a
proper assessment of ska requires an understanding of ska's jazz
roots, a subject explored in "Blue Beat, Nyabinghi, Bebop."

Jazz has always been an important aspect of my music consciousness. As a young boy living with my parents in North
London, U.K. in the early '60s, records by the amazing Dinah
Washington spent a lot of time on the Blue Spot stereogram in our
living room. I am certain I heard the cool sounds of Dave
Brubeck's *Take Five* and the be-bop of Charlie Parker. Although I
was steeped in reggae and the music of soul and funk artists such
as Aretha Franklin, Marvin Gaye, Curtis Mayfield, Chaka Khan,
Stevie Wonder, Ohio Players, the O'Jays, and Parliament

Funkadelic, while living in Toronto throughout the '70s, my friend Dev fed me a steady diet of Miles Davis and another friend Lori patiently transformed me into a Billie Holiday disciple.

Back living in Jamaica during the early '80s, I was inside uptown Kingston's Little Theatre when Sonny Bradshaw's Big Band of Jamaican musicians played a fusion of reggae and jazz on a bill with African-American jazz artists including trumpet player Donald Byrd and reeds man Byard Lancaster. My most memorable Jamaican jazz moment, however, was witnessing the original line-up of the definitive '60s Jamaican ska band the Skatalites (minus Don Drummond) play a lengthy, exhilarating, and jazz-fuelled set of their ska classics at Herbie Miller's Blue Monk Jazz Gallery. That was a truly historic concert because the Skatalites had just reunited after an eighteen-year absence from the scene and the band's performance was stunning. Investigating the jazz scene in Jamaica revealed to me that Bradshaw was crucial in maintaining a jazz tradition on the island and that the Skatalites' legacy went beyond the 2-Tone ska of British punk and new wave. I expand on these themes in the essays "Blue Beat, Nyabinghi Bebop" and "Eastern Standard Time."

Returning to Toronto in the late '80s, I began to explore a different side of jazz—in a sense, the alternative "dub" side of jazz played by musicians such as tenor saxophonist David Murray, jazz vocalist Cassandra Wilson, and alto saxophonists Steve Coleman and Henry Threadgill. This exploration of various kinds of avant-garde jazz became crucial to my research of Jamaican jazz musicians other than Wynton Kelly, a sideman with Miles Davis and John Coltrane, or Jamaican-American singer Carmen McRae. It provided me with a framework to understand the music of Jamaican-born Chicago-based reeds man Douglas Ewart, British-Jamaican saxophonist Kenny Terroade, who played with Archie Shepp and jammed with Count Ossie in Jamaica, and, most important, the great Jamaican alto saxophonist Joe Harriott, who is now viewed as a key figure of European free jazz. Harriott's importance is considered in "Blue Beat, Nyabinghi, Bebop" as a significant part of the essay's treatment of Jamaican jazz history.

In 1998, I purchased the Skatalites live album *Stretching Out*, just released on CD. Herbie Miller produced the album and wrote the liner notes. I knew that Herbie Miller, a Jamaican producer and artist manager in the music business, was equally immersed in the jazz world of New York as he was intricately involved in the Jamaican reggae scene. In the *Stretching Out* liner notes, Miller describes a series of Skatalites concerts in which jazz musicians such as Charley Palmieri and Arthur Blythe on separate occasions shared the stage with the ska band, while other important jazz personalities such as David Murray and the late Lester Bowie were in attendance. Miller's role in linking the Skatalites to the New York jazz scene made him an important contact for advancing my understanding of what I call Jamaican jazz, a term I initially used in my article "Blue Beat, Jazz and Joe Harriott" published in the May 1999 issue of Toronto urban culture magazine *Word* to describe Jamaican musicians fusing nyabinghi, ska, calypso, mento, and reggae with jazz.

This was also the year I first met and interviewed British-Jamaican jazz bassist Gary Crosby. We connected at an appropriate location, the Alpha Boys' School in Kingston, Jamaica where Harriott, Drummond, McCook, and other Jamaican jazz musicians received their music education. I discovered that Crosby is not just a talented jazz musician but also a serious student of jazz, Jamaican jazz, ska, and reggae. In fact, Crosby contributed an engaging preface to *Fire in His Soul*, Alan Robertson's biography of Joe Harriott.

Miller's involvement in connecting the worlds of Jamaican ska and jazz and the vital role played by Gary Crosby's U.K. band Jazz Jamaica in extending the ska and Jamaican jazz tradition into the new millennium are both considered in the essay "Eastern Standard Time." The main thrust of that essay, however, is its analysis of the life, career, legacy, and iconography of Don Drummond.

The Jamaican careers of Marcia Griffiths and Judy Mowatt as solo recording artists and performers were already in full swing during the late '60s when I first heard their recordings. Women are almost never discussed as serious contributors to the advancement of reggae. Even when Griffiths, Mowatt, and Rita Marley became backup singers for Bob Marley, I still viewed them as substantive and influential artists placing their solo careers on hold to work with the Wailers. The "Reggae Sistas' Stories" essay is written from a perspective that considers the significance of women such as Griffiths, Mowatt, Rita Marley, Millie Small, Phyllis Dillon, and producer Sonia Pottinger and their contributions to the art of reggae.

Dennis Brown's stature as an extraordinary singer in the studio or in concert has an overarching presence in reggae. I was fortunate to be in the audience for one of Brown's best live performances in Jamaica on Kingston's National Arena stage as part of the excellent Reggae Superjam '83 festival. Dennis Brown, as headliner on one night of the three-day festival, followed the stellar work by Jamaican reggae balladeer Beres Hammond and an exciting performance by U.K. roots reggae band Steel Pulse, who were red hot in Jamaica at that time.

Brown worked so hard that he not only proved his worth as the headliner but also earned three genuine encores. I can verify those encores were genuine because I was there joining everyone else shouting, banging on the seats to encourage Brown to get back on stage. I have always been amazed at the mesmerizing effect Brown's voice and charisma had on audiences. His popularity during the '70s, '80s, and '90s, in Jamaica and in the Caribbean diaspora was probably unparalleled. It is surprising that someone who is so important to the music has not been the subject of study and examination until now. The "Visions" essay evaluates Brown's influence as a reggae singer. The essay frames its discussion in the context of assessing the diversity in reggae singing by also examining the important voices of John Holt, Delroy Wilson, Leroy Sibbles, Burning Spear, and Toots Hibbert.

Every essay in *Dubwise* explores the cultural interconnections between Jamaica and the Caribbean diaspora. "Blue Beat, Nyabinghi, Bebop" looks at the impact of Jamaican jazz musicians in the U.K. and in America, while "Eastern Standard Time" tracks the legacy of Don Drummond and the Skatalites in the music of British-Caribbean band Jazz Jamaica. There are three *Dubwise* essays, however, that place a special emphasis on the work of artists of Caribbean heritage living in the diaspora territories of Canada, the United States, and Britain. "One-Drop Dubs the Maple Leaf" discusses the history of roots reggae and dub poetry in Canada. "Dub Fire" investigates the rise of diasporic reggae in the U.K. and the United States and "Raggamuffin Rap" provides an overview of how dancehall and hip-hop interact in the context of the Caribbean diaspora. In many ways, my personal history places me in a unique position to provide fresh insights about reggae in the Caribbean diaspora.

My journey of experiences in ska and reggae starts in the U.K., where I was born in the early '50s. During the early '60s, through exposure to parties, sound-system dances, and records my parents or my aunts and uncles played on their home stereos, I was not only familiar with the Wailers and Skatalites but also Prince Buster and Derrick Morgan as solo vocalist and as duet partner with Patsy Todd. When my parents moved back to Kingston, Jamaica in 1965, we lived in the middle-class community of Pembroke Hall, which became home to a variety of names in the reggae industry including Clement "Coxsone" Dodd, Donovan Germain, producer for internationally recognized reggae deejay Buju Banton, the vocal duo of Keith and Tex, Cynthia Schloss, Pat "Satchmo" Thompson, and bass guitarist Peter Tulloch. Wailers bassist Aston "Family Man" Barrett lived on Anglesea Avenue just one road south of our house on Petherton Avenue.

I spent my first school year in Jamaica at St. Anne's Senior school on Percy Street in the heart of downtown Kingston between Oxford and Bond Streets. My cockney accent—an obstacle preventing my desperate attempts to fit in—announced to everyone that I was from the U.K. I became friends with a fellow student named Walter, who once walked me through nearby Trench Town while he discussed poverty and its effects on a particular St. Anne's student and Trench Town resident who he claimed subsisted on cornmeal porridge for breakfast, lunch, and dinner. My initial reaction to St. Anne's and its ghetto surroundings was one of extreme trepidation, but eventually my experiences there formed an important aspect of a growing social and cultural awareness that started my transformation from an English youth of Jamaican heritage to being accepted as a Jamaican. Since that time, I have lived with two co-existing identities: one Jamaican, the other as someone from the English-speaking Caribbean diaspora.

St. Anne's was also a short distance from the business places of the two most influential record producers of the '60s. "Coxsone" Dodd's record shop Muzik City was on Beeston Street and Arthur "Duke" Reid's Treasure Isle record store, liquor store, and studio resided on two floors of a building at the southern end of Bond Street. I don't remember seeing Coxsone on my regular visits to Muzik City, but I did see King Stitt, a seminal deejay toaster who worked for Dodd. Duke Reid, an ex-policeman, was impossible to miss as his tall, large, imposing frame—positioned on a chair—hulked over a cash register situated on the sidewalk in front of the liquor store. Reid struck a daunting pose with a gun belt slung around his waist with a revolver in it.

During my high-school years at Campion College I came across fellow students who were connected to significant achievements in reggae. Michael Murray and Robbie Peart both spoke with me about their aspirations as reggae musicians. Michael Murray eventually moved to Toronto and became a member of Ishan People, possibly the first Jamaican-Canadian reggae band. Robbie Peart became a foundation member of Chalice, a successful reggae band in Jamaica during the '80s.

The first time I heard the Abyssinians' "Satta Massa Gana" blasting out of a ghetto rum-bar through the speakers of a jukebox in 1969, I knew that it was a special groundbreaking record of the early reggae period. The song's heavenly minor key vocal harmonies, its spacious daunting bass lines, the mournful sound of its heralding horns, and its lyrics partially sung in the Ethiopian language of Amharic meant that it was too innovative for '60s radio but perfect for the dancehall. "Satta Massa Gana" is now considered a classic roots reggae anthem.

In those days, youth culture in Jamaica was divided into soul and roots. Soul youths sported big Afros, wore bell-bottom pants, shirts with oversized collars and grooved to the sounds of funk, soul ballads, and rugged reggae. Roots youths covered sprouting dreads with a wool tam or cap, bopped bad-*bwoy* style in ankle-hugging flood pants and Clark's "desert boots." They confronted bass booming at their chests from huge speakers at dancehall sound systems spewing a steady stream of raw exclusive reggae. Some soul youths wore buttons displaying the Black Panther symbol of the radical African-American organization. Roots *man* wore buttons depicting the photograph of a regal looking Ethiopian Emperor Haile Selassie manufactured by the neighbourhood Rastaman. For teenage boys, the soul party was far more conducive to meeting, socializing, and dancing with girls. My *bredren* Chris and Tony and I reflected the in-between nature of our community by enjoying the best of both worlds. We had Afros but wore pants that narrowed towards the ankles. We attended a lot of house parties where 'soul sets' served an exciting rotation of reggae including U-Roy's "Wake the Town" and the Wailers' "Small Axe," the funk of, say, Sly and the Family Stone's "Thank You (Falletinme Be Mice Elf Agin)," and Aretha Franklin's "Rock Steady," and soul bal-

Derrick "Duckie" Simpson of Black Uhuru in Toronto, October 1981.
Photograph by Isobel Harry.

lads such as the Emotions' "So I Can Love You" and the Originals'
"Baby I'm For Real." We also checked out dancehalls where sound
systems such as Tippertone and King Tubby's Hi-Fi thrived on
exclusive reggae dub-plates and pre-releases including the original
"Tribal War" by Little Roy and various versions of "Satta Massa
Gana." For me, this meant not only juggling Jamaican and diaspora identities but also negotiating alternating identities of soul and
roots. A negotiation that recognized a certain kind of musical diversity typified by the Jamaican scene.

In early 1972, I was seated in the Carib cinema in Kingston
when the Jamaican film *The Harder They Come* had its first public

screening. Chris and I considered ourselves budding film critics even though our film universe was mainly confined to spaghetti westerns and other macho action movies. Our growing Black consciousness, piqued by our reading of James Baldwin's *Fire Next Time*, newspapers of the Black Panther Party, coupled with an empathy for Rasta's Afrocentric theology, meant that our screen heroes did not just consist of Clint Eastwood or Sean Connery. We were interested in so-called Black films like Sidney Poitier's *The Lost Man* and *Uptight* starring African-American actor Raymond St. Jacques because both movies told fictional stories about Black revolutionaries, like the Black Panthers, who militantly confronted racism in America. Neither film was outstanding and their depiction of Black radicals was distorted. In that context, *The Harder They Come*, as an independent Third-World film about Black Jamaicans and reggae culture, offered us a new satisfying cinematic experience. As the first Jamaican film, it possessed all the elements of early '70s rebel Jamaican youth culture, it grappled with issues of race and class exploitation, incorporated a sympathetic portrayal of Rastafari and skanked to a *wickid* reggae soundtrack.

When I left Jamaica for Toronto, Canada in the fall of 1972 to attend university, I arrived with a rudimentary sense of radical politics that developed to maturity as a result of discussions, study of radical literature, and a participation in community-outreach activities fostered by the University of Toronto's Black Student Union, "Home Service" on Bathurst Street, the Universal Negro Improvement Association on College Street, and the Harriet Tubman Centre at Robina and St. Clair. By 1974, young radical Blacks of my generation began shifting their Black consciousness to the left by merging Black Power and Afrocentricity with Marxism. Dionne Brand's lyrical essay "Bathurst" in her book *Bread Out of Stone* provides a good sense of the Black radical tradition as it existed in those days. My activism and the "equality and justice" lyrics of Bob Marley, Peter Tosh, and Burning Spear complemented each other. In some ways progressive social commentary reggae was the '70's soundtrack for many radical Caribbean diaspora youths. The main Black community newspaper then was *Contrast* and my favourite column was "Cream Off the Top" written by Norman "Otis" Richmond, whose columns married a social consciousness to his music analysis that considered reggae, calypso, and African in addition to soul, funk, and jazz.

In 1978 while I worked at a pop-bottling plant in East York, an Indo-Guyanese co-worker named Azim introduced me to the music of British-Caribbean roots reggae band Aswad. I listened as Azim played tracks from *Hulet*—Aswad's debut album—on his powerful home stereo, tracks that at the time sounded so unusual to me, I was not quite sure how to assess them. I continued to listen as Azim's speakers conveyed the creative interpretation of Burning Spear's rustic reggae rockers by Aswad as backing band for Burning Spear's 1977 concert at the Rainbow in London, U.K. As we listened to *Burning Spear Live*, one of roots reggae's best concert albums, I appreciated the innovative U.K. reggae impulse, maybe because it energized a Jamaican reggae context that I understood. Azim was excited about what he called the "musicality" of Aswad's reggae and its stylistic differences with Jamaican reggae. For me, it was an initial encounter with the distinct reggae of the English-speaking Caribbean diaspora.

By the end of that decade, as I was preparing to move back to Jamaica, I had my first exposure to the growing Canadian reggae scene. Ato, a visual-artist friend, invited me to a Regent Park community centre to hear a rehearsal of Truths and Rights, a band he was managing. My first exposure to dub poetry occurred during that time through a reading delivered by Lillian Allen. I was so impressed by Allen's poetry, flow, and use of Jamaican language that I introduced myself and talked with her about her work and the young dub-poetry movement.

I arrived back in Jamaica in May 1980 shortly before the announcement that elections would be held sometime that year. The violent clashes between supporters of the incumbent People's National Party and the opposition Jamaica Labour Party that accompanied Jamaican elections of the '70s reached a particularly vicious fratricidal peak that year. The crippling election violence of 1980—in which at least seven hundred and fifty people died—was followed seven months later by another historic tragedy: the May 1981 death of Bob Marley. While some analysts in America began discussing the death of reggae as if Bob Marley was its sole representative, I experienced a cultural scene in Jamaica that was very much alive, creative, and vibrant.

During the initial post–Bob Marley era of the early '80s, a wave of exciting roots reggae recording artists began to establish their presence in Jamaica and on the international scene. This wave included Judy Mowatt, Dennis Brown, and Black Uhuru. When Black Uhuru's Duckie Simpson, Michael Rose, and Sandra "Puma" Jones ran out on stage in front of drummer Lowell "Sly" Dunbar and bass guitarist Robbie Shakespeare and their band, as the last performers for Reggae Sunsplash 1983, it was already Sunday afternoon and we had been in Montego Bay's Jarrett Park since 7:00 the previous evening. Duckie and Michael were dressed in black leather and the raw mid-day sun immediately soaked them in perspiration. As the Sly and Robbie band blazed the "Shine Eye Gal" *riddim*, Duckie looked supercool in his sunglasses, barely nodding his head while casually skanking in one spot. Michael leaped what looked like six feet off the stage. Sandra "Puma" Jones—the group's feisty female member wearing a thigh-length white dress—twisted and gyrated her body in exciting, "cultural," Afrocentric dance moves. Black Uhuru was on fire and succeeded in energizing an exhausted bleary-eyed audience.

British-Caribbean reggae bands such as Aswad and Steel Pulse were a crucial aspect of reggae's second wave of the early '80s. Oddly enough, my initial encounter with a live performance of each of these U.K. diasporic reggae bands took place in Jamaica. Steel Pulse has the distinction of being one of the few reggae bands not indigenous to the island to have a really significant impact on the Jamaican music scene during that time. The attraction to the band certainly had a lot to do with the quality of their music, lead singer David Hinds' distinct silky tenor, his charismatic persona, and his unique look characterized by clumped dreadlocks standing upright on his head. Another factor may well have been that Jamaican fans warmed to the music of their cousins from the diaspora. In an interview on Jamaican radio in 1983 when the band was in Kingston for their first concert in the capital, David Hinds was asked where in the U.K. he was from. Hinds' response was a priceless diasporic reply. He said that he was from a community called Handsworth in Birmingham, a community that was like Jamaica in the U.K.

The relationship between Jamaican reggae fans and Caribbean diaspora reggae artists can also be complicated. I attended the 1984 edition of Bunny Wailer's Youth Consciousness reggae festival on the night when Aswad, a favourite of Wailer, performed a tight set displaying an exceptional musicianship. For some strange reason, Aswad did not really connect with the audience that night. Maybe

Aswad's sound was too rooted in a '70s dub sensibility, still relevant in U.K. reggae but already old school in Jamaica. Maybe it
was that Aswad front man Brinsley Forde, on that particular night,
did not express the charisma necessary to spark the Jamaican
crowd. As Aswad frantically attempted to generate an audience
response while their performance drew to an end, the remark of a
humble ghetto youth sitting directly in front of me reflected the
audience's ambivalence: "Onoo good you know, but you naah talk
to me." Aswad, however, did have enthusiastic fans in Jamaica
and I was one of them.

During those first years of the '80s in Jamaica, I experienced the
process that eventually led to the dominance of the dancehall style
over roots reggae. The two deejay giants of that period were
Yellowman chatting secular themes laced with X-rated "slackness"
lyrics, and Brigadier Jerry, flowing rhymes and phrases of social
commentary and Rasta theology. Yellowman's unassuming charisma in performance on stage allowed him to dispatch even the most
ribald risqué deejaying in a way that clothed his sex stories in an
inoffensive comic veneer. Brigadier Jerry, on the other hand, was
the MC on Jahlovemuzik International, the most popular sound
system of the time. I was present at many of the Jahlove dances,
held at the Hope Road headquarters of the Twelve Tribes Rasta
organization, which overshadowed any other sound system's
attempt to attract dancehall fans.

I witnessed the rise to maturity of dub poetry as a reggae
genre, whose leading practitioners became recording artists and
concert performers. Mutabaruka's "Every Time Ah 'Ear Di Sound"
was the first dub-poetry recording I heard and I remember experiencing the combination of Muta's defiant voice, a rough roots
rhythm, and his provocative verse as a revelation of a new form of
reggae on vinyl. I also have fond memories of Jean Breeze's inim-
itable and dramatic poetry performance and the way it weaved
itself around the fractured saxophone jazz of Hugh "Pappy" Pape
in a room at the Mutual Life building in New Kingston.

In 1985, I was present at the Tom Redcam Library for the
launch of the Land of Africa project, a benefit for Ethiopian famine
relief by reggae artists. Land of Africa, though it provided a modest contribution to the famine relief effort, in its own way underscored the lack of a reggae and African music presence in Bob
Geldof's 1984 Live Aid recording, concert, and film projects.

Geldof completely ignored the fact that Rasta reggae artists view Ethiopia as their spiritual homeland. David Hinds' description of Live Aid as "Jive" Aid was made in that context and seemed accurate when it is considered that Geldof's main criteria for artist selection was chart position and record sales. On the other hand, Sun City, the 1986 anti-apartheid project of Steve Van Zandt—who played Silvio Dante on *The Sopranos* but whose first claim to fame was as guitarist with Bruce Springsteen's E Street Band—proved that a benefit recording and film project could be successful and include activist musicians who may not have achieved gold or platinum record sales. On the project's recordings that insisted on a boycott of the South African tourist resort of Sun City, Van Zandt—in addition to progressive mainstream rockers such as Bob Dylan, Bono of U2, Springsteen, and Bonnie Raitt—included reggae artists Jimmy Cliff, Big Youth, and Linton Kwesi Johnson and from Africa, the Malopoets and Sonny Okosuns.

Ibo Cooper of Third World initiated the reggae artist's relief efforts that were focused around generating proceeds from a recording called *Land of Africa*. The artist selection for participation on the recording was very inclusive in a reggae context reflecting a progressive mix of roots artists Freddie McGregor, Gregory Isaacs, Bunny "Rugs" Clarke, Ibo Cooper, Cat Coore, and, in fact, all the members of Third World, dancehall's Edi Fitzroy and Tristan Palma, and dub poetry's Mutabaruka. Marcia Griffiths, Judy Mowatt, and Rita Marley as the I-Three ensured the substantial participation of women in the project. U.K. reggae performers of Caribbean heritage were represented by Hinds, Steel Pulse drummer Steve "Grizzly" Nesbitt, and Aswad's Brinsley Forde. *Land of Africa* also represented a significant collaboration between Jamaican and diaspora reggae artists.

When I returned to Toronto in March 1986, hip-hop was breaking out on its own terms. Though I had purchased early rap recordings such as the 12" vinyl of Sugar Hill Gang's *Rapper's Delight* and Kurtis Blow's *The Breaks* when they were first released, during the music's second phase of the late '80s, the first hip-hop album I owned was Public Enemy's masterpiece *It Takes a Nation of Millions to Hold Us Back*. Initially, I was caught up in the creativity of artists such as Run-DMC, Public Enemy, MC Lyte, Eric B and Rakim, Boogie Down Productions, and Queen Latifah, but I eventually became interested in hip-hop's fascination with reggae.

Michael Rose of Black Uhuru kicks up the energy at the 1983 Reggae Sunsplash in Jamaica.

Reggae remained a significant aspect of my cultural life. At the time, Lance Ingleton's LIP promotions staged some of Toronto's most memorable reggae performances, which mainly alternated between Concert Hall and the Copa, two downtown concert venues that no longer exist. At those venues, I checked out different LIP concerts featuring performances by Burning Spear, Third World, Maxi Priest, Shinehead, and Dennis Brown. Brown usually appeared on the Saturday night of most Caribana weekends during that period. LIP provided a forum for Caribbean-Canadian reggae as artists such as Errol Blackwood and deejay Kid Fareigna displayed their talent on LIP stages. Ingleton's creative booking strategy presented cutting-edge African diaspora talents like Senegal's Youssou N'Dour as well as Brazilian star Gilberto Gil and Ivory Coast's Alpha Blondy, who both infused reggae into their music. Eventually, Allan and Denise Jones as "Jones and Jones" emerged as prominent promoters of dancehall concerts and sometimes roots reggae shows.

The Toronto scene reflected a creative balance of international-ly recognized Jamaican reggae acts and reggae artists of Caribbean heritage from Canada, the United States, and the U.K. I enjoyed some great reggae shows at the Copa, Concert Hall, and main-stream venues such as the Forum in Ontario Place, another distinc-tive Toronto outdoor concert venue that has been dismantled and replaced by the Molson Amphitheatre. The Forum, with its sloping grass embankments, its slowly revolving stage, and consequently great sight lines played host to the annual Reggae Sunsplash festi-val, which presented a one-day version of the Jamaican festival. The Forum also presented Canadian reggae of bands such as Messenjah and the Sattalites. In the summer of 1990, I experienced two legendary artists at the Forum on one bill: Jimmy Cliff open-ing for the incredible Fela Anikulapo Kuti, who gave a transcen-dent performance.

The essay titled "The Writing About Reggae Must Skank to an Authentic Rub-a-Dub Bass Line" reveals the characteristics of the insider perspective through a comparison of some of the more high profile reggae books written by outsiders with the insider perspective of pioneer Caribbean documenters of Jamaican music. My initial efforts in researching the music's history began when I was living in Jamaica during the early '80s with an investigation of the existing books about the music. I read two books on reggae his-tory: *Jah Music* by U.K. based Trinidadian Sebastian Clarke and *Reggae International* an anthology of essays edited by Americans Stephen Davis and Peter Simon. I then read two books with a focus on Bob Marley: American writer Timothy White's *Catch a Fire* and *Bob Marley: Reggae King of the World* by Jamaican-American Malika Lee Whitney and Dermot Hussey, the only author among that group of writers living and working in Jamaica at that time.

Jah Music was initially published in 1980 before Bob Marley died and before the other books mentioned here. At the time, I found *Jah Music* refreshing as a compact history of Jamaican music that described Wailers Bob Marley, Peter Tosh, and Bunny Wailer as the "Three Modernists." *Jah Music*'s main asset is its prominent consideration of reggae's journey in the U.K. and its documentation of British reggae's initial years. *Reggae International* contains a number of decent essays written by authors from Jamaica, the U.K., and America that cover ska, rocksteady, roots reggae, the dancehall deejay, and the influence of ska and reggae in the United States and the U.K. The late Timothy White's *Catch a Fire*, with a narrative clearly influenced by a literary non-fiction approach is probably the best writing of the early non-Jamaican meditations on reggae. Though White's descriptions and fluid novelistic approach are sometimes compelling, I found his use of Jamaican language disconcerting and at times annoying, particularly where he repeatedly punctuates quoted Jamaican patois phrases with the exclamatory "ta raas." I understand that *Catch a Fire* is a Bob Marley biography, but I did not understand why White minimized or ignored the important contributions of Count Ossie and Don Drummond and the impact those contributions imparted to Marley's art.

Malika Lee Whitney's *Bob Marley: Reggae King of the World* reads as a Jamaican-American Rasta woman's impressions of Bob Marley's career and ideology. The book differentiates itself through the interviews she incorporates with important women in Marley's life including his mother Cedella Booker, his wife Rita, his colleague Judy Mowatt, and his lover Cindy Breakspeare. Dermot Hussey's contribution to *Reggae King of the World* can be found in the book's preface in which he attempts to squeeze sixty years of Jamaican music history into a handful of pages. In addition to a very interesting narrative about a Jamaican folk music called mento, Hussey recognizes that rocksteady was not exclusively the domain of soul-style romantic ballads and discusses it as music of protest and rebellion. Hussey also breaks with convention by writing about Don Drummond as a visionary and indicating that Bob Marley was Drummond's successor.

Dermot Hussey, an eloquent journalist as writer and broadcaster is an expert on Jamaican music and a jazz aficionado who today works at XM satellite radio in Washington, DC. During the several decades he worked in Jamaican radio, Hussey combined the mechanics of the radio disc jockey with his skills as a broadcast journalist. He used a quasi-documentary style to provide the appropriate context, history, and incisive analysis of lyrics and music to accompany the roots reggae, jazz, Latin, and African music that he played. The radio show Hussey hosted during the early '80s was a weekly two-hour program called the *Inner Ear*. If the *Inner Ear* was like a non-academic college level class on popular musics of the African diaspora, then I was an avid student in attendance most weeks. On one show he played two hours of the Wailers' ska material. On another, he featured Miles Davis. Other programs focused on the music of Brazil's Gilberto Gil, Steel Pulse, Jamaican jazz pianist Monty Alexander and another on the female voices of jazz. On a show that did not focus on a single artist, he would play an eclectic mix that might have included dub poet Oku Onuora, U.K. dancehall deejay Smiley Culture, Paul Simon, Steely Dan, and the African reggae of Sonny Okosuns. The *Inner Ear* introduced me to Gilberto Gil, reacquainted me with Miles Davis, Billie Holiday, and Charlie Parker, and left me with a deeper appreciation of reggae and ska.

The most influential work that I read during that time were essays published in the '60s or '70s by Garth White and Verena Reckord, Jamaican scholars living and working in Jamaica, and by Guyanese academic Gordon Rohlehr. These essays—G. White's "Rudie Oh Rudie" and "Master Drummer," Reckord's "Rastafarian Music" and Rohlehr's "A Look at New Expressions in the Arts of the Contemporary Caribbean"—expressed an understanding of Jamaican music culture that reflected my sense of the social and cultural milieu of ska and early reggae. These essays began to shape my perspective as one that I now refer to as an insider perspective. "Notes on the History of Jazz and Its Role in Jamaica" by James Carnegie, another Jamaican writer, introduced me to U.S.-based Jamaican-born trumpet player Dizzy Reece and alto saxophonist Joe Harriott, both important jazz musicians. Carnegie also discusses how Skatalites' Don Drummond, Tommy McCook, and Roland Alphonso expressed their take on jazz through ska.

Garth White became a kind of mentor to me. He was generous enough to answer all my questions, queries, and probes about reggae. He possesses an encyclopedic knowledge of Jamaican music and his analytical skills and conclusions are informed by his role as a keen inside observer of the scene and was on good terms with "Coxsone" Dodd, Bob Marley, and the Skatalites. In fact, as he once told me, it would be easier to say which of the ska, rocksteady, or reggae artists that he didn't know.

In 1992, six years after I returned to Toronto, Phil Vassell and

Donna McCurvin launched *The Metro Word*, a new, hip, Black culture magazine that eventually dropped "The Metro" in the title
and substituted the word "urban" for "Black." *Word* displayed the
writing of a number of talented Black writers and in so doing,
underscored the lack of opportunities for writers of colour. *Word's*
alumni reads like a who's who of Toronto's Black writers and
includes *Globe and Mail* contributor Donna Bailey Nurse, fiction
and non-fiction author Nourbese Philip, filmmakers Alison Duke
and Sudz Sutherland, *Toronto Sun* columnist Nick Davis, *Source*
contributor Kim Fraser, McLean Greaves, Zoe Dille, *NOW* contributor Dalton Higgins, Marva Jackson, film critic and film festival
programmer Cameron Bailey, Norman Richmond, playwright
Maxine Bailey, and acclaimed science-fiction novelist Nalo
Hopkinson.

I wrote several pieces for *Word* in its inaugural year including
one in which I reviewed Bob Marley's *Songs of Freedom* box set. In
my review "Marley on the Box," I critically assessed essays by
Timothy White, Rob Partridge, who was ex-press director at Island
Records, and American keyboardist John "Rabbit" Bundrick, a
contributor to the Wailers' *Catch-a-Fire* album. At the same time
that the *Word* issue with my article hit the streets, Roger Steffens
happened to be in Toronto. A few weeks later, I received a phone
call from Phil Vassell in which he enthusiastically informed me
that the U.K.-based Partridge had sent a letter passionately
defending himself from my critique. Before Partridge's response
could be published in the *Word*, I noticed that Steffens had penned
his own review of *Songs of Freedom* in *The Beat* an L.A.-based magazine of which he was the founding editor. His article, cheekily
titled "The Last Word on the Marley Box Set," implicitly insinuated that his assessment of the anthology was definitive, ultimate, or
final as compared to mine, though my article was not explicitly referenced. Steffen's review, however, also criticised the essays of
Partridge and T. White, but reserved its most pointed attack for
Derrick Morgan, a Jamaican singer prominent during the ska and
rocksteady eras. On the other hand, Steffens lavished praise on
Bundrick's contribution. I wasn't sure whether to be pleased or
dismayed that my review generated so much attention. Those
direct and indirect responses to my article strengthened my
resolve that voices with a different perspective deserved to be
heard within an environment of varying points of view in which

discussion would not be dominated by the notion of a final word on reggae and its history.

In 1995 I began a journey to construct a new perspective for telling the stories of reggae and ska. I realized from the start that there should be some attempt at raising the level of the quality of the writing about reggae in terms of the depth of analysis and style. I felt that the quality of the writing should reflect the best examples of the music. In terms of perspective and analysis, the writing of Rohlehr, G. White, Reckord, Richmond, and the radio shows of Hussey initially influenced me. In terms of how depth of analysis is creatively expressed, I admired the journalism of African-Americans Greg Tate, Lisa Jones, and Joan Morgan, all writers whose words breathed a hip-hop sensibility. I also enjoyed the inventive incisive jazz commentary of Stanley Crouch, Gary Giddins, and Amiri Baraka. The work of those American writers, however, reflected a jazz aesthetic. The closest equivalent of those writers in reggae, for me at that time, was certain dub poets and the fiction of someone like Michael Thelwell in his novelization of the reggae film *The Harder They Come*.

At lunch hour one day in the fall of 1998, I was browsing in the book section of a leading retailer of CDs and DVDs at the corner of Queen and Yonge streets in downtown Toronto when I came across a book of poetry titled *Wheel and Come Again: An Anthology of Reggae Poetry*, edited by Kwame Dawes. As I flipped through the book's pages, I realized that I was familiar with a lot of the poetry, but discovered that the preface, written by a fiction writer named Colin Channer, boasted a style that integrated a witty use of Jamaican language, skillful use of metaphor, and a gregarious sense of humour that strived to discuss the serious issue of how Caribbean literature resisted the influence of reggae. Dawes, an academic, poet, and fiction and non-fiction writer, writes an accessible, fluid and engaging introduction that discusses reggae as an important resource for Caribbean writing and, specifically, for the poems he selected for the anthology. I immediately contacted Dawes and began a continuing dialogue about reggae writing and the history of reggae. Eventually, I contacted Channer and spent a fair amount of telephone time discussing writing craft, reggae, dancehall, and film with him in an exchange of ideas that influenced my work.

The journey of writing this book about ska and reggae con-

Bob Marley on stage at Massey Hall in Toronto, 1976.
Photograph by Isobel Harry.

vinced me that while celebrating the genius of Bob Marley, I should also celebrate the historic innovations of Count Ossie, Don Drummond, and Louise Bennett. The journey confirmed that my perspective must consider crucial intersections of the music with jazz, funk, soul, rock, hip-hop, African, and Latin without losing sight of the fact that those intersections are guides to a better understanding of Jamaican popular music. This journey convinced me that reggae is not simply a Jamaican art form but one that has been creatively enriched by musicians, singers, poets, deejays, and rap artists in the Caribbean diaspora, particularly in cities such as New York, London, and Toronto. In a sense, *Dubwise* contains a viewpoint of reggae that is Jamaican and at the same time represents a perspective of the Caribbean diaspora. It is the first work to treat reggae and ska of the diaspora with the importance they deserve. *Dubwise* is the first book to seriously consider women's contribution to roots reggae. It also breaks new ground by discussing the influence of roots reggae singer Dennis Brown. The chapter on Bob Marley attempts to provide a fresh assessment of his music, lyrics, and the influences that shaped his art. The essay on reggae's relationship to hip-hop is also pioneer work in its attempt to weave together parallel histories of dancehall deejays and hip-hop MCs as it features the rise of raggamuffin rap, a

Caribbean diaspora phenomenon. The chapter on the *Insider Perspective*, though it may be controversial in its critical review of the work of prominent reggae experts, is mainly concerned with uncovering the insider perspective of writers operating in the music's seminal period of the '60s and '70s.

Dubwise does not try to be definitive or comprehensive, it is simply my version of reggae's history as someone who is a U.K.-born, middle-aged, Jamaican *yout'* living in Toronto.

X-Ray Dub

By Klive Walker

Roots reggae
born as a heartbeat
pumping
spacious
thick
bass notes
into the life-blood
of Jamaican culture

Plump
sensual bass tones
passionately kissed
by percussive
one-drop
trap-drum licks

Inspired by
funde and repeater hand drums
conversing in voices of
thunder
as they sit between the legs of
Rasta
congo
bongo-I

Roots reggae
learned its sense of syncopation
from clap han' beats
that assist
the slap and shake of tambourines
to rattle
the neighbourhood Church of God building

Reggae heard
its sense of timing
in the enhanced
rhythmic breathing
of dark-chocolate coloured
Jamaican women
wearing white dresses
and white turban-like head-wraps
as they wheel and spin
wheel and spin

Women
whose Christianity
finds comfort
in African spirit worship
as they jump
poco
in revival time
on a street corner
in downtown Kingston

In a pulsing roots reggae dancehall
exposed to a Jamaican night's
star-filled
navy blue skies

strategically placed speaker boxes
shaped like
tall, overbearing refrigerators
exhale urgent dubs

that compel
couples of man and woman
facing each other
in a slow-dance embrace
to rub
a series of
deliberate
waist and thigh movements
that lock their groins

in a french kiss
rocking
to the heave
of the reggae dub
in
rub-a-dub style

Solo dancers
skank in slow motion
sway hips and waist
in sympathy
with a bass line
that intoxicates
like a
long draw
of high-grade
ganja weed

Roots Souljah

Reflections on Bob Marley's Life and Art

Fat imposing sounds of reggae bass thunder out of the large compound at 56 Hope Road. Rugged bass lines wrapped around a trap drum's offbeat one-drop syncopation rumble along the asphalt roadway in different directions intent on disturbing the neighbouring residents in this uptown, middle-class suburb of Jamaica's capital. Tuff Gong became the official name of this large colonial-style house and compound that was Bob Marley's home and workplace.

The sun's probing rays beam sizzling heat that seems to focus special attention on the grounds of the compound. In one corner of the Tuff Gong yard, sweat drips off Bob Marley's narrow nose as his well-toned five-foot-six frame launches into action to tame a soccer ball. Dressed in a white T-shirt, black track pants, and soccer boots, Bob Marley plays "keeping up" with a small group of *bredren* who formed a circle.

"Keeping up" is a soccer training drill that requires each participant to use any part of their body, except their hands, to prevent the ball from falling to the ground. Marley keeps up the ball like a juggler; delicately kicking it in the air knee-high with the instep of his right foot, then with the instep of his left. When the ball again connects with his right, he propels it high above his head. As gravity pulls the ball downward, his ripe-plantain-coloured forehead meets the ball. The effect of heading it back up in the air, just a few inches, causes his rust-tinged dreadlocks to shimmer and shake. Marley bounces the ball off his forehead twice before letting the ball fall to his right foot that passes it to a *bredren* in the circle.

At times, the Tuff Gong compound took on the social setting of a sanitized uptown version of a downtown ghetto tenement yard in West Kingston's Trench Town, the urban bowel that nurtured Marley during his adolescent and early adult years. The compound was a place where Marley's family, friends from Trench Town, ghetto gunmen, the slumming sons and daughters of the Jamaican upper-class elite, foreign and local journalists, record company executives, and philosophical Rastafarians congregated in clusters.

It is April 1978, only days before the One Love Peace Concert where Bob Marley and the Wailers are scheduled to be the headlining band. Bob Marley, the first Third-World superstar, flexes like a regular *bredren*. He walks around the yard of his home with a rhythmic bop in his step accentuated by his bowed legs and by the proud, almost arrogant posture he assumes as he "bigs-up" his chest in a way that looks like a soldier at attention.

That day Marley exchanges words with White Jamaican impresario Chris Blackwell, the owner and founder of Island Records, the U.K.-based international record company that issues and expertly markets the Wailers' albums. Marley also lectures Canadian photojournalist Isobel Harry in a terse combative tone about not interrupting him when he and his *bredren* are deep in conversation. Marley tells her to be patient if she wishes to score an interview.

A meeting of the Central Peace Council is in progress in a room of the Tuff Gong house. The Central Peace Council emerged in 1977 to facilitate and broker the fragile ceasefire between gunmen unofficially representing each of the island's two major political parties. The One Love Peace Concert represents a superstar reggae event designed to sanction and publicize the historic ceasefire.

Marley walks into the small room that is dark and intimate because it has no windows and because the space not occupied by the mainly male Peace Council members is filled by the gray-blue smoke of ganja. Everybody is standing against the room's available walls. Marley situates himself as a tangential participant of the discussion by calmly lying on his back on top of a table pushed up against one wall. Marley closes his eyes giving the impression to an outsider, like the Canadian journalist observing the situation, that he might be asleep. Like a lead guitar taking its opportunity to lace a reggae rhythm with a fervent blues solo, Marley interjects his thoughts into the unity talks swirling around him when a break in the rhythm of the dialogue permits him the opportunity to speak.

It is interesting that wherever British imperial rule established itself, national disunity, usually outfitted in violence, established deep roots: religion was the catalyst in both Ireland and India, language and ethnicity the divisive factors in Canada, while race became the pretext in Guyana. That kind of post-colonial tribalism, in a Jamaica that earned its formal independence in August 1962, assumed the form of political association. Deadly clashes between gangs of gunmen affiliated with either the socialist Cuba-friendly People's National Party (PNP), the government of the day, or the conservative pro-American Jamaica Labour Party (JLP) reached crisis levels in the '70s. During that time, lethal gunshots devastated ghetto communities identified by nicknames including "Tel Aviv," "Dunkirk," and "Angola," which were really the names of places that at some point in recent history had experienced war, terror, or both. The gunshots of political tribalism spelled terror for innocent ghetto residents. They lived with the consistent promise of death or mutilation within a climate of intimidation that was like a perpetrator of repression using the heel of his army boot to *cotch* the neck of a ghetto preteen who is face-down on the ground.

The objective of this intimidation was to force voters to change their allegiance during an election campaign. The climate between election campaigns favoured intense cold-war incidents that frequently ignited into violent flashpoints. If the generals of political tribalism's troops were to be found at the highest levels of the island's political parties, then the lieutenants leading operations in the actual theatres of death were sons of the very ghettos where vengeful bullets chewed up vulnerable flesh. These lieutenants were *bad-man* like the JLP's Claudie Massop and the PNP's Aston "Bucky" Marshall who decided to end the cycle of bloodshed in 1977 by declaring a truce; a truce celebrated by residents of those virtual war zones; a truce treated with suspicion by some politicians because a permanent ceasefire would alter their ability to manipulate voters. This truce produced the Central Peace Council, whose meetings were sometimes hosted by Bob Marley at his Tuff Gong headquarters.

As a progressive Rastafari, Marley viewed political tribalism as having a destructive effect on poor African-Jamaicans. Marley's relationship to the peace process was strengthened by the fact that the Peace Council's chairman was his friend Trevor "Bones" Phillips, a tall, slim, grassroots intellectual with a South-Asian heritage that accommodated an African racial mix. The soft eyes and fine facial features of Bones the dreadlocked Rastaman was secured by Isobel Harry's camera as he stood beside Bob Marley, both *bredren* holding opposite edges of a photograph of Emperor Haile Selassie of Ethiopia, the Jah or God of most Rastafari. Bones, Bucky, Claudie, and Bob sometimes discussed the business of peace and unity at 56 Hope Road.

Marley's stake in the anti-tribalism pro-unity initiative was not just a product of his Rasta principles or his friendship with Bones.

Bob Marley and Trevor Phillips holding a photo of Haile Selassie at 56 Hope Rd.

It also reflected his own rites of passage in Trench Town, which itself was balkanised into two sections—the PNP-aligned Concrete Jungle and the JLP-associated Rema. Marley's promotion of rights and justice for the poor and disadvantaged through his music grew out of his lived experience. That may be the reason why the emotion of Marley's wailing vocal is able to seep into the consciousness of listeners across the planet with its penetrating sense of truth. Marley integrated a simple Rasta greeting of unity—"one love, one heart"—into the lyrics of "One Love/People Get Ready" intended in the original ska recording as an antidote to divisive tribalism and gang war in specific communities of '60s Jamaica.

Marley songs written in the '70s were more precise in dealing with ghetto violence. "Johnny Was," from 1976's *Rastaman Vibration* album, for example, drew a graphic picture of a mother in distress over the death of her son killed by a stray bullet. "Top Rankin'," from 1979's *Survival* album, spoke directly to the political gang leaders, the "top rankin'" ghetto gunmen, as it wondered whether they were really serious about "coming together." In one rebellious string of words, the song bravely communicates: "They don't want to see us unite ... all they want us to do is keep on killing one another."[1] The unmentionable "they" also seems to refer to certain elected politicians and their foreign supporters and allies. The song does not specifically name Jamaica or Kingston, so the message is easily transformed into a universal one. The universal appeal of Bob Marley is an important factor in assessing his contribution to reggae's international recognition.

Marley's music drilled way below the surface of Western popular music tastes. Marley's reggae burrowed so deep that its rhythms and words erased barriers of language and culture, so that even the globe's most marginalized citizens embraced the Rastaman's vibration. The Aboriginals of Australia, the Maoris of New Zealand, and the First Nations of the United States and Canada recognized the roots reggae of Bob Marley as a kindred musical spirit. His prominent profile in Europe, North America, and Japan must be weighed against the fact that '70s reggae, in many ways, was still treated by the mainstream music industry, much of the status quo media, and even some of the hip alternative-rock press as a cute ethnic curiosity that they did not quite understand. Mainstream radio's resistance to reggae meant that Marley was forced to explore alternate avenues of finding, then capturing a loyal audience. A hectic schedule of concerts through several nations and continents became his connection to an ever-expanding fan base.

Marley's riveting concert performances combined his own dramatic dance movements and gestures, the trance-inducing reggae rhythms of the Wailers' band, the angelic harmony of the three women backup singers known as the I-Three, and his own wailing tenor vocal. Marley's movements and gestures on stage translated into dance the neo-African spirituality, which is at the root of African-Jamaican culture. Marley's knee lifts reflected the dancing of Rastafari to intense hand drumming at a nyabinghi gathering. The gesture of Marley concealing half of his face with his hand as the unconcealed eye rolls back suggested to the observer that he was in the grip of a spirit, or when he placed his forefinger on his temple, his eyes closed, his brow furrowed, as if a spirit freely moved inside his body placing him in a trancelike state both reference the image of a Pentecostal church member trembling uncontrollably under the influence of spirit possession. His waist movement, which traced a circle such that his body pivoted back and forth, mirrored the way that practitioners of Afro-Christian religious sects like Pocomania and Kumina reacted to a distinctive style of hand drumming often differing from the syncopation of nyabinghi percussion. Marley's great skill was his ability to present this deeply spiritual and very sensual body language as an intensely dramatic piece of reggae theatre within the context of what was really a rock-style concert format.

After 1976, Marley hit a peak in popularity assaulting the pop charts in England and Germany, and performing at major venues such as a soldout one-hundred-thousand-seat soccer stadium in Milan, New York City's Madison Square Garden, and five nights in London's Hammersmith Odeon. South America did not meet Marley in person, but his music touched a sensitive chord in many of that continent's countries. Brazil developed a close relationship with reggae and Marley's music. African-Brazilians, particularly residents of Salvador Bahia, included reggae as a vital aspect of their carefully constructed cultural mosaic, interlocking spiritual and musical elements that reflected possibly the most authentic retention of African culture in the diaspora. Bob Marley's connection to the African continent itself began with his transformation to Rastafari.

Africa is central to the theology of Rastafari. The movement views the continent as the original homeland of all Africa's descendants, and Ethiopia as the promised land. Marley's plea for continental unity in his song "Africa Unite"—from the *Survival* album—is expressed from the perspective of an African living in diaspora, wanting to repatriate: "Unite for the Africans Abroad / Unite for the Africans a Yard ... Cause we're moving right out of Babylon / And we're going to our Father's land."[2]

Marley's activism through the medium of his music, with its emphasis on disadvantaged people and those throughout the African diaspora, received official recognition when the African Nations at the U.N. awarded him a Peace Medal. Marley won admiration from the all-important African man and woman on the street, as well as African politicians and royalty who indulged the hero of their citizens. Marley loved Africa. Africa loved him back.

In Zimbabwe, Marley's music played the role of a catalyst accompanying the final phase of the liberation struggle fought during the late '70s in what was then Rhodesia. His song

"Zimbabwe," recorded for the *Survival* album, inspired rebel free-dom fighters with lyrics like "Every man have a right / to decide his own destiny ... Africans a liberate Zimbabwe."[3]

The liberation war against White-settler rule in Rhodesia con-cluded in favour of the African freedom fighters. Marley's popu-larity throughout southern Africa and his reputation as an impor-tant figure for Africans on both sides of the Atlantic made him an obvious choice as the diasporic brother to assist a reborn nation observe the death of racist Rhodesia, the country's aging evil per-sona. He would help celebrate the birth of a young and inexperi-enced Zimbabwe that continues to struggle in the shadow of its colonial alterego. Bob Marley stood like a giant on the stage in Rufaro Stadium, located in Zimbabwe's capital, Harare, as a Third-World reggae icon pouring his voice into a microphone that trans-ported the words relating his audience's struggle for independ-ence beyond the stadium's walls. The rhythms of Marley's song "Zimbabwe" acted like a magnet that pulled the guerrillas stand-ing outside the filled stadium towards the entrance.

The triumphant sounds of "Zimbabwe" inspired the freedom fighters to storm the stadium gates.

The dreadlocked Jamaican Rastaman who sang and danced on that stage in Zimbabwe was once a peasant boy from the village of Nine Miles, in Jamaica's northwest coast parish (province or state) of St. Ann—a mulatto peasant boy Jamaicans would describe as red-skinned or half-caste. A boy abandoned by a deadbeat White father, loved and encouraged by a Black mother and Black grand-father, whose ancestors were Africans. Africans like the ecstatic Zimbabwe audience adoring every vocal inflection, every dance gesture of the once humble country boy who became possibly the most acclaimed diasporic African of his generation.

The arc of Bob Marley's life is like a road of success potholed with severe setbacks. Marley's life as a musician, singer, and recording artist is intricately intertwined with the history of Jamaican music. Bob the peasant youth, born in Nine Miles in 1945, absorbed rural folklore and trained his young voice with melodies drenched in a Jamaican calypso known as mento. Relocation to Kingston initiated Bob's transformation to *rude-bwoy* teenager of Trench Town who wailed ska tunes in a harmony sex-tet called the Wailers. Bob had two Trench Town–based mentors during that period of the '60s: Mortimer Planno and Joe Higgs.

Bob Marley was one individual in different gatherings of progressive youth who assembled at Planno's Trench Town yard to hear his words of wisdom. Born in 1920 and reborn as a Rastafari in 1939, Planno was a significant personality of a movement that promoted Afrocentrism, the radical idea that God is Black and living in Ethiopia—a movement opposed to racial and class discrimination against African-Jamaicans. In 1961, Planno travelled to Ethiopia, Nigeria, Ghana, Liberia, and Sierra Leone with a Jamaican delegation that included two other Rastafarians: Filmore Alvaranga and Douglas Mack. The business of the delegation's African tour involved investigating the possibility of creating relations between Jamaica and those African nations, but, more important, it was an official response to the Rastafari movement's call for repatriation to Africa. Planno became a mentor to a younger generation of Black Power radicals, cultural *rude bwoys*, and quasi-Rastas from the urban ghetto, as well as rebels from the middle-class. He dispatched intellectual thoughts about Black consciousness, Rasta theology, and the centrality of Africa to his young disciples with a deep charismatic voice that resonated with the pace of nyabinghi hand drum rhythms. Planno was like a Jamaican Malcolm X to urban ghetto youth in '60s Jamaica. His influence extended to Kingston's loosely knit radical arts movement. Singers such as Bob Marley, Rita Marley, and Donald Manning (a member of the Abyssinians— a harmony trio whose groundbreaking recordings "Satta Amassa Gana" and "Declaration of Rights" remain classics of the roots reggae era); intellectuals such as reggae historian Garth White and poet Robin "Bongo Jerry" Small; visual artist Ras Daniel Hartman; and soccer player Allan "Skill" Cole—who had a profile in Jamaica at that time that was larger than any reggae singer—were all participants of Planno's reasoning sessions.

Singer/songwriter, vocal arranger, and voice coach Joe Higgs gave Bob Marley and the Wailers lessons in vocal harmony. The Wailers earned folk-hero status among poor African-Jamaicans by distilling the ideas of Black liberation and unity among ghetto residents into lyrics accompanied by crisp rhythm and blues–style harmony and Bob's thin wailing vocal that sang lead on the original "One Love," "Rude Boy Ska," and #1 hits such as "Simmer Down."

Most of the Wailers' ska tunes were recorded for Clement "Coxsone" Dodd, the most prolific and possibly the most creative producer of the day. The Skatalites provided the music on those

Wailers' ska singles. The Skatalites' most celebrated soloist was gifted jazz trombonist Don Drummond, whose legacy could still be heard in the music of reggae's roots era of the late '70s, a decade after his death. Drummond's trombone voice had a lasting impact on Marley as a teenager in the recording studio with Drummond and the Skatalites. This impact can be heard years later on "Running Away," a track from the 1978 *Kaya* album on which the talented Vin Gordon's moaning trombone voice and Marley's edgy vocal, channel Drummond's signature melancholy tone.

As a young man in his early twenties, Bob with his wife Rita endured a sufferer's existence as a rocksteady vocalist in a Wailers that was pared down to himself and his two close *bredren* Peter Tosh and Bunny Livingston. A decline in the Wailers' fortunes propelled Bob into the belly of America where he landed a job operating a forklift on the night shift in a Delaware warehouse. The labour grind obstructed his commitment to developing his skills as a songwriter and reggae artist so Bob returned to Jamaica and the Wailers a few months later. During the music's rocksteady and incipient reggae era, the Wailers were overshadowed by the popularity of harmony trios such as the Heptones, the Paragons, and the Maytals, but still managed to produce memorable singles such as "Hypocrites," "Stir It Up," and "Nice Time."

By the time Bob was twenty-five, a revitalized Wailers, in collaboration with innovative producer Lee Perry, created classic leading-edge rebel music such as "Duppy Conqueror," "Small Axe," "Soul Rebel," and "Don't Rock My Boat." "Duppy Conqueror" and "Small Axe" dominated the radio airwaves and the popularity charts. "Soul Rebel" and "Don't Rock My Boat" rocked the underground dancehall scene. In many ways, the Wailers, possibly the most innovative harmony trio of the early roots reggae era, were unique in enjoying commercial radio access while maintaining underground rebel status at the same time.

In the immediate post–Lee Perry period, the Wailers continued to produce quality hits such as "Screwface" and "Trench Town Rock" on their own Tuff Gong label. Trench Town was the kind of community that everybody wanted to keep their distance from. Marley never turned his back on Trench Town, a community often feared, devalued, and despised. Trench Town is featured in the lyrics of Bob Marley songs such as "Concrete Jungle" and "No Woman No Cry," songs that portray the complexities of ghetto poverty, while at the same time humanizing its residents as people with the same hopes and aspirations as anyone else. Even Marley's last album, *Confrontation*, released two years after his death in 1983, contained an emotional love letter to that community in a recording simply titled "Trench Town."

"Trench Town Rock"—recorded and released in 1971—was immediately adopted as Trench Town's unofficial anthem. That year, the community's relatively new eight-year-old high school had an all-star soccer team that was expected to win that season's Manning Cup high-school soccer competition. Whenever Herbert "Dago" Gordon, Devon "Dread" Lewis, Leroy "Kill-o" Cephas, Nehemiah "Shitty" Branch, his brother Theophilus "Toto" Branch, and the other Trench Town Comprehensive High School players stepped on to the pitch at the National Stadium in their faded chocolate-brown gear to display their sublime skills, the students and community supporters of the team would proudly sing Marley's "Trench Town Rock." It was the first time that a cheer from a high school in a ghetto community completely outclassed the arcane Latin chants and phrases harmonized by supporters of the more established high schools. Trench Town Comprehensive High School supporters were not just cheering on a soccer team, they were representing their entire community. They were rejoicing in the knowledge that positive, creative, and artistic achievements in music and sports could emerge from the depressed ghetto environment of Trench Town. Marley's "Trench Town Rock" offered the community a vehicle to express their humanity.

When Bob was twenty-seven, the Wailers secured an international deal with Island Records, which released *Catch a Fire*, *Burnin'*, and the groundbreaking *Natty Dread* in successive years to critical, if not popular acclaim. The two famous tracks on the *Burnin'* album are "Get Up, Stand Up," which has now become a human rights anthem, and "I Shot the Sheriff," which was covered by Eric Clapton. On *Burnin'*, Marley and the Wailers established their connection to the rhythmic roots of reggae through the "Rastaman Chant" recording. "Rastaman Chant" attempts to highlight the ingredients of pure Rasta music: chants accompanied only by the percussive pulse beats of funde, repeater, and bass hand drums.

The man who developed, nurtured, and championed this kind of Rasta music was the late master drummer Oswald "Count Ossie" Williams, an iconic figure in Jamaican music who would

Bob Marley performs at Maple Leaf Gardens, Toronto, November 1979.
Photograph by Isobel Harry.

have been influential to Marley and the Wailers as a musician and
Rasta elder. He was also respected by the great jazz musicians of
ska, as well as by hand-drum ensembles of the roots reggae era
such as Ras Michael and the Sons of the Negus.

Jamaican reggae historian Garth White, a seminal figure in the
research and documentation of Jamaican popular music, considers
Count Ossie, Don Drummond, and Bob Marley to be three individuals whose innovations have had an immeasurable impact on the
course reggae music has taken over the past forty years. If it is at
all possible to make a rough comparison between reggae's key
innovators and the heroes of jazz, Ossie would be Jamaican
music's counterpart of Louis Armstrong; Drummond, Jamaican
music's Charlie Parker; and Bob Marley, its John Coltrane.

Count Ossie's drum ensemble created the foundation of a
multi-layered syncopation from which much of Jamaican music
receives its rhythmic sustenance. Count Ossie's influence can be
traced quite easily to Lloyd Knibb, the Skatalites' trap drummer,
who has acknowledged that he tried to capture and interpret
Ossie's syncopation within a ska context. In turn, Sly Dunbar, possibly reggae's most inventive trap drummer, has named Knibb as
one of his influences.

Drummond created a distinct Jamaican jazz language through his unique approach to trombone playing that was revolutionary in the way it provided a vehicle for his genius to convey the raw emotion of injustice, poverty, and oppression suffered by African-Jamaicans through bleak brooding trombone notes.

Bob Marley's major contribution came through the artistry and honesty of his poetic lyrics rooted in Drummond's themes and elevated by music that distilled the history of musical influences reinterpreted from the work of icons who preceded him. "Running Away" and "Rastaman Chant" are two examples of how Marley creatively interpreted the influence of Don Drummond and Count Ossie. Count Ossie, Don Drummond, and Bob Marley represent the tradition of three important artistic components of Jamaican popular music and its international impact: distinctive nyabinghi hand drumming, jazz-inspired reeds and horns, and reggae poetry as song lyrics.

Bob Marley always worked with first-rate producers and musicians in his climb to international notoriety. During the ska era, he worked with Clement Dodd and the Skatalites. As rocksteady transformed into early reggae, the Wailers were produced by Leslie Kong, the man responsible for recording international hits such as Desmond Dekker's "007 (Shanty Town)" and the Melodians' "Sweet Sensation." The Wailers' celebrated collaboration with Lee Perry and the Upsetters band followed.

When Peter Tosh and Bunny Wailer departed the Wailers, Marley convinced the most talented female roots reggae singers of the day to join him. At the time, Judy Mowatt—already a major talent on the local Jamaican scene—had the vocal skills, intelligence, and beauty to accomplish her international career goals as a solo artist. Mowatt's groundbreaking album *Black Woman* was recorded and released while she operated as part of the I-Three. Marcia Griffiths, as part of a duo with Bob Andy, had already tasted international success three years earlier with a cover version of Nina Simone's "Young, Gifted and Black," a chart-topping hit in the U.K. and Europe. Although Rita Marley, Bob Marley's wife, did not have the same profile as Mowatt or Griffiths back in the '70s, she proved her potential during the early '80s after her husband died, through the international popularity of her single "One Draw."

The experience of having collaborated with some of the most talented artists prepared Bob Marley for the Wailers' emergence on the international scene, particularly when he began his solo career without Peter Tosh and Bunny Wailer. This meant that during the Island years, Marley had a keen sense of how he wanted to arrange and organize his music—how he wanted his reggae to sound. Marley's tenure with Lee Perry would have been an inspiration for Marley to operate on the creative edge, to push beyond the perceived musical limits of roots reggae.

At the age of thirty-one, Marley was well on his way to superstar status with his *Rastaman Vibration* album experiencing brisk international sales. That year, 1976, unknown assassins carrying automatic weapons invaded his Hope Road residence, squeezed off multiple rounds of miserable bullets that grazed Marley, injured his wife Rita, and seriously wounded his manager Don Taylor. Fortunately, neither Marley's wounds nor the injuries suffered by Rita or Taylor were lethal. Whatever the intentions of the assassins, their bullets were on a deadly mission to kill Bob Marley.

Marley climbed out of a deep valley of adversity, yet again, emerging with a diasporic and international profile that cast a bright spotlight over developing countries like Zimbabwe. It was there on April 17, 1980, at thirty-five years old, where he sang his way to a permanent place in the history of the African continent by performing at the Zimbabwe independence celebrations.

A year later, the cancer that had locked Marley's body in a prison of pain and suffering, gradually sucked away his life, sending him on a voyage to immortality. His turbulent life combined heady successes with sublime tragedy in a tense and tightly interweaved relationship, much like an intense rub-a-dub Wailers' rhythm—the kind of dramatic tension between percussive trap drumming, implosive basslines, and precisely timed pregnant spaces. The drama of Bob Marley's entire life seemed to skank to an ominous dubwise rhythm.

Marley's creative body of recorded work has produced an international impact that is crucial to understanding the man's musical legacy. His songs have been covered by significant artists; two examples are the interpretation of "Guava Jelly" by incomparable American vocalist Barbra Streisand, and the version of "I Shot the Sheriff" by exceptional U.K. rock guitarist Eric Clapton.

In the context of the African diaspora, Marley's lyrics and the Wailers' rhythms have been sourced by major stars such as African-American blues singer Taj Mahal in his cover of Bob

Marley's "Slave Driver," African-Brazilian singer-guitarist Gilberto Gil's version of "No Woman No Cry" (or "No Chore Mais" as the song is called in Brazilian Portuguese), and Ivory Coast's Alpha Blondy, the West African musician and singer who channelled Marley's rhythmic and vocal style in his music.

A very important aspect of Bob Marley's music legacy is his influence on the Caribbean diaspora. The work of reggae artists of Caribbean heritage—artists born or socially shaped in the U.K., the United States, and Canada—has been inspired by Marley's social-commentary lyrics, music, and vocal approach. His reggae was certainly the foundation for important British-Caribbean reggae bands like Steel Pulse and Aswad. Aswad enjoyed a mainstream profile in the U.K. throughout the '80s with recordings such as "African Children," a song that investigates issues of ghetto living and poverty just like Bob Marley's "Concrete Jungle," except that "African Children" references the U.K., not Jamaica. David Hinds, the lead singer of Steel Pulse—the first diasporic U.K. reggae band to achieve mainstream prominence in the U.K. during the late '70s—developed a singing style influenced by Marley's approach to reggae vocals.

Today, over twenty years since his passing, Bob Marley's legacy, in terms of how his catalogue has been marketed, is slanted in favour of accommodating his so-called "softer" side. This is reflected on compilation albums such as *Legend* and recordings like "One Love/People Get Ready," whose original meaning has been seriously diluted so that it translates into a kind of smarmy "can't-we-all-get-along" anthem. Despite the attempts to hijack Marley's legacy and conceal the full range of his work, his writing on human rights, equality, and revolution is just as important as his discourses on love, introspection, and spirituality.

On *Natty Dread*, the 1974 album that qualifies as Marley's first "solo" work after Bunny Wailer and Peter Tosh departed the Wailers, Marley teases out his vision of rebel reggae with potent poetic lyrics and music that extends beyond the creative limits of '70s roots reggae. *Natty Dread* is a riveting concept album whose individual songs are connected by themes of poverty and rebellion, sometimes filtered through the prism of apocalyptic Rastafari theology.

The opening lines of "Them Belly Full" depict this theme by immediately establishing the dialectic between the satiated appetites of the "haves" and the poverty and anger of the "have-nots": "Them belly full but we hungry / A hungry mob is a angry mob."[4] The song's purpose is to highlight the suffering and rebel attitude of people who do not possess the basic necessities of life.

In "Rebel Music," a different aspect of poor people's subsistence is explored as the lyrics reveal the roadblocks to freedom of movement when curfews and police spot checks in ghetto communities challenge the already limited rights and freedoms of ghetto residents. The most telling lines in "Rebel Music"—told in a poignant first-person voice—reflect the sentiment that possession of a little herb stalk of ganja might be the pretext, but disadvantaged individuals who are harassed by the authorities possess little of anything except their lives: "Take my soul and suss me out / Check my life if I am in doubt."[5]

"No Woman No Cry," the only track on *Natty Dread* that references Jamaica, does so through the phrase: "... in a government yard in Trench Town." While Jamaica is readily recognized in all the other tracks, they are skillfully written in a way that makes them both location-specific and universal at the same time. "No Woman No Cry" is also interesting because a female ghetto resident is the subject of the song's lyrics and she is consoled and reassured in a way that seems to empathize with her situation without any overt sexual or romantic motives.

"Talkin' Blues" continues Marley's detailed sketch of disadvantaged individuals with its portrayal of a homeless person who sleeps outdoors and wears shoes too small for his feet. Unlike "Them Belly Full," which discusses poor people coping with their circumstances by using music and dance to ward off oppression ("forget your troubles and dance"[6]), the homeless character of "Talkin Blues" talks about bombing the churches of lying preachers and joining the freedom fighters when the revolution begins.

"Revolution," *Natty Dread*'s final track, advances the position without any ambiguity that "It takes a revolution to make a solution."[7] An apocalyptic Biblical warning about the truth of Revelation precedes that line and maintains the balance or, more correctly, the merger of the spiritual and the rebellious that is a crucial feature of reggae crafted by Rastafari.

Many of the Wailers' Island studio albums, starting with *Natty Dread*, have an over-arching theme or concept. The theme of the *Natty Dread* and *Rastaman Vibration* albums is overcoming poverty through rebellion. Half of *Exodus* fuses spirituality and rebellion, while the other half works a theme of love—particularly romantic love. *Kaya* continues the love theme, but also investigates introspection. *Survival* is clearly Marley's Afrocentric manifesto linking the social issues of Jamaica to the struggles in southern Africa of the late '70s with the African diaspora as a whole.

Uprising's theme is reflected in the borderline pessimism and despair of recordings such as "Bad Card," "We and Dem," "Real Situation," "Work," and "Pimper's Paradise." The album is tempered with positivity in "Forever Loving Jah" and the exceptional "Redemption Song," a tune that may be Marley's most uplifting anthem (read Kwame Dawes' book *Bob Marley: Lyrical Genius* for an insightful evaluation of *Uprising's* lyrics).

"Redemption Song" can be read as a reggae poem with an epic sweep and incisive depth of historical analysis. The song skillfully discusses the Atlantic slave trade and the dangers of the nuclear age, while promoting the crucial idea that Africans in the diaspora and on the continent must emancipate themselves from mental slavery.

Natty Dread is a concept masterpiece because of its words, but also because of the music that provides an appropriate vehicle for the lyrics to have maximum impact. Aston "Family Man" Barrett's bottom-heavy soul-searching bass lines and his brother Carly's rickety-tick, on-the-one, one-drop trap drumming embrace like passionate lovers on each and every track. The album's undiluted roots reggae rhythms were only one characteristic that provided the music on the album with a distinct persona. What takes it to an altogether different level of creativity is its use of the blues. In some ways, *Natty Dread* is a blues album in a sublime roots reggae context. The gorgeous playing of African-American lead guitarist Al Anderson and the appropriate use of harmonica—another prime instrument of the blues—are the obvious indicators of a blues sensibility on *Natty Dread*. Bob Marley's vocals and the I-Three's call-and-response harmony provide the album with a reggae interpretation of a blues feel—a kind of reggae blues. The key thing to understand in this analysis of *Natty Dread's* music is that the Wailers are not really trying to fuse blues and reggae in a simplistic way. The album's music offers something much more organic; it offers a blues that adapts itself to the objectives of roots reggae.

This mix of blues and reggae works because of the very nature of reggae itself. The Barrett brothers' spacious roots rhythms leave ample room on recordings such as "Lively Up Yourself" that allow

Al Anderson to inject crying blues chords. Anderson's guitar riffs act like a second wailing vocal, supportive of Bob Marley's ragged blues-soaked tenor. Anderson's blues snake intermittent piercing notes and moody solos throughout "Them Belly Full" that negotiate the thunder clap of nyabinghi hand drums and the Jamaican gospel-inspired harmony of Marcia Griffiths, Judy Mowatt, and Rita Marley. From the opening bars of "Rebel Music," a whining harmonica introduces itself as the featured sound of the blues on this classic Bob Marley track. Lee Jaffe's purring harmonica places its stamp by negotiating the crevices of space between Marley's vocal, Tyrone Downie's atmospheric organ, and the Barretts' rollicking rhythms. Anderson's guitar chords, given much less room here than Jaffe, noodle around the track's roots rhythms until they are allowed the opportunity to present an understated, yet uplifting blues solo.

On most of Bob Marley's Island studio albums, the listener can detect a certain musical concept, a creative way of expressing the reggae that provides nourishment to the album's lyrics. *Rastaman Vibration* operates within a musical framework of stripped-down dub-style rhythms in which Carly Barrett's militant snare and petulant drum rolls tussle with his brother Aston's menacing bottom-heavy bass on tracks such as "Positive Vibration," "Roots Rock Reggae," "Want More," "Crazy Baldhead," and "War." *Kaya* features keyboards and a lot of brassy Latin-inspired horns—in fact, it is the first Wailers album to actually credit its trombone, saxophone, and trumpet players. The first half of *Exodus*, with dub-laden tracks such as the haunting "Natural Mystic" sounds like it belongs thematically and musically to *Rastaman Vibration*. The second half of *Exodus*, with tracks such as "Jamming" and "Three Little Birds," prominently featuring keyboards, could just as easily have incorporated *Kaya*'s title track and "Easy Skanking."

Kaya is an interesting album in terms of how it sounds. The first five tracks "Easy Skanking," "Kaya," "Is This Love," "Sun Is Shining," and "Satisfy My Soul" are given a bright and bubbly pop-style sound mix, seasoned with sweet horn harmony, courtesy of saxophonist Glen DaCosta, trumpet player David Madden, and talented trombonist Vin Gordon.

Most of these songs were originally recorded and produced by Lee Perry. The Lee Perry originals avoided joyful upbeat horns and instead delivered ominous bass lines energized by serpentine keyboard and melodica riffs. The rugged reggae on the originals, and the way the lyrics were voiced, seemed intentionally incongruous with the words of these love songs in a way that expressed a raw hungry feel. The Island versions are songs of exile, recordings reworked when Marley was living in England after the assassination attempt on his life. They were love songs that also allowed Marley, no longer a resident of the ghetto, to reflect, in a mellow frame of mind, on his love for the island nation of his birth. The Lee Perry versions were far from mellow musically; they conveyed Marley's mindset as a man of limited means still living the rough existence of the ghetto. On "Sun Is Shining," for example, Marley spits the words "sun is shining, weather is sweet"[8] as if he is talking about a dark dreary thunderstorm. The music and Marley's vocal on the original versions seem to tell us that the weather may have been sweet, but ghetto life remained bitter. That is a contributing reason why the early '70s roots reggae dancehall–style music of the Lee Perry–produced "Sun Is Shining" and "Don't Rock My Boat" (renamed "Satisfy My Soul" for the *Kaya* album) was much more raw, much darker than the poppish production quality of the Island versions.

The second half of *Kaya* shifts tone. Marley's vocal on "She's Gone" reflects the tragic sentiment of the lyrics despite the insistence of employing a bright sound-mix. "Crisis," with its initial bass bluster, dramatic guitar chords, and Marley's singing spiced with jazz-like vocal improvisation certainly has different intentions than the album's main sonic theme. "Running Away," possibly the best track on *Kaya* from a lyrical *and* musical perspective, opens with a mournful piano, sheepish hi-hat trap-drum signatures, and slow-paced bass chords that create a moody and reflective rhythmic backdrop. Marley's haunting vocal offers an introspective mix of talk and singing that perfectly complements the song's psychoanalytical words. The horn arrangements for saxophone, trumpet, and trombone on "Running Away" convincingly convey the emotion of the song's sadness and anxiety. In particular, Vin Gordon's moaning trombone underscores Marley's troubled vocal by delivering a solo that conveys a deep sense of melancholy and pain.

Musically, *Kaya*'s "Time Will Tell" track is all about guitarist Julian "Junior" Marvin's delicate twelve-string folk styling that dutifully consoles Alvin "Seeco" Patterson's sombre hand drumming. Another outstanding example of "Junior" Marvin's lead-

Peter Tosh at Convocation Hall, Toronto, March 1979.
Photographs by Isobel Harry.

guitar work is that economical, crying, blues-rock wail he creates for the visceral solo on the *Exodus* track "Waiting in Vain." In many ways, however, it is Tyrone Downie's keyboard work on *Exodus* that sets a tone and mood that breathes character into the collection of tunes contained on that album. On "Jamming," for example, Downie's keyboard speaks in accents of bouncy organ tones and jazzy acoustic piano grooves that paint vibrant colours over the song's laid-back rhythm. Downie's atmospheric introduction to "Waiting in Vain" establishes the song's pensive mood. His fun-filled organ sounds define the delightful "Three Little Birds'" intended playful pop feel.

The *Exodus* title track is all about the primacy of a smouldering, densely layered groove; a compelling groove that seems to knit together all the sounds of each of the band's instrumentalists without anyone taking centre stage. A clipped horn harmony fanfare and the controlled wails of Marvin's lead guitar add fuel to a groove peppered with hand drums and powered by steady rocking, but understated combination of trap drums and bass. This infectious groove insists that the listener imagine the journey expressed by the hook of the song that speaks of the movement of *Jah people*. Even in that polyrhythmic context, Downie makes his instrument reasonably conspicuous especially in the song's musical intro, which opens with scratchy rhythm-guitar sounds, repeated like an echo, infiltrated by Downie's popping bubbly keyboard injections flavoured with a cluster of distinguished chords sounding like they emanate from a grand piano.

Survival and *Uprising*, the last two studio albums released by Island while Bob Marley was still alive, are in many ways a musical departure from the Wailers' previous work. The music on these albums reflects the sound of an expanded band format that was less concerned with guitar or keyboard soloing. It seemed to favour creative ways of constructing different kinds of reggae grooves. This musical approach had a lot to do with the way in which Marley expanded the Wailers at that time.

Prior to the recording of *Survival*, the Wailers studio band included a variety of lead guitarists: Peter Tosh and the psychedelic rock flavour of American Wayne Perkins on *Catch a Fire*, Peter Tosh on *Burnin'*, Al Anderson on *Natty Dread*, "Junior" Marvin on *Exodus* and *Kaya*, and African-American blues specialist Donald Kinsey and Jamaican Earl "Chinna" Smith on *Rastaman Vibration*.

Perkins' appearance on *Catch a Fire* and the presence of Smith and Kinsey on *Rastaman Vibration* were really like special-guest performances, as none of these guitarists became permanent Wailers band members.

For the recording of *Survival*, the Wailers studio band boasted two permanent lead guitarists "Junior" Marvin and Al Anderson, who reunited with the band. Earl "Wia" Lindo, who had not been a part of the Wailers since *Burnin'*, also returned to the band joining Tyrone Dowie as a second keyboard player. The Wailers experience was now reshaped, in studio and on stage, into a configuration boasting two quality lead guitarists and two keyboardists, in addition to the core rhythm section of Aston "Family Man" Barrett, his brother Carly, and percussionist Alvin "Seeco" Patterson. Trombonist Ronald "Nambo" Robinson and Dean "Youth Sax" Fraser on saxophone were also brought in to add their talents to the *Survival* album, while DaCosta and Madden became part of the Wailers band in studio and in concert.

The band's expansion and Marley's constant quest to use creative sonic textures in his reggae, made these albums different in the way each instrument was arranged—the way each instrument was apportioned in the sound mix. *Survival*'s rhythmic foundation can be found in the rumble of a fat bass integrated with steady nyabinghi drumming that expresses, in music, the album's themes of Black liberation and the centrality of Africa. One important distinction of *Uprising* is the deliciously elaborate musical introductions on almost every track, particularly "We and Dem," "Work," and "Zion Train." *Uprising*'s final track, "Redemption Song," does not take advantage of the Wailers' expanded band format. In fact, the song has none of the obvious musical trademarks of reggae. No bass, no one-drop trap drumming, no *cheng-eh, cheng-eh* guitars, or bubbly keyboards excite this tune. It features just Marley's voice and his acoustic guitar, and seems like a Bob Dylan–style folk song. But reggae is an important part of the tune. Although Marley's guitar playing offers a hint of mento, it is the way he uses a Jamaican accent to trace the song's melody that gives the tune reggae attitude. The way in which Bob Marley voices "Redemption Song" allows him to seduce the folk form into surrendering to the charms of the reggae aesthetic.

A complete focus on Bob Marley as someone whose most important work was about social protest and revolution is just as shortsighted as attempts to categorize Marley as mainly a purveyor of romance and love. His songwriting investigated a variety of themes with the same depth and passion as his songs about romance or protest including themes of spirituality and Rasta theology as found in songs like "Natural Mystic" and "I Know." In the song "Running Away" from the 1978 album *Kaya*, Bob Marley crafts a particularly outstanding work with a different thematic perspective that combines understated social commentary with poignant self-analysis. This song is an introspective meditation on Marley's departure from Jamaica following the assassination attempt on his life. The lyrics reveal much more than a slice of autobiography. It captures Marley's self-analytical, reflective frame of mind as it expresses how his identity is intertwined with the social problems in the land of his birth through the brilliant line: "You running and you running but you can't run away from yourself."[9]

In "Running Away," Marley responds to the critics of his self-imposed exile through a narrative that illustrates his mental anguish in pitting his instinct to survive against a choice to either remain or take flight from the conditions and characters that threatened his life. The song's words "Every man thinketh his burden is heaviest" provide a sense that Marley is working through some serious issues. While the lines "You must have done something wrong / why you can't find where you belong" reflect a sense of longing and alienation regarding his inability to return to his homeland. "Running Away"'s sharpest response to critics of his exile are found in the following lyrics: "... I'm not running away, don't say that ... I've got to protect my life." The unwritten real-life epilogue to the song witnesses Marley's return to Jamaica several months later for the One Love Peace Concert.

A total of nine Bob Marley–penned romantic love songs appear on only three of the eight studio albums that the Wailers recorded for Island Records between 1972 and 1980. *Catch a Fire* includes "Baby We've Got a Date," "Kinky Reggae," and "Stir It Up." *Rastaman Vibration* has "Cry to Me." *Exodus* features "Waiting in Vain" and "Turn Your Lights Down Low." *Kaya*, the album most associated with love songs, contains three: "She's Gone," "Is This Love," and "Satisfy My Soul." Four of those nine songs are included on *Legend*, a compilation that has been marketed quite aggressively since Marley's passing in 1981. This marketing strategy has created the impression, among certain listeners, that Marley is more lover than rebel.

The truth is that the overwhelming bulk of Marley's work is engaged in various kinds of social commentary. In fact, some of the more outstanding Wailers' Island studio albums such as *Catch a Fire*, *Natty Dread*, and *Survival* were noted for their rebellious themes and music. On the other hand, *Kaya*—which was seen as an album of ballads, if not a work of mainly love songs—was not well received at the time of its initial release, neither by rock critics in Britain and the United States nor by fans in Jamaica. An acclaimed album such as *Exodus* may have been noted for the wonderfully performed "Waiting in Vain," but the album's success was also driven by the popularity of its title track about repatriation to "our father's land" from the African diaspora and the spirituality of "Natural Mystic," as opposed to straight-forward romantic love song "Turn Your Lights Down Low" or the playful "Three Little Birds."

Romantic love songs may constitute a small section of the Bob Marley Island Records catalogue, but their significance resides in the way some of them were crafted. "Waiting in Vain," for example, does not conform to a simple boy-meets-girl, girl-falls-in-love-with-boy romantic love song format. Although told from the man's viewpoint, the song is really about a woman determining the path of a relationship on her own terms. We are told that she, for reasons not mentioned in the song's lyrics, is unable to return the man's romantic intentions. The man's narrative clearly depicts his love for the woman to the extent that he is willing to wait. He tells us through the lyrics that "It's been three years since I'm knocking on your door."[10] This indicates that he is a very patient man and that his efforts to win the woman's love may possibly be futile. The lines "Tears in my eyes burn / While I'm waiting for my turn" suggest he is pained by the woman's other romantic relationships. The interesting thing about the story told in "Waiting in Vain" is that as listeners, we are not quite sure of the true personalities of the characters depicted in the song. Is she just spiteful and uncaring? Or is she completely justified in spurning his affection because of past history? On the other hand, is he really emotionally wounded by the rejection? Or is he using this as a ruse to win her affection?

Kaya's "She's Gone" opens with the tragic declaration: "My woman is gone."[11] The song's male character is moved to tears by the woman's departure, but the note she leaves hanging on the door clearly explains why she must move on. In many ways, this song is the opposite of "Waiting In Vain" in the sense that it discusses the woman's motives in detail. We are told that the woman feels imprisoned and under pressure in the relationship. While it can still be argued that "She's Gone" is written from the man's viewpoint, it is clear that Marley is able to write a multi-dimensional female character. In "She's Gone," Marley skillfully illustrates the complexities of why a woman may opt to leave a relationship. This is a mature piece of writing that is distinct from many of Marley's song narratives about women.

"Is This Love" is another interesting, atypical, romantic love song penned by Marley that portrays a man of limited means who does not have much to offer in terms of luxury and material possessions. He offers only love, the humility of a single bed, and food provided by the grace of Jah.

Songs such as "No Woman No Cry," "Johnny Was," and "Pimper's Paradise" all discuss the plight of women in non-romantic contexts. As discussed earlier, "Johnny Was" and "No Woman No Cry" depict women caught in the web of poverty or violence of the urban ghetto. *Uprising*'s "Pimper's Paradise" is, in a sense, a departure for Marley in its judgemental accusatory attitude towards a woman who smokes weed, indulges in cocaine, and generally parties and has a good time. The refrain "pimper's paradise" suggests that the woman is a whore involved in questionable sexual escapades. In a tone of pity, the lyrics describe the woman of "Pimper's Paradise" as a victim, which suggests that her redemption may be possible. The song's hint of redemption cannot save itself from its rather nasty attack on the woman's character. A curious and hypocritical attack when it is considered that Bob Marley himself was fairly open about his weed smoking and his womanizing. If the lyrics are assessed in the context of Marley's behaviour, then the message seems to be that women should not have the freedom to indulge these "vices" as opposed to the idea that these practices are morally incorrect for everyone. In this sense, the lyrics take on a kind of sexist edge. The song's narrative appears to be out of character for Bob Marley's compositions about women written during the Island years, when his songwriting matured and fermented. Marley's songs composed during that period were usually more thoughtful and sensitive to issues facing women. The overall thematic mood of *Uprising* may have reflected Marley's frame of mind as he battled the cancer that began its own nasty attack on his body.

Bob Marley was not perfect, but he was someone who really cared. His care extended beyond just simply writing lyrics and singing songs about injustice. He cared enough to return to Jamaica—after an assassination attempt on his life—for the cause of a peace that he understood may have only meant, if only for a brief moment of history, that some lives of poor ghetto residents might be spared.

It is April 1978, and the One Love Peace Concert is in progress. Many high-profile Jamaican reggae artists such as Dennis Brown, Jacob Miller, Althea and Donna, Big Youth and Ras Michael, and the Sons of Negus sing, drum, chant, and deejay for peace. The lighting to illuminate the specially constructed stage in the National Stadium is poor, particularly for those individuals seated in the stadium's grandstand and bleachers sections. The chairs reserved for politicians, including PNP prime minister Michael Manley, JLP leader of the opposition Edward Seaga, other VIPs such as Mick Jagger and Keith Richards of the Rolling Stones, plus the international press were situated on the stadium soccer pitch at stage level that provided much better sight lines.

Reggae superstars Peter Tosh and Bob Marley are scheduled to appear as the last two performers of the concert. Peter Tosh steps onto the stage and takes command of it like a man on a mission to present the case of injustices inflicted on African-Jamaicans over the past four hundred years. Tosh articulates the details of race and class oppression on the island, while he points a proverbial accusatory finger at Manley and Seaga who sit in the second row in front of the stage. Peter Tosh the "Steppin' Razor" "... drape up / two top-ranking politishan / one wid 'im left han' / the other wid 'im right / Then head buck dem with a torrent of truth / Not about peace / just equal rights and justice."[12]

Bob Marley's One Love Peace Concert gesture is just as historic and controversial. As the Wailers' set winds down during a relentless rendition of "Jamming," Marley sings a diplomatic plea that becomes more urgent, forceful, and demanding as it is repeated: "Show the people that you mean them right, show the people they should unite." Marley marries that suggestion to a tactful offer to Jamaican prime minister Michael Manley and leader of the opposition Edward Seaga that was impossible to refuse in front of the thousands gathered: "Come up on stage, right here ... shake hands, show the people (that you mean it)."[13]

After more coaxing and encouraging by Marley, Edward Seaga then Michael Manley flank the reggae icon. Seaga stands to Marley's left and Manley to his right. The odd gathering of this trio assumes an even more bizarre dimension when armed henchmen, who are the unofficial bodyguards of the political leaders, join the three principals on stage. Bob Marley's goal is to show grassroots Jamaicans that the leaders they are willing to fight and die for can put aside their differences and at least shake hands. Manley and Seaga are very tentative about making any gestures of unity. But in front of their partisan supporters, the forces of anti-political tribalism, and the international press, they have no alternative but to accept the hand of the Trench Town Rastaman who is about to force them to clasp each other's right hand. Creating an image captured for posterity in photographs and on video, Marley hoists the joined right hands of Manley and Seaga over his head. Almost simultaneously, Marley thrusts his free right arm straight at the audience—palm up, fingers pointed at the sky. With this metaphoric body language, Marley seems to be commanding the violence and disunity to stop dead in its tracks.

The One Love Peace Concert, Peter Tosh's animated critique of injustice, and Marley's symbolic unifying of Jamaica's political leaders were events that actually marked the beginning of the end for the peace process. Jamaican politics of the '70s could not coexist within an environment of peace. If Jamaica began to take on the characteristics of a "banana republic" during the '70s, it did so as a nation struggling with its identity as an island within the United States' sphere of influence. Left-of-centre and radical critics pointed to CIA intervention, while the pro-U.S. right-wing perspective claimed that Cubans interfered in the island's affairs.

The Wailers' concert lighting technician, Neville Garrick, whose art decorated some of the Wailers' album covers, has commented that the image at the One Love Peace Concert of Marley standing between Manley and Seaga was like the Dread between the two thieves. Garrick's comparison, intended as a "Christ-on-the-cross-flanked-by-two-thieves" analogy, is more appropriate than he may have realized in the sense that the peace was crucified, killed off, in favour of the most vicious and bloody election violence imaginable in Jamaica; an election that voted the JLP into power in 1980. Peter Tosh's mantra promoting equality and justice, as opposed to an empty unsubstantial peace proved deeply prophetic.

Despite the short-lived peace—the brief cessation of political tribalism in the ghettos of Kingston for a few months in 1977 and 1978—the importance of a Rastafari reggae singer named Bob Marley, acting as a broker for peace in a climate of violence that almost took his life only two years before, cannot be diminished or devalued in any way.

Rain a Fall, Dutty Tuff

The Relationship between Louise Bennett's Mento Verse and Bob Marley's Reggae Poetry

Bob Marley's lyrics assume the form of quality reggae poetry. In "Concrete Jungle," Marley's poetry employs a vivid metaphor to describe the Jamaican ghetto sufferer's experience when he tells us that neither the sun nor moon smiles in the ghetto. Without using words like "unemployment," "money," "poverty," and "exploitation," Bob Marley accurately depicts how ghetto residents subsist in the concrete jungle: "No chains around my feet, but I'm not free."[1] Marley tells us that life and love—two fundamental human requirements—cannot be found in the concrete jungle.

"Concrete Jungle" is about the ghetto in Jamaica, or the ghetto in any country, as seen through the eyes of someone who faces its daily tribulation. The immediacy of Marley's words and the poignant images they sketch are directly connected to Marley's own experience as a resident of Trench Town—one of Jamaica's worst concrete-jungle ghetto communities.

Bob Marley's poetry is immersed in Jamaican language and Jamaican proverbs. The lyrical verse of Marley's "Talkin' Blues" tells the universal story of a homeless character. Unlike "Concrete Jungle," "Talkin' Blues" is told in the first person using Jamaican language: "I've been down on the rock for so long / I seem to wear a permanent screw."[2] The "screw" to which Marley refers is a term used by Jamaicans, particularly in the '60s and '70s, which meant the contorted facial expression of an exaggerated frown—an expression that twists a face into a grimace of destitution and anger. A *screwface* evolves naturally as a response to the pressure of abject poverty. It often becomes the mask of rebellion. Marley underscores this rebellion by having the homeless character of "Talkin' Blues" spit angry words about blowing up the churches of lying preachers and joining freedom fighters when the revolution is in process. "Talkin' Blues" does not contain any easy sloganeering, but it employs the use of Jamaican language to provide depth of meaning to the song's poetry.

Bob Marley's use of Jamaican language was as political and rebellious as his themes of revolution and liberation. This is because sections of the island's upper-class elite and elements of the Jamaican middle-class opposed, and continue to oppose, the use of Jamaican language in favour of the "proper" English of the colonial "mother country"—Britain. When Jamaica won its independence from Britain in 1962, its political independence and especially its economic independence was still very much a work-in-progress. In arts and culture, particularly in the popular music of ska, lower-class Jamaicans seized and directed their own cultural destiny. They fundamentally changed the way Jamaica and the world related to a vibrant creative African-Jamaican culture fiercely independent of Britain and critical of slavery, colonialism, and post-colonial class and race disparities. The bold conscious use of Jamaica's rich language, folklore, and musical traditions by Bob Marley and many other roots reggae artists, during the '60s and '70s, represented a post-colonial identity for African-Jamaicans and, in fact, all Jamaicans.

Many of the songwriters of the roots reggae era including Marley, drew directly from the reservoir of rich African-Jamaican poetic wordplay that had been defended and nurtured by Louise Bennett, the godmother of Jamaica's folklore during the thirty years leading up to the island's independence from colonial rule. Bennett, in many ways, gave that initial post-colonial roots reggae generation permission to be proud of Jamaican language and its poetic usage.

Jamaican language has evolved as a mix of English, the island's colonizing language, and African, the language of Africans brought to Jamaica through the Atlantic slave trade. This unique combination of English and African words tempered by the retention of African grammar and syntax was spoken with an accent similar to the rhythm of mento, a Jamaican form of calypso, from at least the early twentieth century until the '60s. The musicality of Jamaican language, the rhythm with which it is spoken, has evolved in step with the constantly changing rhythms of Jamaican popular music. Bob Marley's reggae poetry, in some ways, is like the post-colonial successor to Bennett's mento poetry. Bennett, more than any other individual, is responsible for maintaining a foundation for the language and poetry of the peasant and working-class Jamaican. In its own way, Bennett's poetry rebelled against colonialism in form as well as in its often-revolutionary political content.

Louise Bennett.

Some of the best poetry Louise Bennett wrote in the '40s and '50s are collected in the anthology *Jamaica Labrish: Jamaica Dialect Poems.* The themes of many of these poems reflect issues characteristic of the time. Poems like "Invasion" and "Italy Fall" documented Jamaican reactions to events of the Second World War. The aborted attempt at a federation of the islands that constitute the West Indies is discussed in the poem "Dear Departed Federation." "Jamaica Ant'em" grapples with some issues involving Jamaica's struggle for independence from colonial rule.

Some Bennett poems from this collection exhibit a clear thematic affinity with the post-colonial Black Power and Black-liberation poetry of a new generation of Jamaican poets and reggae artists who emerged during the '60s and '70s. The poem "Pinnacle" was also the name of a Rasta community established in the hills of St. Catherine, a parish to the immediate west of Kingston, the island's capital city. In those days, Rastafari was a despised, oppressed, anti-colonial movement.

The Pinnacle settlement existed for over a decade and a half as a community separate from mainstream society. In the early '50s, the Jamaican government used the police to finally destroy Pinnacle after several earlier attempts. The poem describes the negative and brutal attitude of the authorities towards the Rasta movement, using a particular Rastaman's story during an earlier police raid of the settlement. The final verses of "Pinnacle" express a sincere empathy for the man and his Rasta aspirations and dreams. These sentiments of empathy are quite revolutionary considering the poem was written in the '40s, at least two decades before more positive depictions of Rasta reached critical mass. It was not until the '60s that positive sentiments about the movement began to seep into the consciousness of the Caribbean mainstream through the work of high-profile Rasta poets such as Bongo Jerry and poetic Rasta lyricists such as Bob Marley.

Louise Bennett's "Colour Bar" tackles the perennial Jamaican preoccupations with race and racial bias on an island where, to many, brown, red, fair, or White skin colour still denote superiority or social advantage in relation to darker shades of Black skin. In this poem, Bennett's words read like a prelude to the viewpoint of the militant Black Power and radical Rastafari movements of '60s Jamaica. Bennett accomplishes this with her reference to Jamaicans as having African ancestors and her observation of some Jamaicans who refuse to be classified as White. The final militant line of the poem invokes the fire imagery—usually employed by Rastafari—to depict racism's destruction as the burning down of the colour bar.

In "Bans O' Ooman!" Bennett discusses the launch of the Jamaican Federation of Women, which the poem tells us was open to women of all classes and races. In "Registration," Bennett documents the campaign of the federation to register bachelor fathers who the poem implies do not meet the responsibilities of their children. With these poems, Bennett provides not only a sense of the tradition of Jamaican women seeking rights and freedom from gender discrimination, but also her own support for the cause. Although the Rasta and Black Power movements in Jamaica were very much male-centric, it was left to talented female poets of the '70s and '80s such as Jean Breeze and Lillian Allen, and innovative roots reggae lyricists such as Judy Mowatt and Marcia Aitken to

Bob Marley at Maple Leaf Gardens, Toronto, November 1979.
Photograph by Isobel Harry.

revisit the struggle of Black Jamaican women with feminist verse and an activist tone that shares a kinship with Bennett's poetry.

"Bans O' Killing," possibly Bennett's most militant and aggressive poem, carries within it the pain and burden of having to consistently oppose the constant attacks from several critics voicing the ideology of the colonial status quo in its attempts to invalidate Jamaican language and, by extension, African-Jamaican culture as a whole. "Bans O' Killing," written early in Bennett's career in 1944, demonstrates her "early sense of purpose and literary courage," as Jamaican sociologist and cultural critic Professor Rex Nettleford accurately describes. The poem is a brilliant polemic that begins its response to the critics of Jamaican language like this: "So yuh a de man ... say yuh gwine kill dialect." Bennett's incisive verse places "proper" English under the microscope of historical analysis revealing that the English language, revered by these critics, is built on a latticework of dialects. She informs the critics that to kill Jamaican dialect they must first put to death fundamental aspects of English: "Yu wi haffi kill de Lancashire / De Yorkshire, de Cockney ... Yuh wi haffe tear ... out Chaucer, Burns ... an plenty Shakespeare (and) ... ef yuh drop a 'h' yuh mighta haffe kill yuhself."[3]

"Bans O' Killing" is not simply a polemic or an eloquent defence of Jamaican language, but, as Nettleford suggests, the poem represents Bennett's belief in "the power of the language she uses to express the essential passions of the people's heart."[4] This belief, and its centrality in Jamaican culture, is at the core of Bennett's legacy.

If Bennett championed the rights and culture of African-Jamaicans as a significant cultural figure on the island, then Marcus Garvey was a champion of Black culture as an important political activist during the colonial era. Garvey, maybe the most influential Jamaican political leader of the twentieth century, returned to Jamaica in 1927 from the United States where he built the Universal Negro Improvement Association (UNIA), possibly the largest African-American organization of its kind. Garvey's ideology, which guided the UNIA and his activities in Jamaica, was Afrocentric, promoted pride in the Black race, and economic self-reliance. Garvey's activities in Jamaica reached their peak between 1929 and 1934. During these years, he organized the anti-colonial quasi-socialist People's Political Party. Garvey's philosophy on race, class, and Africa had a profound influence on the Black Power and Rastafari movements of '60s Jamaica and the lyrics of reggae artists like Bob Marley and Burning Spear.

Louise Bennett was not the only poet with an impact on the language and politics of post-colonial poets in the Caribbean. The verse that Edward Kamau Brathwaite published in the '60s was a vital component of post-colonial Black Liberation in Caribbean poetry of that time. Brathwaite influenced various dub poets in the Caribbean diaspora. Dub poets emerged in the early '70s as spoken-word artists writing and performing a certain kind of reggae poetry. Jamaican dub poet Mikey Smith associated with Brathwaite, while dub poets such as British-Jamaican Linton Kwesi Johnson, Antiguan-Canadian Clifton Joseph, and Jamaican-Canadian Afua Cooper have indicated that they were inspired by Brathwaite's poetry. Born in Barbados, Brathwaite—a historian, in addition to being a groundbreaking poet, who taught in Jamaica at the University of the West Indies for several decades—used a jazz voice as the initial vehicle to communicate his poetry. Bennett's major contribution to poetry in Jamaica and the Caribbean diaspora distinguishes itself from the contribution of someone like Brathwaite because her work expressed the social concerns of grass roots African-Jamaicans using the people's own language, wit, humour, and irony submerged in the indigenous rhythm of mento.

It is true that Louise Bennett did not invent Jamaican language or its spicy metaphors and proverbs, but she must be credited for elevating it to an art form. Bennett's formal education, which included studies at the Royal Academy of Dramatic Arts in the U.K. during the late '40s and early '50s, was placed in the service of her research, documentation, creative writing, and performance involving Jamaican language. She taught drama in Jamaica at social welfare agencies and at the University of the West Indies. Her ongoing research of Jamaican folklore took the form of discussions and close interaction with grassroots communities across rural Jamaica. She collected and documented words, phrases, verse, stories, songs, and ring games, dating back several generations, that were passed down through the African-Jamaican oral tradition. One of Bennett's greatest achievements was her ability to crystallize the fruits of her research into the art of poetry, storytelling, plays, and pantomimes *and* communicate them through performance to the broadest cross-section of Jamaicans. This communication assumed the form of spoken-word performance on radio, television, and in pantomimes mounted in theatres accessible to grassroots Jamaicans. Through this ubiquitous activity, Bennett assumed an omnipresent persona of gigantic proportions. In other words, Bennett's popularity at the grassroots level was huge in the immediate post-independence decades. It was virtually impossible for a child to grow up in Jamaica during the '50s, '60s, and '70s and not be intimately familiar with Bennett's work in creating art out of the people's language. As a result, the roots reggae generation of poets and songwriters, during their youth, breathed in Bennett's verse like oxygen. Whether or not these poets and songwriters were consciously aware of Bennett's influence, her work was a natural part of their cultural makeup.

This post-colonial roots reggae generation of poets and songwriters used verse and lyrics to trace gritty stories about their own lives, about the lives of their contemporaries, and about social issues on the island. In many ways, these stories updated Bennett's work for a new age: the *rude bwoy* as gunman in the Slickers' reggae recording "Johnny You Too Bad" echoes Bennett's poem "Dead Man"; the uplifting portrayal of Rastafari in Bob Marley's

"Positive Vibration" can be linked to "Pinnacle"; and the discussion of racism and exploitation in Bob Andy compositions such as "Unchained Melody" and "Fire Burning" can be related to "Colour Bar." Furthermore, the examination of the struggles of Black Jamaican women as they rebelled against slavery in the lyrics of Judy Mowatt's recording "Black Woman," as they survived rape in Lillian Allen's dub poem "Nellie Belly Swelly," and as they negotiated mental illness in the roots reggae verse of Jean Breeze's "Riddym Ravings" find a kinship with Bennett's "Bans O' Ooman!" and "Registration."

There were occasions when Bennett's poetry of the pre-independence period reached into the future and embraced a postcolonial reggae aesthetic in theme and rhythmic metre. Although written several decades before reggae's birth, sections of Bennett's poem "Dutty Tough," particularly the first and last verses, possess a rhythmic metre that seemed more in line with a steady nyabinghi Rasta hand drum beat. Bennett's reading of these parts of the poem is not couched in the "sing-song" tones of mento but in the halting haunting speech patterns that produce a much more ominous tone than usual—a tone that predicts the attitude of the dub poet. "Dutty Tough"'s opening line: "Sun-a-shine but tings noh bright"[5] is echoed in the lyrics of Bob Marley's "Concrete Jungle": "No sun will shine in my day today."[6] Comparatively, the lines: "A rain a fall but dutty tuff / A pot a cook but the yood (food) noh nuff"[7] in Bob Marley's "Them Belly Full (But We Hungry)" are a rearrangement and update of two lines from "Dutty Tough": "Rain a-fall but dutty tuff / Doah pot a-bwile, bickle noh nuff."[8] Louise Bennett's poetry not only serves as sustenance for reggae but is also one of its integral building blocks providing the very language with which it communicates.

It is difficult to say whether Marley's lyrics would have been very different without the existence of Louise Bennett. Bob Marley, however, constantly sampled Jamaican folklore in his compositions, folklore harvested and promoted by Louise Bennett. On 1964's "Simmer Down," the Wailers' first Jamaican hit single, Marley uses a number of unique Jamaican proverbs including "chicken merry hawk de near" and "sweet nanny goat ah go run yuh belly"[9] (literally: sweet goat mutton will give you diarrhea) both meaning that joy can quickly transform to fear and sorrow. Near the end of his career, on 1979's *Survival* album, despite his

Bob Marley at Maple Leaf Gardens, Toronto, November 1979.
Photograph by Isobel Harry.

international status, Bob Marley's recordings still plundered the colourful selection of grassroots proverbs at his disposal. The track "Wake Up and Live" also deploys a variety of Jamaican proverbs including "one-one coco full basket,"[10] conveying the idea that patience is a virtue or, more specifically, patient step-by-step saving or work towards a goal is virtuous.

The lyrics of roots reggae, reggae-influenced poetry, and dub poetry all cribbed from the speech of Rastafari. This Rasta-talk—a derivative of Jamaican language—increased its rebellion against standard English by a deconstruction of certain English words to create new ones. The phrase "I and I" is a profound expression that identifies the dialectic between the individual and the collective. In simple terms, "I and I" can mean "us" or "we" or the spiritual unity of individuals and the creator. "Ital" is moulded from "vital," but means something that is wholesome and healthy, like salt-free vegetarian food for example. "Irie" means nice, positive, uplifting. Rasta-talk began as a form of communication among Rastafari, but eventually many of the words and phrases of this speech became integrated into Jamaican language and accepted by the larger Jamaican population by the '60s. Rasta-talk, particularly its use in chants and poetry, was spoken in the rhythm of the Rasta nyabinghi hand drum. The rhythm of Rasta-talk teased out a tone of speech much more uncompromising, rebellious, and messianic than a mento tone.

As the post-colonial generation looked for a new version of Jamaican language to express their poetry and lyric writing, Louise Bennett's work remained the foundation, while Rasta-talk, Rasta chants, and Rasta poetry were a vital component, a bridge to that new post-colonial voice of reggae and reggae-influenced poetry. The '60s verse of someone like Rasta poet Robin "Bongo Jerry" Small not only promotes the Black Power politics of its time, but also establishes a clear voice of Rasta speech: "right, now I and I underfed / no clothes, no food, not even a draw to get red / Dem want I dead? / Going dread / Dread / But mus'."[11]

The Rasta influence on grassroots poetic traditions as demonstrated in that verse from Bongo Jerry's poem "Sooner or Later" is post-Bennett but pre–roots reggae. "Sooner or Later" was published in December 1970 when reggae was barely two years old and dub poetry was at least two or three years away from its gestation period. In theme and voice, poems like this one drew from the energy of early reggae. At the same time it pointed the way to a new poetry, speaking in a modernized Jamaican language and consciously immersed in the rhythms and social commentary themes of roots reggae.

The work of gifted Jamaican dub poet Mikey Smith, who died in 1983, brings together the influences of Louise Bennett and Rasta, while crafting verse that was fresh, innovative, and relevant to the concerns of the roots reggae generation. Take, for example, the powerful opening verse of Smith's poem "I an I Alone": "I an I alone / a trod through creation / Babylon on I right, Babylon on I lef / Babylon in front of I an Babylon behind I / I an I alone in the middle / like a Goliath wid a slingshot."[12] Smith uses the Rasta term "Babylon"—meaning exploitation and oppression or an imperialist power—as a character and constructs a kind of imposing claustrophobic scenario built with Rasta terms and phrases and seasoned with strong Biblical references. In "Me Cyaan Believe It," Smith borrows the line: "(Oh) what a night" from the mento song "Carry Mi Ackee (Go Linstead Market)" and riffs on it like a jazz improviser to produce verse—with Louise Bennett–style mento undertones—that really converse in a flurry of reggae bass lines: "what a night what a plight / an we cyaan get a bite / me life is a stiff fight / and me cyaan believe it."[13]

Although Louise Bennett has been referenced as a clear influence on dub poetry, there is evidence to suggest that Bennett's legacy has infiltrated the lyrics of roots reggae and dancehall reggae. Like the current crop of dancehall deejays—as rappers are known in the reggae world—who have reintroduced mento into the rhythm of the language and use traditional folklore phrases in a way that gives them a fresh new spin, Bennett's poetry is also designed to create excitement through humour and its overblown sketches of the day-to-day existence of its audiences. Like the art forms that it has impacted, Bennett's writing offers insightful commentary on how the Jamaican psychology grapples with social inequality. Like Bennett, Bob Marley's poetic lyrics and Jamaican music's golden age of '70s roots reggae have had a crucial influence on Caribbean novelists like Colin Channer and Michael Thelwell and on reggae poets such as Kwame Dawes and Lorna Goodison.

Lorna Goodison's poetry is directly related to the Louise Bennett tradition, but carries within it the creative and political edge nurtured by artists of the initial post-colonial generation, born in the '40s, who came of age in the '60s. In that sense, Goodison is an artistic contemporary of Bob Marley and other important roots reggae lyricists like Bob Andy. If Bennett heard mento when she was constructing her verse, Goodison hears ska in her poem "For Don Drummond," rocksteady in "Upon a Quarter Million" and "What We Carried With Us," and roots reggae and dub in "Jah Music." These Goodison poems are not just about music, but they skillfully demonstrate how the music must be referenced to make her discussion about the condition of grassroots African-Jamaicans more meaningful.

The verse of Kwame Dawes—a poet born in the post-independence period of the early '60s—is significantly inspired by the poetic lyrics of Bob Marley and the roots reggae rhythms of the '70s, the era in which he came of age. Some of Dawes' poetry is concerned with the poetic quality and thematic intentions of Marley and other roots artists such as Burning Spear. Dawes' poems such as "Light Like a Feather, Heavy As Lead," and "Guiltiness, Rest on Your Conscience" eloquently riff off phrases from Bob Marley songs as they travel on a roots reggae bass line on their journey to make sense of Jamaican politics and culture, and attempt to unravel the emotional and social significance of the reggae rhythm itself.

The politics of poetic social commentary, the use of Jamaican language, and the use of the once-despised rhythms of mento and roots reggae in the metre of Caribbean poetry live an active and healthy life today because the legacies of Bob Marley and Louise Bennett remain important components within them.

Reggae Sistas' Stories
The Women of Roots Reggae

A trio of female singers, known collectively as the I-Three, occupy a section of a concert stage that is not the focus of attention. The central attraction is Bob Marley. The concert venue is packed with reggae fans who, from time to time, are pleasantly distracted by those three attractive women on the right side of the stage.

The I-Three are high-quality *brawta*. They provide the Wailers with extra, yet essential vocal flavour. The I-Three are also a visual treat for those who care to look. They wear white ankle-length dresses and multicoloured head-wraps. Rays of red (*ites*), green, and gold-yellow light wash over the stage, one colour at a time, in quick succession. The Wailers band—operating behind Marley, who acts like he owns centre stage—churn out a reggae rhythm like thick molasses, a rhythm that fills the room and intoxicates the audience. As some fans look toward stage right, they witness the magic of how the light paints the I-Three's outfits in rich Rasta hues—first *ites*, then green, then gold. Each one of the I-Three— Judy Mowatt, Rita Marley, and Marcia Griffiths—move toward their designated microphone stands using steps that are synchronized like the harmony they produce, as each of them breathe smooth vocals into separate microphones. The voices of Judy, Marcia, and Rita massage Bob Marley's lucid tenor. Their voices fabricate a harmonic tour bus that comfortably transports his soulful wail straight to Zion.

The I-Three were vital in nurturing Bob Marley's iconic persona as recording artist and live performer. They were an important element of the Wailers at a time when the band enjoyed its greatest popularity. The story of the I-Three is the story of three female vocalists nurturing and decorating the music of a man. The stories of Judy, Rita, and Marcia describe the substantive careers of three unsung female reggae pioneers whose contribution to the music is as notable, in its own way, as that of Bob Marley, Burning Spear, and Peter Tosh.

The narrative charting the course of women in reggae ferments by the time it confronts the plot lines of Mowatt, Griffiths, and Rita Marley. The story of women in Jamaican popular music begins ten years before Bob Marley recruited the I-Three. These stories begin in 1964 with the explosive introduction of a twenty-two-year-old vocalist named Millie.

Chris Blackwell, the founder of Island Records, took Millicent Small to London, England for the purpose of recording a Jamaican ska song. Millie Small's debut single, the pop-oriented "My Boy Lollipop," showcased her thin brash vocal, cooing bubble-gum lyrics: "My Boy Lollipop / you make my heart go giddy-up."[1] The record became the first international hit of a Jamaican popular music that was barely a toddler. Small's version of a 1958 rhythm and blues recording softened the edge of the more rambunctious examples of Jamaican ska, and flaunted a jagged harmonica interlude rather than a jazzy saxophone or trombone solo. During the summer of 1964, the single did "giddy-up" the British charts to #1 and occupied the #2 position on the American hit parade.

American Bob Marley biographer Timothy White has found it easy to dismiss "My Boy Lollipop" as simply a novelty tune that provided Small with fluke fame. The achievements of female artists have been routinely minimized, marginalized, or ignored by most reggae analysts, whether these achievements were novel or groundbreaking. The irrefutable fact is that a female Jamaican artist named Millie Small was the first to enjoy mainstream success on both sides of the Atlantic using the island's distinct popular music. "My Boy Lollipop" primed the British market for a batch of male singers from Jamaica including Wilfred "Jackie" Edwards, Owen Gray, and Jackie Opel, who all moved to London and developed careers there. Ernest Ranglin, guitarist and musical director on the "Lollipop" recording session, also benefited from the popularity of the tune while he was in England advancing his status as an accomplished jazz guitarist.

"Lollipop" has much deeper implications for Jamaican music's sustained international prominence over almost forty years. Six million copies of "Lollipop" were sold, making it the initial success of Chris Blackwell's Island Records. In many ways, it was the popularity of the so-called "My Boy Lollipop" "fluke" and the revenue it produced that gave Island Records the kind of profile in the British music industry that led to the signing of English rhythm and blues singer Steve Winwood and a number of major rock acts. It was the success of Millie Small's hit that eventually allowed Island Records to sign reggae stars Jimmy Cliff and Bob Marley.

Reggae women Rita Marley (left) and Marcia Griffiths (right). Undated.
Photograph by Monica DaSilva.

Small's tours of Ghana and Nigeria took her deeper into pioneer territory, which meant that she performed on the African continent before Cliff and Marley. Despite the attempt at formulaic follow-up recordings, "Sweet William" and "Oh Henry," one single defines Millie Small's career. The significance of "My Boy Lollipop" is that it represented the initial international breakthrough for Jamaican popular music.

Island Record's biggest seller before "Lollipop" was the 1962 ska recording "Housewives Choice," a single that prominently features the substantial voice of a woman named Millicent "Patsy" Todd, together with male singer Derrick Morgan in a duet credited on the record as Derrick and Patsy. The originally untitled record apparently acquired its name after being frequently requested by women on a morning show on Jamaican radio. "Housewives Choice" also became popular in U.K. nightclubs that played Jamaican music and at sound-system dances organized by Caribbean immigrants in the U.K.

Unlike "Lollipop," "Housewives Choice" delivers an edgier ska sound with its boogie-blues piano phrases and its hot saxophone solo, propelled by a feverish syncopated ska beat. Patsy packs enough emotion into her thin but muscular voice to match Derrick's earthy vocal as they each sing "I love you" lyrics to each other.

The underground success of "Housewives Choice" in England did not really alter the fact that the ska era in Jamaica was not very kind to Patsy or any female Jamaican recording artists. In those days, it was rare for women to record as solo acts. Women were mainly ghettoized as junior duet partners alongside male singers who often enjoyed solo recording careers.

Marcia Griffiths and Rita Marley both voiced their first recordings in 1964 in duet partnerships. Rita was paired with Bunny Wailer, while Marcia joined forces with Tony Gregory. Talented female singers sang on a number of popular ska recordings in the early '60s: Enid Cumberland on "Worried Over You" with Keith; Patsy Todd on "When You Call My Name" with Stranger Cole; Paulette on "Can't You See" with Delroy Wilson; Norma Fraser on "We Will Be Lovers" with Lord Creator; and Millie Small on "We'll Meet" with Roy Panton. Other important female singers involved in duets were Doreen Schaefer with Jackie Opel, and the impressive Hortense Ellis with Lascelles Perkins.

Millie Small's rise to international fame as a solo artist proved to be an exception, as the second-class status of Jamaican female singers during the ska days remained unchanged. Many of these women fought a quiet struggle to build solo careers. Some succeeded in partially opening the door to greater opportunities during the era of rocksteady, the name given to the slow, sensual, bass-driven beat that shifted the frenetic ska beat from the centre stage of Jamaican popular music in the summer of 1966.

Dawn Penn is an example of one woman who attempted to initiate a career as a solo rocksteady artist. Penn's 1967 tune "You Don't Love Me" seized whatever notice it could mainly through rotation at sound-system dancehall parties. The bass lines of this song communicate a cool and deadly sensuality as they arrive decorated with slightly echoed choppy piano riffs. Before the second drum intro is complete, Penn begins to layer the rhythm with a tense fluid vocal. She adopts an edgy tone that fuses with the bass line's evocation of dread. The lyrics of the song were typical of the material women were given to perform in those days: "You don't love me, yes I know now ... I'll do anything you say boy / If you ask me ... I'll get on my knees and pray."[2] With the assistance of a

Judy Mowatt and the I-Three, Toronto. 1984. Photograph by Isobel Harry.

hardcore dancehall rhythm, Penn sings the lyrics with such a confident and empowering style that she succeeds in gutting the intent of the tune's words about a woman prepared to grovel in front of a man who does not love or want her.

Penn re-emerged in the early '90s out of a self-imposed exile from the music scene to re-record the song. "No, No, No," the name of the reworked version, established a new life for itself as a favourite in New York City clubs. More than twenty years separated the underground dancehall popularity of "You Don't Love Me" and the hit status of its alternate personality "No, No, No." Penn spent many of those years in the Virgin Islands, away from Jamaica and away from a music business unfriendly to female artists.

Norma Fraser's journey was similar. After two successful recordings she left Jamaica for the United States. During that time, Fraser was encouraged by her parents to attend college and pursue a more conventional career path. She now holds a master's degree in gerontology. Like Penn, Fraser resumed a recording career in the early '90s following a lengthy absence from the scene. Her career began in 1961 when "We'll Be Lovers" ruled the Jamaican charts. Fraser's version of "The First Cut Is the Deepest," released in 1967, displays her melodic voice negotiating a well-crafted Jamaican interpretation of Cat Stevens' words, soaked in an animated rocksteady rhythm. "First Cut" created ripples in London, U.K. where the singer was named in one music poll as the "Best Female Newcomer." Fraser, however, discarded her career as a reggae singer for twenty years.

Patsy Todd survived the duet ghetto to make her mark as an important solo singer during the rocksteady era. Todd poured a passionate and mature vocal over two significant singles: a potent version of Miriam Makeba's South African township classic "Pata Pata," appropriately powered by the African-inspired percussion of Count Ossie's hand drum ensemble, and a gregarious rock-steady interpretation of a calypso tune "Fire in Your Wire." Both recordings earned heavy rotation on Jamaica's radio stations.

The initial solo careers of Penn, Fraser, and Todd terminated abruptly when all three departed the music scene after showing serious promise. The already small representation of women in Jamaica's music industry during the '60s was effectively reduced. Throughout the rocksteady and reggae phases of the music, several female singers made decisions to abandon a vocation as recording artists; decisions influenced, to some degree, by the fact that these women were not taken as seriously as their male counterparts. The attitude of some male producers toward women in the business is reflected in these comments attributed to Clement "Coxsone" Dodd, possibly the most important record producer in Jamaica during the '60s: "(Hortense Ellis) was one of the best that I had. But she had too many children ... she was never able to dedicate herself to the music."[3]

Discrimination against women in the workplace, especially single mothers, is not specific to that time, industry, or just specific to Jamaica's labour relations. Inequality within the island's music industry, however, seems to have meant that a female artist's career was not adequately shaped, supported, and properly promoted. A record company that had a complete disregard for the specific circumstances of its female singers, in relation to family and children, was an obstacle impeding the progress of the women on its roster. The dialectic of balancing career and family has, in many ways, defined women who choose to do both—women who struggle against the odds to be successful at a career and the job of caring for children and family. Judy Mowatt and

Marcia Griffiths were able to sustain long and outstanding solo music careers as single mothers or as mothers with a male partner who may not have been supportive of their role as the most talented female personalities in roots reggae.

This "natural" disadvantage for female singers competing for the highest quality management, production, and marketing is directly related to why, historically, there are so few women in the Jamaican music industry. Too many of the women who do enter a music profession, for which success is elusive, even for male artists, often leave. Any success for a woman in the business is really an extraordinary achievement.

Phyllis Dillon was one female artist whose extraordinary, if not sustained, success is an important reggae *sista*'s story. If Alton Ellis and Delroy Wilson were the kings of rocksteady, then Dillon was clearly considered its queen. No account of Jamaican music's rocksteady era is complete if it does not discuss Phyllis Dillon. The skilled vocalist, originally from the town of Linstead in St. Catherine, possessed an easy flowing, yet robust tone. Dillon's vocals, as heard on her signature ballads like "Perfidia" and "Don't Stay Away" placed her on the front line of the best singers of that time. On the classic rocksteady track "Don't Stay Away," Dillon employs a voice that is convincing in its attempt to seduce her boyfriend character in the lyric not to leave her for another woman. A less assured reading of the lyric could have sounded trite. The way Dillon inhabits the lyric with her sinuous delivery is not at all "girlish," as Chang and Chen—the Jamaican authors of *Reggae Routes*—suggest. It reflects the feelings of a vulnerable woman who is confident that she will not be crushed if the boy does, in fact, stay away.

Like Dawn Penn, the dignity of Dillon's voice shines through on songs that are not written as tomes of female empowerment. She easily negotiated the transition to early reggae with outstanding vocal performances on popular Jamaican singles "One Life to Live" and a duet with Hopeton Lewis on "Right Track." Even though she was under-recorded, Dillon's impact on reggae is indelible. Her gifts as a vocalist can be heard on reissues of her recordings that appear on quality compilations like *The Story of Jamaican Music* (Mango/Island).

Jamaican reggae historian Garth White and English reggae enthusiasts Steve Barrow and Peter Dalton both substantiate

Dillon's impact and popularity as a prominent rocksteady vocalist. The tragedy is that even a superior talent like Phyllis Dillon could not sustain a career in the unforgiving male-dominated landscape of Jamaica's music industry. She did not survive the transition of the music to its roots reggae phase. Like Penn and Fraser, Dillon emigrated to the United States in the early '70s, leaving her homeland and a relatively high profile in the island's music industry.

During the late '60s, women distinguished themselves as more than just recording artists. Sonia Pottinger emerged as the Jamaican recording industry's only female producer, and became one of the few producers to establish a nurturing environment for women artists. Pottinger was the force behind some of the early work of Judy Mowatt, and it was she who produced some of Marcia Griffiths' best recordings.

Pottinger got her start in the Jamaican music industry by assuming control of her husband's recording business. She immediately transformed a competent company into one that existed in a position where popularity, profitability, and cutting-edge artistry intersect. In 1966, the first Pottinger-produced hit, "Every Night" by Joe White and Chuck, positioned her in an arena where only male producers waged an intense competition for the ears and hearts of rocksteady fans.

The popularity of "Every Night" was one of many instances when records on Pottinger's High Note, Gay Feet, and Tip Top labels would upstage music that appeared on Dodd's Studio One label, Leslie Kong's Beverly's imprint, or Arthur "Duke" Reid's Treasure Isle. By 1968, her production of the Melodians' "Swing and Dine" and the Gaylads' "Hard to Confess" established these harmony trios in the top echelon of rocksteady recording artists. Pottinger's production skills also worked magic for the exceptional voices of Ken Boothe and Delroy Wilson as she maintained the integrity of their previous success with "Coxsone" Dodd. In an industry plagued by accusations about producers exploiting musicians and vocalists, Pottinger had a reputation for fairness, as lead singer of the Melodians, Brent Dowe, testifies:

> ... we were at Duke Reid's; we hear that another producer was paying bigger money. So we check it out, and it was Mrs. Pottinger ... she say she do business with us ... word spread that there is money down (t)here; and everybody

started going down to Tip Top, leaving Coxsone. Coxsone must have heard about that because he started to raise (increase) his money.[4]

Pottinger worked successfully with a variety of talented male solo acts and harmony groups, but it is her efforts in developing an artist roster boasting a large complement of female singers that is very significant. Pottinger's production of Patsy Todd's "Pata Pata Rocksteady" is notable because it is a departure from the practice of interpreting the work of American artists. The fact that "Pata Pata" was an international hit may have influenced the decision of Pottinger and Todd to cover it, but Pottinger's use of Count Ossie's ensemble of Rasta nyabinghi drummers to provide the tune's rhythmic underpinning suggests an African diasporic connection to the song.

Pottinger also produced a cover version of Diana Ross' "It's My House" for Lorna Bennett, who had previously hit big in Jamaica and the U.K. with 1972's "Breakfast in Bed." Each of these Pottinger-produced singles captures an assertive vocal performance expressing lyrics that did not undermine the dignity of women.

The late '60s High Note single "I Shall Sing" introduced Judy Mowatt's soul-inspired take-charge vocal. Other tracks Mowatt recorded for Pottinger include "Emergency Call," on which Mowatt's defiant vocal simmers over a raucous reggae rhythm, and "I'm Alone," a Jamaican pantomime show tune written by playwright Trevor Rhone that finds Mowatt working a torch song submerged in a slow dirge-like pop beat.

The existing histories of Jamaican music often fall short of assessing Pottinger's contribution. *Reggae Routes* by Kevin O'Brien Chang and Wayne Chen does not even mention Sonia Pottinger. For Chang and Chen, she simply does not exist. Garth White, in his excellent and groundbreaking series of articles outlining the history of women in the island's popular music that appeared in Jamaican newspaper *The News*, comments, "While one would not put her (Pottinger) in the same league as trailblazers 'Coxsone' Dodd and Duke Reid, she surely ranks with the secondary level of early producers like Leslie Kong in ska days and 'Niney' Holness, Harry Johnson, and Harry Moodie in the early reggae days."[5]

Barrow and Dalton in *Reggae: The Rough Guide* offer a more precise comment: "Perhaps a more prolific output would have ensured that Sonia Pottinger was mentioned as often as Reid and Dodd."[6] Prolific or not, in terms of quality recordings, Pottinger's production credits place her beside Reid, if not Dodd. In terms of developing and nurturing the talent of female artists and proving that women are more than capable of successfully operating as producers and managers in the Jamaican music industry, Pottinger is in a class by herself.

As the early reggae period gave way to the more adventurous roots reggae experiments of a new generation of producers in the early '70s, several pioneer producers exited the scene. Duke Reid and Leslie Kong both died while "Coxsone" Dodd emigrated to New York. The tenacious Pottinger survived the pitfalls that lined the paths of transition from rocksteady to early reggae, and from there to the music's roots era. In the late '70s, Pottinger added a new and exciting chapter to her work by managing recording sessions for important roots albums including Culture's *Cumbolo* and Marcia Griffiths' *Steppin'*.

Naturally and *Steppin'*, the two albums Griffiths recorded for Pottinger as the '70s concluded, reveal the work of a gifted singer engaged in the realization of her potential. If the roots era represents the golden age of the music, then these Pottinger-produced Griffiths albums are essential parts of the framework around which reggae is constructed. Pottinger and Griffiths created possibly their finest work with each other.

Pottinger describes her connection to Griffiths: "Marcia Griffiths is like my relation. We ... have a very good rapport."[7] That synergy is evident in the quality of work found in the collections of songs on *Naturally* and *Steppin'*. On these recording sessions, Griffiths is accompanied by the leading-edge roots reggae sound of the Revolutionaries. Marcia Griffiths' voice, however, is always the undisputed star of her recordings, regardless of the skills brought to the session by her supporting cast of musicians and back-up singers. Griffiths' voice is one of the best instruments in reggae for conveying a range of feeling and nuance. It wears emotions such as yearning, pain, triumph, and love with the elegance of a high-fashion model wearing an haute couture evening gown. Griffiths' singing resonates a supple restrained tone that arrives at the listener's ears as a smooth unfazed flow.

Griffiths can work a dramatic edge into a song when required, but always within the context of an effortless sense of cool. She always seemed to exhibit that same unfazed cool look on her round coffee-coloured face, given character by moody eyes and a mole on the right side of her nose-bridge—a cool look that suggested a mix of innocence and quiet determination.

The songs on *Naturally* are all expertly written. The remarkable songwriter Bob Andy composed seven of the ten songs on the album. Griffiths previously recorded many of these tunes for Coxsone. They reappear on *Naturally* as fresh, mature, fully ripe interpretations. On "Tell Me Now," for example, Marcia's voice floats like a warm Caribbean breeze easing through a busy roots beat.

A revision of another Andy composition, Griffiths' first Jamaican #1 hit "Feel Like Jumping" was restructured by underscoring it with a darker rhythmic edge, while the horn arrangement locks down the happy-go-lucky feel of the original. Marcia's mature vocal immediately informs the listener that the song's subject is now a woman, not a girl having fun by dancing and jumping around.

"Truly," "Mark My Word," and "Stay" are fine examples of how Marcia's vocals are the ideal vehicle for the great sense of melody Andy carefully worked into each of these love songs. Griffiths' singing on these ballads is a good indicator of her abilities as a fine interpreter of romantic reggae ballads that came to be known as "lovers' rock" tunes. John Holt and Leroy Sibbles, two of reggae's leading romantic balladeers from that era, have nothing on Marcia in that regard.

The Andy song on *Naturally* that is most associated with his voice is the Jamaican classic "I've Got to Go Back Home." Only someone with Marcia's talent could even attempt to cover a tune that, in its original form, became more popular, more pervasive as it aged. Pottinger's work on this one is sublime. The rhythm and horn arrangements offer three different moods: the despair of being home sick, the discovery of what caused the desperation, and the joy of arriving at the decision to go back home. Griffiths' vocal immerses itself into each of the tune's moods like a skilled actor investigating the emotional fabric of a script by the way the lines are whispered, shouted, or simply spoken.

Griffiths' interesting interpretation of another roots classic "Dreamland," originally recorded as a reggae song by Bunny Wailer, does not fundamentally depart from the original approach. Griffiths' voice, however, seems more suited to the creation of the soothing ethereal sensibility the song demands.

Although *Naturally* is a showcase of impressive songs by important Jamaican songwriters, Griffiths' second significant Pottinger-produced collection of recordings, *Steppin'*, presents Griffiths' singing her own words on several tracks. The buoyant rollicking beats that drive the title track "Steppin' Out of Babylon" meet their match in Marcia's assured vocal as she sings: "When I think of all the bitter times I've had / Oh God, it doesn't make me sad / Oh no, it doesn't bother me / Strength and honour is all I see ..."[8] Griffiths explains the meaning of her lyrics: "The chorus 'steppin out of Babylon' is not necessarily a movement in the physical . Babylon can be either a situation or a system but, it is a hell to anyone who knows love and light and warmth ... So (when) we step ... its not just a physical step, but an inner evolution."[9]

Griffiths' discussion of "Steppin' Out of Babylon," in one sense, can be taken as a general statement about a variety of social groups contending with injustice. Griffiths' narration of the song's words in the first person link her own personal battles with Babylon and suggest that she is using her lyrics to engage an implicit discussion about the situation of African-Jamaican women, specifically those involved in the music industry. This song is the closest Griffiths came to sounding rebellious, if not militant. Her persona as a recording artist always seemed more comfortable residing in the lyrical territory of male-female relationship songs in which, true to life, women were often treated unfairly.

On another standout track from *Steppin'*, titled "Peaceful Woman," Griffiths hints at deeper problems beyond that of relationships. As a talkative keyboard organ sound bubbles melodic lines over an earthy bass line, Marcia reasons: "Why do they always try to keep me down / Tell me why ..."[10] These words can be read as a metaphor not only for her career, but also her place in the music's history. Marcia Griffiths has been a shadowy figure in many of the existing reggae accounts. Although she is often discounted as merely the "best female" vocalist, Griffiths is the owner of one of the all-time great voices of Jamaican music.

When Griffiths graduated from her first duet phase in the mid-'60s, her first producer, Clement "Coxsone" Dodd, acknowledged her obvious teenage talent by attempting to grow a solo career for her. Dodd, however, instead of matching her voice with the creative cutting-edge rhythms of the day, took a trial-and-error method that tried to match her voice with songs intended to pro-

Sandra "Puma" Jones of Black Uhuru in Toronto, October 1981.
Photograph by Isobel Harry.

duce pop-style recordings. Most of these early Dodd-produced
recordings did not create any real impact. The European-style pop
ballad "I Cried" and the slow rhythm and blues "You Mean the
World to Me" were notable for revealing a promising young singer
and the unfortunate choice of bland non-reggae musical accompaniment. On the other hand, "Truly" and "My Ambition," both
stoked with the slow-burning fire of early reggae rhythms, represented the better examples of Dodd's work with Griffiths.

"Coxsone" Dodd's consistent efforts and Griffiths' developing
talent eventually gave birth to the original version of "Feel Like
Jumping" in 1968. "Feel Like Jumping" emerged from the Brentford

Road hit factory as Griffiths' initial success in collaboration with the lyrics and music of Bob Andy. Griffiths became involved in a professional and personal duet with Andy, who was already a big name in Jamaican reggae as a recording artist and songwriter.

Keith "Bob Andy" Anderson's mature poetic lyrics that fuelled songs recorded during the rocksteady and roots reggae periods situated him as one of the music's gifted songwriters. His strengths were not just in the poetry of his song's words, but also in his ability to craft an attractive melody to convey these lyrics. He wrote tender love ballads like the songs he wrote for Marcia Griffiths, and also wrote significant protest and social commentary songs that he recorded himself.

Andy's classic rocksteady gem "I've Got to Go Back Home" demonstrates the quality of his writing as the "home" Andy discusses can be interpreted in a variety of ways: Rastafarians desiring to go "home" to Africa; individuals from a Jamaican rural community displaced by the harsh urban reality of Kingston wanting to go back home to the country; Jamaican immigrants transplanted to the metropolitan environments of cities like London, Toronto, or New York thinking about going back home, particularly during the cold winter months.

In "Let Them Say," Andy brings together introspection and social commentary with the ease of a talented writer. Using the first-person voice of a hungry homeless person dressed in raggedy clothing, Andy's words are poignant: "People see me acting strange ... But the people don't realize the pangs of hell that I feel."[11]

Andy's "Unchained Melody" uses the system of slavery as a metaphor for the hardship poor Black Jamaicans continue to endure. While lyrics such as "multinationals are really criminals"[12] from "Check It Out" and when the "fires" start burning, "haves will want to be in the shoes of the have-nots"[13] sung in "Fire Burning" are quite explicit, the love ballads that Andy composed and recorded, such as "Honey," were equally as strong.

Despite his superior writing talent, Bob Andy was comfortable recording cover versions. His choices were very different than those of his contemporaries. Instead of, say, Curtis Mayfield, Andy chose to do a version of American Joe South's folk-pop hit "Games People Play"—a personalized account of society's hypocrisy—the kind of song that coincides with Andy's own song themes. It is ironic that Andy's profile, at least internationally, hinges on his recording of "Young, Gifted and Black" with Marcia Griffiths, while his songwriting talents are not widely acknowledged.

In 1970, the duo of Bob and Marcia worked with producer Harry Johnson whose Harry J label released their cover of "Young, Gifted and Black," a song made famous by African-American soul/jazz singer Nina Simone. Griffiths' participation in the Bob and Marcia vocal partnership was quite different from the male-female duets of the early '60s. In this arrangement, Griffiths was not simply a junior partner, she now possessed a reputation as an emerging talent with great potential on the strength of her solo Jamaican hit "Feel Like Jumping." Though Andy had a larger profile at the time, it is Griffiths' appealing delivery that carries this duet's rendition of "Young, Gifted and Black." The song was one of only two singles that achieved international success for Griffiths with Andy, but it was also important that the record featured Griffiths' fine voice, singing conscious Black Power lyrics.

"Young, Gifted and Black" signified a break with the practice of talented female singers like Dawn Penn and Phyllis Dillon, who almost exclusively recorded interpretations of songs about romance and love lost. An African-American woman wrote "Young, Gifted and Black" about empowerment and self-actualization in relation to Black men and women.

By the mid-'70s, reggae singer Marcia Aitken aggressively challenged the male-chauvinist lyrics of "Woman Is Like a Shadow" by roots reggae harmony group the Meditations with a direct militant response in her recording "Narrow Minded Man." Aitken's song is like a cover version of the Meditations' recording with the misogyny completely drained out. Aitken adds her own words to ensure that the Meditations' message is turned inside out so that instead of being demeaning to women, it is empowering.

When Judy Mowatt's solo work of the late '70s arrives a few years later, it offers songs written by her that express a maturation of the female reggae recording artist with themes of independent womanhood that are neither interpreting nor reacting to a male perspective. In this context, Griffiths' participation in "Young, Gifted and Black" can be seen as a turning point for women in reggae.

The hit status of "Young, Gifted and Black" in Jamaica quickly translated to broad-based popularity in Europe through the marketing and distribution efforts of the U.K.-based Trojan company. Griffiths and Andy then toured several major European cities in support of the record's success: "All the places I've been with the Wailers, they were not new to me."[14] The success of "Young, Gifted and Black" also attracted inquiries from Motown and CBS. The failure of Marcia's Jamaican management to come to terms with either of these prominent American companies derailed her aspirations for an international career that would have preceded that of Bob Marley.

Back in Jamaica, Griffiths continued to advance her persona as a creative entertainer in live performances as she thrilled Kingston nightclub patrons with her skillful interpretations of African-American rhythm and blues tunes. Marcia's stature as a quality vocalist with career accomplishments in Europe attracted the services of Judy Mowatt and Rita Marley as backup singers in Griffiths' nightclub act. The trio's repertoire soon developed into an exciting potpourri of songs, some of which could be found on the albums of the Sweet Inspirations, a vocal group that consisted of three African-American females led by Cissy Houston—Whitney Houston's mother.

Although the Sweet Inspirations' records remain obscure, the group's airtight, gospel-seasoned, rhythm and blues harmonies should have been as well known as the Supremes'. There is a strange affinity between Marcia and Cissy Houston. Each of them provided vocal support for male icons: Houston for Elvis Presley and Griffiths for Bob Marley. Neither woman really achieved a sustained hour in the sun of mainstream popularity.

In 1974, Marcia's nightclub act was effectively transformed into the I-Three—Bob Marley's replacement for original Wailers Bunny Wailer and Peter Tosh. The idea that Marcia, Judy, and Rita were substitutes for the departed foundation Wailers is not totally accurate because none of the I-Three were given any solo or even duet duties in a band that, at least in a vocal sense, was completely defined by Bob Marley. Marcia's inclusion in reggae's world-famous band was both a winning lottery ticket and a curse. The proverbial lottery ticket brought her eclipsed fame and more financial fortune than any other time in her career. The curse was that Marcia lost her identity as a substantial solo artist and became first and foremost a member of Marley's backing trio the I-Three, a persona that loomed like a dark shadow over her subsequent solo efforts.

The meagre writing on this subject within various reggae books and magazine articles invariably describe the zenith of

Marcia's career as her time with the Wailers. They are wrong. The apex of Griffiths' tenure as a roots reggae recording artist is her own work on *Naturally* and *Steppin'*. Although the quality of these albums places Griffiths as a significant figure in reggae, she did earn a measure of mainstream acclaim when the dance-oriented pop-reggae track "Electric Boogie"—written by Bunny Wailer—figured prominently on America's Billboard charts in 1991.

When Judy Mowatt's *Black Woman* was released in 1979, the album created reggae history. The very existence of Mowatt's ten-song album was revolutionary because it was produced, written, and mixed by the woman whose urgent searing tone breathes the consciousness of an independent Rasta woman into every song. The female producer in reggae is rare, so it is quite an achievement that Judy Mowatt became the first female vocalist as producer to take a leadership role in an innovative recording project. An important aspect of *Black Woman*'s innovation is that it does not contain any romantic ballads, but is a solid concept album of protest material with a focus on Black women's issues.

"Black Woman," the title song, is the centrepiece of the album. Judy's lyrics tell us that the song is dedicated to Black women like her who have travelled life's rugged paths with the heaviest load. Using a fearless vocal coloured by vulnerability, Judy makes a plea to sisters: "Don't give up now / Just pray for strength now."[15] Mowatt's writing on "Black Woman" is probably her sharpest. She expertly crochets together the present-day situation of Black women with their history of dehumanization during plantation slavery. Mowatt uses her lyrics to paint a portrait of slave women on the plantation, their skin ruptured by the lash of the whip, their experience in chains on the auction block. She also confronts the horrific sexual violence—or carnal abuse as she calls it—inflicted on African slave women. Mowatt speaks directly to her Black sisters when she wails "You have struggled long," and the words "I feel your affliction"[16] are conveyed with such emotional intensity that the listener immediately realizes that her personal tribulations inform the tune's concerns about all Black women who have suffered at the hands of inequality and abuse.

"Black Woman"'s sturdy unhurried bass line is as determined and sincere as the lyrics. The trap drum's one-drop and the chatter of a funde hand drum are in constant discussion with contentious bass lines, while the sound of mournful horn harmonies offset a bluesy lead guitar to feed the song's description of suffering and the will to rebel against it.

Mowatt continues to work the theme established by "Black Woman" with "Sisters' Chant," a song whose most striking line is the unapologetic criticism of the irresponsible behaviour of some Black men: "(Jah) help us to fight when the brothers are out of sight."[17] That sentiment is not asking Jah to bring the brothers back, but seeks the strength to continue the struggle whether the man is present or not. Over twenty-five years ago, that was a bold statement for a Black Jamaican Rasta woman to articulate on record. Mowatt's soul vocal, supported by prominent church organ–inspired notes injects a rhythm and blues/gospel flavour into "Sister's Chant." Gospel is the perfect foil for Mowatt's lyrics that seek comfort, assistance, and strength from Jah for Black women in their struggle to overcome frustration, temptation, and desolation.

The words of "Slave Queen" urge Black women to liberate themselves from the mentality of a Eurocentric ideal of beauty: "Your lips are red, your eyes paint blue / Slave Queen remove the shackles from your mind."[18] The conventional Rasta reasoning of the '70s preached that Black women should wear their hair in natural hairstyles, refrain from wearing make-up and dress modestly. "Slave Queen" and the Rasta ideas of that time have proven to be prophetic in the sense that Rasta dreadlocks and an Afrocentric natural look are now an acceptable fashion alternative for Black women in North America, Europe, Africa, and other parts of the world.

Those three tracks written by Mowatt articulate the African-Jamaican woman's story of struggle for redemption in a way that is in the tradition of the eighteenth century female rebel leader Nanny. There are many heroes of the Jamaican struggle against slavery, but the story of Nanny, leader of the Portland Maroons, has a legendary mythic quality. Nanny's contributions to the freedom struggle, including her establishment of a six hundred acre liberated settlement for freed slaves, were not officially recognized until the mid-'70s when the Jamaican government gave her national hero status. Mowatt recognizes Nanny on her "Warrior Queen" recording from the *Look at Love* album, but, just like the history of Nanny's exploits were honoured long after Jamaica's male heroes, the work of Griffiths, Pottinger, and Mowatt still remain part of reggae's unspoken history. The collection of songs on *Black Woman* is a crucial aspect of that history.

Mowatt wrote three other songs for *Black Woman*. "Joseph," the closest she came to including a love ballad on the album, is, in fact, a love song, but one of sisterly love as opposed to romantic or sexual love. The song is a tribute to Bob Marley that discusses Mowatt's relationship to the reggae star. Mowatt describes Bob Marley—in the context of a rhythm and blues–style ballad whose music does not measure up to the standard of her emotive vocal—as a father, a brother, and a mentor to her, and as someone who she saw as a kind of prophet. The song is notable in many ways, not the least of which is that it was recorded at least two years before Bob Marley died. Unlike others, Mowatt did not wait until after Marley's death to tribute him. The second song, "Many Are Called"—a recording in which the music, arrangement, and singing swing satisfyingly as a decent roots reggae workout—is concerned with obstacles that arise in the struggle for redemption in the form of individual men or women who are really a wolf in sheep's clothing. The third song, "Strength to Go Through," like many of Mowatt's songs, emphasizes the idea that women must have the strength and courage of their convictions in the overall struggle for empowerment. This strength, she argues, is not rooted in material wealth, but through faith in Jah.

In addition to her six compositions, Mowatt chose to interpret three Bob Marley songs that appropriately fit the concept of the album. *Black Woman* includes Mowatt's versions of "Concrete Jungle," "Put It On," and "Down in the Valley." Female reggae singers like Marcia Griffiths usually choose to cover Bob Marley's romantic love ballads. Judy Mowatt, however, chose to interpret his rebellious social commentary anthems that fuel her persona as a conscious rebel sister. Mowatt's version of "Concrete Jungle" hits the target because her tone, though less gritty and more melodic than Marley's, manages to capture the tune's necessary sense of tension and dread. The smooth yet cauterizing quality of Mowatt's voice captures the song's poetic lyricism, leaving no doubt that the song has been turned into a story about women living the dark existence of ghetto life. A perspective that becomes obvious as Mowatt inserts the word "woman" in the following line of lyric: "A woman must do her best to survive in the ghetto."[19]

Mowatt's rework of "Put It On" is used to convey a sense that women will be able to achieve victories in their struggle for empowerment. The term "put it on" as used by Bob Marley in the original Wailers' 1965 recording referenced the behaviour of the *rude bwoy*. The *rude bwoy* of '60s Jamaica can be described as rebellious ghetto youth who either engaged in criminal activities or in revolutionary Black Power activities, often through the creative arts such as poetry, essay writing, popular music, and the visual arts. When the *rude bwoy* "put it on," he can be giving sexual love to a girl, inflicting a beating on an adversary, or delivering a body blow to the solar plexus of the system of oppression. As a woman singing this song, Mowatt places a woman as the subject of all three meanings, particularly the idea that women will "put it on" the system and win the battle against discrimination and inequality.

"Down in the Valley" is a song that Bob Marley himself never recorded, and Mowatt sings the song as if it were written to suit the purpose of the *Black Woman* album, even though the song's words do not specifically mention women. Mowatt's voice is filled with a real sense of conviction and determination that suggest she is referencing the trials and tribulations of women, especially when she sings the words: "We've been down in the valley much too long and we never get weary yet."[20] A stepping reggae rhythm underscores Mowatt singing Marley's verse about moving from the deep valley of Babylon (oppression) on a journey to the Rasta promised land of Ethiopia as energetic horn harmonies herald a response to Mowatt's cries of "Ha-lle-lu-Jah." One of the choice lines of the song—"... they killed Lumumba (leader of the African nation the Congo in the early '60s) for his own land / but they couldn't kill the Rastaman"[21]—seems to suggest that though the oppressor may kill Black heroes, the Rastaman represents a movement and an idea of freedom that can never be killed. Mowatt's embrace of the song suggests that women must be an important part of that movement for freedom.

Freddie McGregor, a popular Jamaican reggae vocalist and, at one time, an intimate partner of Mowatt, wrote "Zion Chant." McGregor is also credited as supplying background vocals and assisting in mixing *Black Woman*'s ten tracks. "Zion Chant" surrounds Mowatt's voice, singing upbeat lyrics about the promised land of Holy Mount Zion where oppression does not exist and Black people will be free, with the intermittent chatter of talking hand drums laced with purring harmonica and whistling flute interjections that prime a soothing rhythm and blues melody. "Zion Chant" is a freedom song that fits comfortably on an album in which Mowatt advocates freedom for Black women.

As a concept album, *Black Woman* creates a special place for itself in reggae history by exhibiting the struggle, spirit, and artistry of Judy Mowatt, an African-Jamaican Rastafari woman. *Black Woman* placed the issues of Rasta *sistren*, Black women, and perhaps all women, front and centre during the so-called golden age of roots reggae. Mowatt's conversion, some years ago, to a more conventional Christianity can never dilute her impact on Rastafari or that of her most enduring work as a recording artist.

One aspect of Judy Mowatt's persona that cannot be over-looked is her physical beauty. During the '70s, Mowatt possessed a slim dancer's body whose waist pulled her torso into a V-shape. Mowatt was the image of a devastatingly attractive Rasta princess. Her long, crinkly, dreadlocked hair framed a light-brown face so naturally smooth and unblemished that even a hint of makeup would have been excessive and artificial. Mowatt had a face—off-set by penetrating lemon-shaped eyes and seductive lips—that even in person looked like an airbrushed photograph. This was the image of Mowatt that lived an active existence in the minds of a variety of Jamaican men of various ages. Mowatt defined a partic-ular image of Jamaican Afrocentric beauty. If she had been a movie star, she would have been a matinee idol who would have boiled the blood of Caribbean men in the same way that Dorothy Dandridge, the cinnamon-coloured film star of '50s America, raised the temperature of many African-American males.

Judy Mowatt's stunning outward appearance was gift-wrapped in a package of several enviable inner talents. She was an articulate speaker, a top-shelf reggae vocalist, and an activist who supported both the struggle against apartheid in South Africa and the island's Jamaica Council for Human Rights organization. Mowatt was also a choreographer and dancer. It was she who worked out the steps for the I-Three's dance routines. In fact her journey in the entertainment field began as a dancer in the mid-'60s.

Mowatt began to tap her skills as a vocalist when the rock-steady era was in full swing. She recorded "I Shall Sing" first, under the pseudonym Juliann for Sonia Pottinger in 1967. The fol-lowing year, Mowatt joined Beryl Lawson and Merle Clemenson as lead singer of the Gaylettes. Their first single "Silent River Runs Deep," released in 1968, exhibits the personality of a Jamaican-style '60s Motown girl-group. Judy's not-fully-realized lead voice still packs as much sincerity as possible into lyrics that are essentially bubble-gum. The group's sweet harmony, an infectious melody, and a sufficiently edgy, upbeat, uptown-type reggae rhythm ensure that the tune is credible for the time. "Silent River" went straight to #1 on the Jamaican charts.

The Gaylettes followed up with "Son of a Preacherman"—a version of a song made famous by English rhythm and blues singer Dusty Springfield—and "I Like Your World." Both recordings were popular in Jamaica. On "Silent River" and "I Like Your World," the power and emotion of Judy's singing is much more evident.

Mowatt eventually left the Gaylettes in favour of a solo career. Initially, she voiced Three Dog Night's "Joy to the World" and then returned to work with Pottinger to record "Emergency Call" and "I'm Alone" in the early '70s.

Judy Mowatt's Rasta consciousness began to develop at that time as she moved through the transition from a pop-reggae singer sporting big, fluffy, afro hair to a dreadlocked roots artist, placing her power vocals in the service of her own songs of female empowerment and as a member of the I-Three with Bob Marley's Wailers. After Marley's death, Mowatt was able to focus exclusively on her solo career. Several notable Mowatt albums were released during the '80s including *Working Wonders, Love Is Overdue,* and *Look at Love.*

Although Mowatt did not experience a major international breakthrough, her profile was significant enough to warrant Grammy and NAACP Image award nominations in the late '80s. She also appeared on NBC's *Night Music*—hosted by saxophonist David Sanborn—an excellent and groundbreaking American late-night television show featuring musicians and singers from a variety of music genres such as jazz, blues, rhythm and blues, reggae, world beat, punk, and alternative rock.

Mowatt was one of the many reggae celebrities associated with the Twelve Tribes of Israel Rastafari organization. Judy Mowatt, in many ways, was the most prominent face of the independent Rasta woman. A persona reflected in the lyrics of her songs and her actions. In the late '70s, she even formed her own record label Ashandan. Mowatt can be compared to Miriam Makeba or Aretha Franklin in terms of her stature in Jamaican music because she is an outstanding and innovative contributor to reggae.

Rita Marley is not usually assessed seriously in terms of her contribution to Jamaican music. Marcia Griffiths and Judy Mowatt have both been described as the queen of "something to do with reggae," while certain analysts have strictly defined Rita within the context of her marriage to Bob Marley and the sons and daughters produced by that union.

During Rita's fifteen-year marriage to Bob, she was often a sideline spectator to the intriguing melodrama involving her husband's multitude of lovers and the many children these affairs produced. These extramarital romantic episodes unfurled in such a public manner in the Jamaican and international media that Rita battled indignities related to her husband's infidelities. In an interview in Jeremy Marre's Bob Marley documentary *Rebel Music*, Rita indicates that she rebelled against Bob's affair with Cindy Breakspeare—a Jamaican beauty queen who won the Miss World Beauty contest in 1976. She did so by refusing to join the I-Three in providing harmony for the recording of "Turn the Lights Down Low," a song Bob wrote about his relationship with Breakspeare.

After Bob Marley's death, Rita continued to face challenges related to various claims by different interests on the Bob Marley estate. The real issue behind the estate dilemma was not necessarily the contending factions, but the fact that Bob Marley failed to write a will. Rita eventually emerged victorious from the legal entanglements of the estate dilemma in her efforts to secure a future for herself and her children. Immediately following Bob's death, Rita skillfully negotiated the delicate balance of establishing her individuality while promoting his iconography.

Rita's best achievement as a solo recording artist is "One Draw," her playful celebration of ganja smoking, released as a single in the year of Bob's death. The tune's lyrics only care about the mind-altering effects of weed: "I want to get high / so high."[22] The bouncy beat, though rootsy but not intense or dark, is more concerned with serving the melody's objective of presenting a fun-filled semi-comic portrayal. "One Draw" made an impression on the international pop music scene.

American independent record company Shanachie issued Rita Marley's strong album *Who Feels It Knows It*, which included the herb anthem. In some ways, the collection of songs on the album reflect a joyous celebratory mood that seem to underscore Rita's new lease on life as an independent woman striving to achieve

success on her own terms. The title track is Rita's competent interpretation of an original Wailers' recording written by Bunny. She
brings a fresh approach to voicing the melody that lends unique
character to a version in which the musical support is adequate.

"I'm Still Waiting," a second Wailers cover, is not as interesting
as the original or Delroy Wilson's superb restructuring, while
"Thank You Jah" offers an earnest soul vocal that is definitive Rita.
On the latter track, she proves that she knows how to use her tone
to read the emotion of each line of lyric. The rhythmic support,
spiked with a pedestrian guitar sound, is solid and unobtrusive.
Rita's singing on "Good Morning Jah" is measured to complement
the rhythm's drama, creating an insidious daunting environment
for the up-tempo mood of lyrics praising Jah. "A Jah Jah," a song
written by Bob especially for Rita, is perhaps the best track on the
album. The tune is introduced by the seductive syncopation of
nyabinghi hand drumming that eventually infiltrates the entire
rhythm. Rita's skill as a vocalist is clearly evident here, her voice
engaging a fluid melody as it rides the crevices of the hand
drum–driven beat with ease.

Who Feels It Knows It is to Rita what Naturally is to Marcia and
what Black Woman is to Judy in terms of how it defines Rita's place
in the world of reggae. Who Feels It Knows It was co-produced by
Rita and provides an early indication that she is about to take
charge of her own career, the careers of her children, and the family business. Despite the arrival of the Harambee album in 1982,
Rita's focus since "One Draw" and Who Feels It Knows It has been
on the business side of the music industry equation. Rita Marley
must be given the lion's share of the credit, especially in the months
and years immediately following her husband's death, for ensuring
that the Tuff Gong Studios and record manufacturing plant, established by her husband, continued to successfully operate.

As previously mentioned, Rita entered the music business in
1964 as one half of a male-female duet. By 1965, she was singing
with Marlene Gifford and Constantine Walker in a group called
the Soulettes, the first harmony trio to feature women. The work
Rita created with the Soulettes remains obscure to this day. Rita's
marriage to Bob Marley in 1966 set the tone for her future career as
a singer. Her growth as an artist independent of her husband
seemed to end. Unlike Judy and Marcia, Rita was sometimes an
unnamed contributor to the Wailers' experience since the group's

early days, while Peter and Bunny were still part of the group. Rita's solo efforts such as the mid-'60s single "Play, Play" did not make an impression when it was initially issued. The one glimpse of Rita's presence as a reggae artist prior to "One Draw" was the extraordinary "A Jah Jah" originally released as a single in 1979. An assessment of Rita as a vocalist can only speculate how she would have developed if given even the limited scope that her *sista* artists Marcia and Judy secured for themselves.

In 1977, a Rasta band from the small island of Jamaica exceeds expectations in record sales and sold-out shows on the European continent. A large concert venue that makes its home in some major European city is playing host to the Wailers that summer. As the I-Three await their cue to spice the musical proceedings with Jamaican-flavoured gospel harmony, they respond with their bodies to the dub rhythm spinning out from Aston "Family Man" Barrett's bass guitar and his brother Carly's drum set.

That night, Rita stood in the middle, Judy to her right, and Marcia on her left, the three of them looking comfortable, relaxed, and ready to work. *Ites*, green, and gold fabric is neatly wrapped around each of their heads, like pretty ornate bandages, so that their hair is completely hidden. The three of them wear the same hunter-green cotton T-shirts tucked into fitted skirts that are the same shade of green. Each woman wears a belt of a different style and colour that seemed to suck in their stomachs in an unrestrictive sense. Crimson letters *E-X-O-D-U-S* blush as they sit on the section of the T-shirt that caresses each woman's breasts. The band's name—*BOB MARLEY AND THE WAILERS*—in smaller yellow lettering was positioned just above the red letters that spell the name of the group's latest album. The movements of the three *sistas* of reggae are conservative and subtly sensuous. As they dance, Judy turns her head to her right, Rita shifts her face in the opposite direction, and Marcia looks down giving the impression her eyes are closed.

Judy, Rita and Marcia work the night shift for Bob Marley as the I-Three. But we now know them as more than mere backup vocalists. We now know them as the *sistas* of roots reggae who laid a foundation for many of the successful reggae women who followed; artists such as Sandra "Puma" Jones of Black Uhuru, Sister Carol, J. C. Lodge, Nadine Sutherland, Lady Saw, Patra, Diana King, and Sasha. We now know them as individuals who, with half a chance, might have been superstars themselves.

Blue Beat, Nyabinghi, Bebop

The Jamaican Roots of Ska

Ska, the music that unleashes a hectic energetic beat spiked with boisterous horn riffs, started life in '60s Jamaica as a jazz-influenced popular music. The Jamaican pronunciation of the word ska is "sk-yah." By the time ska energized the '90s pop music of American bands such as No Doubt, non-Jamaicans had already been pronouncing it "skah" as though it rhymed with "blah." Fans that discovered ska as interpreted by punk or pop bands of America or the U.K., probably know little or nothing about the Jamaican origins of the music. Young hip-hop heads and some Caribbean diasporic *rude bwoys* and *rude girls* of the dancehall reggae scene may think of ska as a kind of offbeat variation of a certain type of rock music. They are probably unaware that ska is the mother of roots reggae and the grandmother of dancehall reggae.

Ska has energized certain kinds of rock and pop since the '80s in the same way as the blues was at the core of '60s rock. Icons like the Rolling Stones, Eric Clapton, and Led Zeppelin were disciples of African-American blues legends such as Robert Johnson, Howlin' Wolf, and Muddy Waters. 2-Tone and punk-ska outfits of the late '70s and '80s like the Specials, Selector, and Madness out of the U.K.; America's the Toasters and Fishbone; and Canadian bands like the Arsenals, King Apparatus, and One are directly or indirectly linked to the Jamaican creators of ska.

The following Jamaican jazz musicians are the fathers of the international ska phenomenon: trombonist Don Drummond, tenor saxophone players Tommy McCook and Roland Alphonso, alto saxophonist Lester Sterling, trumpeter Johnny "Dizzy" Moore, a rhythm section composed of the two "Lloyds"—drummer Lloyd Knibb and acoustic bassist Lloyd Brevette—rhythm guitarist Jah Jerry, and pianist Jackie Mittoo. These Jamaican musicians were all members of the Skatalites, the definitive ska band. Jazz guitarist Ernest Ranglin—an important figure in Jamaican ska history—was a frequent guest with the band.

During the early '60s, the innovative ska beat represented the rhythm of the first indigenous Jamaican popular music and interpreted elements of American blues and American rhythm and blues in a very Jamaican way by accenting the second and fourth beats. This interpretation of an American rhythm combined the Jamaican sensibility of Rastafarian nyabinghi hand drum syncopation with hints of mento, a Jamaican folk music. A distinct signature riff played by the rhythm guitar or the piano, which the word *ska* attempts to mimic, also underscored the music's unique character. Finally, Latin influence is found in the harmony arrangements for horns. Solos articulated by trombone, trumpet, saxophones, and guitar conveyed mature musical phrases with a technical proficiency only associated with jazz. This jazz aesthetic is an integral ingredient of Jamaican ska. Much like a Jamaican attempting to speak English with an American accent, the contribution made by the band's horn section to the Skatalites' music represented a distinct Jamaican interpretation of jazz.

Understanding the history of jazz in Jamaica is therefore an important aspect of understanding the roots of Jamaican ska. Jazz seems to have had a presence in Kingston since the '20s, though evidence suggests that the music surfaced on the island at least a decade prior. By the '30s, jazz became Kingston's popular music and continued as such through the '40s and early '50s.

In those days, British colonial rule in Jamaica meant that the privileged upper classes were mainly White, while the working class and those sections of the society living in poverty were mainly African-Jamaican. Indigenous folk-music forms such as mento, burru hand drumming, and the music associated with Afro-Christian religious practices like pocomania and kumina were the popular music forms of African-Jamaicans in the island's rural communities. The Jamaican upper class found their cultural connections in the classical music of Europe and in the popular forms of American music. They did not regard the indigenous music culture of African-Jamaicans as being legitimate. Jazz, however, was able to gain fans across all classes.

During the '30s, local jazz bands such as King's Rhythm Aces and Rhythm Raiders assumed a significant place in Kingston's cultural life. At the same time, tenor saxophonist Bertie King, pianist York De Souza, and trumpet players Leslie Thompson and Leslie "Jiver" Hutchinson proved that they had the skills to play jazz at the highest level. They migrated to the U.K. and enjoyed lucrative careers in Europe with some of the major jazz names of the day. When American jazz stars toured outside the U.S. in those days,

The All Stars Big Band. Organized 1947–49 annually by dance promoter Count Buckram (right) at the Progressive Lawns North and Church Streets downtown Kingston. Musicians (from left) standing: Baba Motta—piano, Ken Williams—drums, Sonny Bradshaw—trumpet, Sonny Grey—trumpet, Von Mullo—trombone, Ben Bowers—vocals and M.C. Front seated: Joe Harriott—alto sax, Little G McNair—tenor sax, Bobby Gaynair—alto sax, Tommy McCook—tenor sax, Wilton "Bra" Gaynair—tenor sax. Absent are bassist Noel Gillespie and Fitz Hugh Collash—guitar and arranger. This band is the forerunner to the present Jamaica Big Band conducted by Sonny Bradshaw.
From the Sonny Bradshaw Collection.

they did not travel with the entire roster of musicians in their band, if at all. King, De Souza, Thompson, and Hutchinson were often enlisted to support these high-profile jazz musicians on their tours of the U.K. and sometimes on the European continent. Thompson shared the bandstand with musicians led by Fletcher Henderson and Louis Armstrong. Bertie King played with the bands of Django Reinhardt, Stephane Grappelli, Coleman Hawkins, and Benny Carter. Despite the fact that the careers of King, De Souza, Thompson, and Hutchinson were mainly focused outside the island, these musicians were the pioneers of Jamaican jazz.

Local swing bands satisfied the hunger of jazz fans of all classes throughout the '40s. Big bands like those led by Whylie Lopez, Ivy Graydon, and George Alberga offered their interpretation of jazz exclusively to patrons of high-society functions. The big-band ensembles of Sonny Bradshaw, Eric Deans, and Roy Coburn played to audiences across the class and race divide.

A new generation of jazz artists—who began their rise to prominence on the island in the mid-'40s—would have heard about the faraway exploits of King, De Souza, Thompson, and Hutchinson, but were mainly influenced by the American musicians they heard on records brought in from the United States or on radio. Jamaica's only radio station, ZQI, did not air the kind of music that could satisfy serious jazz fans. Aspiring jazz musicians found ways to tune into American stations like the Armed Forces Radio Service, WLAC in Nashville, WINZ in Miami, stations in New Orleans, and sometimes the BBC in the U.K. in order to hear the music of Charlie Parker, Dizzy Gillespie, Count Bassie, Stan Kenton, and others.

Many from this '40s generation of Jamaican jazz musicians were the recipients of rigorous music training from Alpha Boys' School, the institution in Jamaica that produced the greatest volume of gifted musicians. Although Alpha was conceived as a school for "difficult" boys, some potential students were eager to attend the school because of its reputation for offering high-quality music education. By the late '40s, these young talented musicians began their professional careers in the bands of Deans, Bradshaw, and Coburn. Most of the outstanding players including tenor saxophonists Tommy McCook, Wilton Gaynair, and Harold "Little G" McNair, trumpeter Alphonso "Dizzy" Reece, and alto saxophonist Joe Harriott were past students of Alpha. The school also produced Thompson from the previous generation, plus Skatalites' Johnny Moore, Lester Sterling, and Don Drummond.

The '40s generation of jazz musicians who did not attend Alpha included trumpet players Sonny Grey, Roy Burrowes, and Sonny Bradshaw; guitarist Ernest Ranglin; and tenor saxophonists Andy Hamilton and future Skatalite Roland Alphonso. Whether they were Alpha graduates or non-Alpha alumni, they all possessed the skills to successfully negotiate the difficult terrain of bebop, the complex, new, post-war jazz created by Charlie Parker and Dizzy Gillespie. Like the previous generation of jazz musicians, these Jamaican bebop artists eventually looked beyond the island's shores as a way to mature their artistry and advance their careers.

McCook and Ranglin left home to play gigs in the Bahamas for a few years, but eventually returned to Jamaica and found themselves making crucial contributions to the development of ska. Ranglin is generally considered one of ska's originators. Gaynair, McNair, Grey, Burrowes, Reece, and Harriott permanently migrated from Jamaica during the late '40s and early '50s to seek their fortunes in the U.K., other countries in Europe, and America. All of them succeeded in making an impact. Gaynair, with quality recordings like *Blue Bogey*, had a prominent profile on the German scene. McNair, while based in the U.K., played in the bands of Quincy Jones, Ginger Baker, and "Philly Joe" Jones. Grey traded notes with Dexter Gordon. Burrowes, as a U.S. resident, was a member of the great Duke Ellington band in the early '60s.

Dizzy Reece experienced significant success in the jazz world. He migrated to England in 1948 and established a reputation on the scene there. Reece, also a writer of books, children's stories, and screenplays, was able to translate the recognition of his talent by American jazz musicians into a move to the United States. One of Reece's most enthusiastic supporters, Miles Davis, once remarked that "he (Reece) has soul, originality, and above all he is not afraid to blow with fire."[1] Reece enjoyed a career in America punctuated with several recordings as leader of bands featuring Donald Byrd and Ron Carter and as sideman with Dexter Gordon.

Although the artistry of Harriott, Reece, Gaynair, McNair, and Grey served an American art form, the fact that these musicians distinguished themselves as major talents in the U.S. and U.K. made them the source of pride among jazz fans in Jamaica and in Caribbean diasporic communities of America and the U.K. In terms of artistry, if not mass popularity, the Caribbean diasporic profiles of Harriott, Reece, and Gaynair—as gifted jazz musicians and bandleaders in the '50s and '60s—are in some way comparable to the Caribbean diasporic profiles of '70s roots reggae artists such as Bob Marley, Peter Tosh, and Burning Spear. Harriott predated Marley by at least fifteen years as a great musician and innovator in an international context. Since 1998, the reissue of Joe Harriott's groundbreaking recordings on CD has prompted a flurry of new writing in books and articles by British and Caribbean diasporic intellectuals about Harriott's iconography as the "father of European free jazz." In terms of excellence in craft and creativity, Harriott was the leading jazz figure in the U.K. during the '60s.

Harriott's gifts as a saxophonist were initially developed at Alpha with his contemporaries McCook, Gaynair, and McNair. After leaving Alpha, he participated in a variety of bands including Eric Deans, Sonny Bradshaw, and by virtue of his talent, gained repeated selection to Count Buckram's All-Star Big Band in the late '40s.

In 1951, Harriott arrived in London, England as a seasoned twenty-three-year-old bebop artist and a member of Ossie DaCosta's band that was on tour in the U.K. at the time. When the tour ended, Harriott decided to remain in England. Like most young altoists, Harriott was inspired by Charlie Parker. Throughout the '50s, Harriott contributed his superior technical ability and urgent lyrical alto tone to various U.K. jazz combos including those led by Ronnie Scott, Pete Pitterson, and drummer Tony Kinsey. By 1959, Harriott recorded *Southern Horizons*, his first album as leader, with a quintet that played at the San Remo Jazz Festival in Italy that same year.

Harriott's quintet featured outstanding Jamaican bassist Coleridge Goode. Goode began his career in the U.K. in the time of King, De Souza, Thompson, and Hutchinson. In the mid-'40s, Goode contributed supple bass notes as part of the rhythm section of jazz bands led by violinist Stephane Grappelli and guitarist Django Reinhardt. Goode studied electrical engineering at Glasgow University in the '30s, but it was his jazz artistry on the upright bass that eventually brought him notoriety. Harriott's main foil in the quintet was trumpet and flugelhorn player Ellsworth "Shake" Keane. Born in the Caribbean island of St. Vincent, Keane studied English Literature at London University and wrote commendable poetry, but he is known first and foremost as a jazz musician. His virtuosity on the trumpet encouraged British jazz writer Ian Carr to comment: "His excellent technique and good range were at the service of a brilliant and unpredictable imagination that could handle anything from bebop to contemporary classical ensemble playing to austere and total abstraction."[2] The remaining members of Harriott's ensemble were two Englishmen—the competent pianist Pat Smythe and the excellent Phil Seaman, who has been described as the foremost big-band drummer of the day. Caribbean diasporic jazz musicians, however, formed the band's main axis.

In 1959, Harriott conceived a new creative approach to jazz while in hospital recovering from tuberculosis. He formulated the concept and wrote musical compositions, of an improvised jazz that did not require the safety net of set rhythmic and harmonic patterns. Once Harriott was discharged later that year, he began rehearsing these compositions with his quintet. The first recordings of this experimental work appeared on the 1960 album *Free*

Form. The album was released after Ornette Coleman's seminal 1959 avant-garde album *The Shape of Jazz to Come.* At the time, some commentators suggested that Harriott was merely following in Coleman's footsteps. Today, there is no doubt Harriott's work was conceived before he was aware of Coleman's album—before Coleman's record hit the U.K. streets. Different creative notions inspired the non-structural approach of the two altoists. Coleman's was solidly rooted in a blues aesthetic. Harriott's, while still grounded by jazz's core blues element—Goode and Seaman knew how to swing and did so on *Free Form*—merged it with African-Caribbean sensibilities and aspects of European avant-garde. Prominent American jazz magazine *Downbeat* favourably reviewed the album.

The Joe Harriott Quintet's 1962 album *Abstract* and the 1963 release *Movement* continued to explore a different jazz language. Harriott's recordings were revolutionary for the more convention-al U.K. jazz enthusiasts, but in a strange way gave him a certain underground status in America among certain avant-garde jazz fans. Thirty-five years after Harriott's free jazz explorations, American alto-saxophonist Ken Vandermark transcribed some of Harriott's compositions, and along with a trombonist, bass player, and drummer, performed tunes from his "Joe Harriott Project" at Chicago's Empty Bottle Festival of Jazz in May 1998. The follow-ing year, Vandermark released an album titled *Straight Lines* inter-preting seven Harriott tunes that appeared on either *Abstract* or *Free Form.*

Only three years after *Movement,* Harriott began a collabora-tion that produced another new innovation in U.K. jazz. In 1966, the Joe Harriott Quintet merged with a five-man band led by clas-sical violinist John Mayer that constructed Indian rhythms and melodies with tabla, sitar, tambura, flute, violin, and harpsichord. The resulting double quintet recorded three albums *Indo-Jazz Suite,* *Indo-Jazz Fusions I,* and *Indo-Jazz Fusions II,* and subsequently went on tour together.

The union of these bands produced an exciting fusion that combined Indian music, played by Anglo-Indian musicians, with an avant-garde jazz, played by a band whose chief soloists were British-Caribbean. The unity of two bandleaders originally from the "colonies" could only be described as a cultural anomaly that, during the '60s, was way ahead of its time. The Calcutta-born John

Mayer recalls "Joe was just as good as them (John Coltrane and other American greats), but he came from the colonies ... in those days the Caribbean and India were still considered British. We'd just got our independence but it was too soon for us to just be ... well, ourselves."[3]

Despite Harriott's great skill on the saxophone, and despite his gifts as a creative composer, in the decades since his passing in 1973, his legacy has fallen into an obscure crevice between his satisfying ruggedly sweet sax notes and the sour dissonant tones of little or no recognition. Harriott was simply too great, too early in a country where British artists of Caribbean descent, such as dub poet Linton Kwesi Johnson and roots reggae bands such as Steel Pulse and Aswad, only began receiving a measure of mainstream respect more than a decade after the peak of his career.

The next wave of British-Caribbean jazz musicians emerged in the U.K. and eventually on the international jazz scene two decades after Harriott's signal achievements of the '60s. Many of these U.K.-bred jazz lions, influenced by Jamaican reggae greats and American jazz giants, were inspired by Harriott as an important British-Jamaican jazz innovator who laid the foundation for their arrival in the mid-'80s. Tenor sax man Courtney Pine, alto saxophonist Steve Williamson, and bassist Gary Crosby all clearly understood Harriott's legacy, and each of them have achieved the kind of national and international recognition in the jazz mainstream that eluded Harriott in his lifetime.

Joe Harriott died at the age of forty-five. The cancer that killed him also ended a career that was itself ravaged by the terminal disease of no recognition. Why was Harriott's genius not recognized during his career or, at least, in the years immediately following his death? Why did it take more than thirty years for his recorded work to be reissued? Why did it take twenty-five years after his death for him to be remembered as the "father of European free jazz"? These are controversial questions when it is considered that Harriott's contemporaries, British jazz musicians like Johnny Dankworth, Tubby Hayes, Ronnie Scott, and others have been venerated as important figures in U.K. jazz. Harriott's superior and groundbreaking work was buried and, in a sense, hidden until recently. Jamaican or Caribbean residents of England during the '50s and '60s who heard Joe play always whispered that he was the best jazz musician of his day and that he was marginalized because he was better than his White counterparts. On the other hand, his close associates, both Black and White, would confirm that though Joe could be the sweetest person, he could also be prickly and contentious, a characteristic offered up as a reason for why his legacy has been hidden. Maybe particular instances of this contentious behaviour were one way that Harriott was able to cope and in some ways rebel against the denigration of his talent in favour of White musicians.

Joe Harriott, however, remains the musician from that era who stands out as an icon for Jamaican, Caribbean, and U.K. jazz artists and fans because he was more than just a gifted musician, he was an inventive artist who developed his own distinct voice and initiated two important innovations in jazz. His importance also involves his decision not to exclude his Caribbean roots from his music. Harriott's composition "Calypso" distinguishes itself from the other tunes on the *Free Form* album. The introduction and conclusion of the piece use obvious mento riffs neatly integrated into the smooth tight harmony created by the instruments of Keane and Harriott. These two horn players again insinuate mento into the dissonant, yet often-melodic conversation between the alto sax and trumpet that crowns the middle of this brilliantly performed tune. The significance of a tune like "Calypso" is that Harriott integrated an indigenous Caribbean folk form into an avant-garde jazz framework at a time when ska—the merger of folk forms, jazz, and rhythm and blues—was still only in its infancy, if not its embryonic form.

Young jazz stars in Jamaica during the late '40s and early '50s consisted of two groups. One group as we have seen left Jamaica and were mainly concerned with interpreting jazz as an American art form and at times, as in the case of Harriott, creating innovations. A separate group placed their jazz skills at the service of the development of ska and the future forms of Jamaican popular music—rocksteady and reggae. Alphonso, Moore, Sterling, and Drummond did not leave Jamaica during this period. Ranglin and McCook, as gifted musicians with career experiences outside of Jamaica, returned to the island—Ranglin before McCook—and were drafted into making contributions to the development of ska in a leadership capacity. Ranglin became one of the originators of the ska beat and a mentor for several musicians including Skatalites' guitarist Jah Jerry. McCook was seen as someone who could be the leader of the Skatalites.

McCook's move to Nassau in the Bahamas in 1954 happened as a result of an invitation to play at the Zanzibar Club with Ernest Ranglin and other Jamaican musicians. But McCook eventually moved his family and remained in Nassau for eight years. During that period of his career, McCook made his first trip to the United States in 1956. A stopover in Miami, Florida brought him in contact with the music of then ascending tenor sax star John Coltrane. The Coltrane of that period had a serious influence on the cool melodic lyricism McCook cultivated in his style of play. McCook returned to Jamaica in 1962, the year of Jamaica's independence from British colonialism, and played regular live jazz gigs in Kingston. McCook's initial connection to the young local recording industry had nothing to do with ska, but with a jazz album produced by "Coxsone" Dodd.

Although ska was a popular music on the rise, Dodd—a big jazz fan—took time out to indulge his own tastes and satisfy the yearnings of local jazz talent to produce two jazz albums. The first album was *I Cover the Waterfront*, a 1962 recording by a quintet identified as the Cecil Lloyd Group. Bandleader Cecil Lloyd was an accomplished Jamaican pianist, trained at the famous arts school Juilliard in New York City. The rhythm section of drummer Lowell Morris and bassist Lloyd Mason never translated their talents to ska, but the two horn players Roland Alphonso on tenor saxophone and Don Drummond on trombone became two of the key soloists in the Skatalites.

The second recording, a 1963 album titled *Jazz Jamaica at the Workshop*, featured the cream of Jamaica's jazz musicians on the island at that time. Lloyd, Mason, Alphonso, and Drummond reappear in an octet that includes drummer Carl McLeod and trumpet player Billy Cooke. Ranglin and McCook complete the group appearing as featured soloists. *I Cover the Waterfront* was essentially an album of jazz cover versions. *Jazz Jamaica at the Workshop* introduced four original compositions, "Serenade in Sound" and "Mr. Propman" by Drummond, "The Answer" by McCook, and Cecil Lloyd's "It Happens." Another recording "Calypso Jazz" was based on a traditional mento and is credited to Iron Bar. Many of the recordings on the album reflect a Jamaican interpretation of jazz, but "Calypso Jazz" in particular, with its seamless mix of a Jamaican folk form and straight-ahead jazz, is highly reminiscent of Harriott's "Calypso," but possesses even more of a calypso flavour.

Don Drummond.

The trombone voice of Drummond on his compositions reflects that unique mournful tone that became his signature. Ranglin's playing on the band's cover of "Exodus" and McCook's soloing on "The Answer" also convey jazz with Jamaican personality. In many ways, *Jazz Jamaica at the Workshop* is an indication that many of these Jamaican jazzmen were to work out a Jamaican jazz language through a particular kind of ska—the Skatalites ska. Although Alphonso, Drummond, Ranglin, and McCook initially came together as session musicians for the album, they eventually became part of the all-star cast of the Skatalites.

McCook's reputation as a skilled jazz musician and as a senior figure—he was a few years older than the other Skatalites—formed the basis for the repeated requests for him to lead the group of musicians who were to become the Skatalites. McCook initially refused these invitations because he was not interested in playing ska; his sole intention was to focus on jazz like his Alpha contemporaries in America and Europe. The catalyst for McCook's decision to join the band was not due to anyone's negotiating skills, but the quality of ska delivered on record by the soon-to-be Skatalites. When McCook heard "Schooling the Duke"—an immensely popular tune in Jamaica at that time—he was immediately drawn to the jazz quotient of the solos by Drummond, Bobby Gaynair (Wilton's brother) on saxophone and particularly the trumpet playing of Moore on that track.

Ranglin, it seems, required less convincing to contribute to the ska beat's genesis. Despite Ranglin's willingness to participate in Jamaica's nascent popular music scene, he continued to operate successfully in the jazz world. Ernest Ranglin is a first-rate jazz guitarist. Even though he was influenced by jazz guitar greats Charlie Christian and Wes Montgomery, he developed a style inspired by saxophone players like Charlie Parker. Ranglin minted a playing style that deployed moderately paced mento-edged notes alongside the attack of a rapid-fire flurry of bold jazz chords. He plays it complex or simple as required. He is just as comfortable adding colour to a melody or groove with his deft comping as he is at skillfully dispatching crisp jaw-dropping solos.

Ranglin's exposure to the art of guitar playing started when he was a young boy. His uncles who had a certain dexterity on guitar and ukulele provided Ranglin with his initial lessons. At fourteen, Ranglin began to study the guitar seriously, and at that age played with Val Bennett's band as a prodigy in the mid-'40s. In the early '50s, he joined Eric Deans' organization where he played until he left for the Bahamas. While performing in Nassau, outstanding guitarist Les Paul heard Ranglin display his skills and was impressed with the young Jamaican's talent.

Ranglin was one of a number of studio session musicians involved in the gradual process of creating the ska beat, which probably began in 1958. Under the guidance of producer "Coxsone" Dodd, these session musicians recorded American-style rhythm and blues tunes modelled on the music of Louis Jordan and Roscoe

Gordon, both major figures in American popular music of the early '50s. Ranglin, bassist Cluet Johnson, plus all the musicians who were to become the Skatalites—with the exception of McCook and Mittoo—played on a variety of these Jamaican boogie blues tunes that eventually evolved into a proto-ska form, then finally full-blown ska. There has been some debate about whether this transformation from boogie blues to ska was conscious or whether it happened accidentally. Both assertions may be partially correct. It is possible that the musicians' natural tendency to interpret American music in a Jamaican way began to change the music's direction, despite the intention to imitate. It is also possible that Coxsone, as a savvy and astute producer, recognized this change as something fresh and exciting and consciously encouraged this new direction. Based on the achievements of Coxsone and Ranglin, it is not inconceivable that their explanation, which suggests that they together with Cluet Johnson devised the ska beat, is correct.

After his quality work on the *Jazz Jamaica at the Workshop* recording, Ranglin was musical director and guitarist on the first Jamaican international pop hit, Millie Small's 1964 ska song "My Boy Lollipop." In the same year, he earned a jazz award in the U.K. As Ernest Ranglin himself tells the story, he sat in with the house band at Ronnie Scott's jazz club in London, England. At one point during the set, the band played a difficult tune assuming that a guitarist from Jamaica contributing to pop tunes would be unable to cope. Ranglin surprised everyone by being more than equal to the task. Club owner and musician Ronnie Scott was so impressed that Ranglin became the resident jazz guitarist at the club for the next several months. The jazz poll of Britain's *Melody Maker* magazine declared the unassuming Jamaican guitarist the winner of their "new star" category for 1964.

One aspect of ska's personality—particularly its melodic sensibility—was clearly the creation of Jamaica's leading jazz artists. The other important elements of ska involving rhythm came from sources and influences that possessed a very strong Jamaican component. The importance of the Skatalites' rhythm section—drummer Lloyd Knibb, acoustic bassist Lloyd Brevette, pianist Jackie Mittoo, and rhythm guitarist "Jah Jerry" Haines—cannot be overstated in its historic accomplishment of setting the tone for the rhythmic future of Jamaican popular music forms of roots reggae and dancehall reggae. Brevette's bass lines reflected a

Jamaicanized blues framework. Haines and Mittoo dispatched ska's distinctive rhythmic accents. Knibb introduced a burru style of trap drumming influenced by the nyabinghi hand drumming of Count Ossie's ensemble.

Oswald "Count Ossie" Williams virtually created Rasta nyabinghi drumming. Ossie's journey as a musician began in 1949, through teaching sessions with a burru hand drum stylist named Brother Job. Burru was an underground sect that kept alive a particular African retention in Jamaican music culture involving hand drumming. Eventually, Count Ossie developed such outstanding skills that he became a master hand drummer and creator of innovative drumming based on burru that is today considered Rasta music or nyabinghi. Ossie's profile as a highly talented musician and Rastafari sage was so prominent that he was a magnet, pulling interested Jamaicans of various races and classes to his humble Adastra Road Rasta camp in East Kingston. The artistry of Count Ossie and his hand drum ensemble was officially recognized by political leaders in government and in the parliamentary opposition during the '60s. In fact, when Emperor Haile Selassie of Ethiopia visited Jamaica in 1966, Count Ossie was one of a select group of Rasta leaders who was allowed to meet with the Emperor. Count Ossie's work was also admired by important figures in the jazz world. There is photographic evidence of Ossie meeting Duke Ellington when Ellington visited Jamaica in the early '60s. The photograph shows the Duke standing beside the Count as the Count gives what appears to be an impromptu performance for a small gathering.

Count Ossie's reputation as an iconic drummer and band-leader also attracted the island's best jazz musicians to his camp to participate in what must have been incredible jam sessions. Most of the future members of the Skatalites lived in East Kingston, and most of them spent a lot of time eating, sleeping, smoking, and improvising a highly charged blend of jazz and nyabinghi music at Count Ossie's communal camp. "Coxsone" Dodd has indicated that he first came into contact with the future members of the Skatalites by attending these Count Ossie jam sessions. Moore, Alphonso, Drummond, Ranglin, McCook—when he came back from Nassau—and Lloyd Knibb were all immersed in these historic sessions. In separate interviews, Knibb mentions that his first instrument was a repeater hand drum, which he played at a Rasta

Count Ossie (Oswald Williams).

camp. He also confirms that Count Ossie was one of the main influences on his style of drumming. The Skatalites' recordings such as "Woman a Come," "Don D Lion," "Addis Ababa," and "Smiling" are examples of Knibb's cacophonic burru style.

The period of the mid- to late-'50s—before the birth of ska and before the maturation of the Jamaican recording industry—witnessed the rise to prominence of mobile discotheques, called sound systems, which played recorded rhythm and blues music. The arrival of rhythm and blues as an exciting new sound meant that the urban popular music status of jazz began to diminish. In particular, live jazz aimed at an African-Jamaican audience began to fade into a secondary position.

Sound-system culture, as we know it today, began to surface in the late '40s as a means of entertaining the Black poor with African-American blues and jazz recordings in a dance environment. By the mid-'50s, when rhythm and blues started its rise as the popular music of the day, sound-system dances were preoccupied with exposing their patrons to the rough-edged gutbucket recordings of Amos Milburn, Fats Domino, Bobby Bland, Johnny Ace, Roscoe Gordon, Louis Jordan, and the Latin sounds of Machito, Perez Prado, and others. Sound systems mainly indulged earthy roots music that had an exclusive underground quality. This kind of "hardcore" music was not featured on '50s Jamaican radio, which favoured the recordings of American pop stars like Perry Como, Pat Boone, and Frank Sinatra. Mento records such as *What Is Catty*, *Penny Wheel*, and *Jamaican Gal* painted these '50s dances with local colour during the final hours of partying. At some dances, Count Ossie's ensemble would perform a midnight concert that involved a more secular style of nyabinghi drumming closer to the sound of the "Oh Carolina" single Ossie recorded with the Folkes Brothers, as opposed to the more traditional Rasta music approach that can be heard in the version on the *Grounation* album. The playing of mento records and the live Count Ossie performances, though not the main music played at sound-system dances of that period, ensured that indigenous Jamaican music still occupied an important place in the urban popular music environment.

The heart of the sound system ticked to an amplifier dispensing big power generated by tubes, not transistors. A turntable, plugged into this power tube amp, spun black vinyl while its needle rode the grooves of rhythm and blues tracks and, eventually, ska recordings. The music on these records transmitted through a nervous system of thick wire that connected the power amp to multiple speakers. The guts of these refrigerator-sized speakers bore cavernous bass woofers that gave full voice to over-amplified, but seamlessly resonant bass of non-Jamaican recordings that were beyond the sonic scope of what may have been intended by the record's producers and engineers. Jamaican recordings were produced and engineered with the prime purpose of being played on sound systems in a dancehall. The emphatic bass of roots reggae and dancehall reggae have continued the tradition of Jamaican popular music's signature low-end sonic thrust. Woofers pushed out bass thunder with such benevolent force that the zinc sheets fencing the perimeter of the large outdoor dancehall would hum, "bzzzz, bzzzz." Several public address–style speakers, called steel horns—sometimes perched high in the branches of trees—produced piercing treble sounds through which the sound system sang in a fine falsetto in counterpoint to the rich baritone offered by the speaker boxes.

Sound systems were a mobile creature that relocated on a regular basis to different venues. Coxsone's Downbeat, Duke Reid's Trojan, and Tom the Great Sebastian were the names of three big early '60s sound systems that provided an identity to match their tenacious nature. These sound systems mashed up venues such as Gold Coast, Liberty Hall, and Chocomo Lawn with a relentless beat. Sound-system dances mainly took place in an outdoor location late at night under the easy gaze of a navy-blue sky ornamented with glistening stars. A brace of bass that hit patrons at chest-level and steel horns that carried the jazzy trombone, trumpet, and saxophone solos of ska to the entire community surrounding the venue brought these dancehall parties to life. Young men, dressed in immaculately pressed short-sleeved cotton shirts and dark-coloured gun-mouth pants that narrowed as each pant leg approached the ankles, danced aerobic ska moves with women wearing crinoline dresses that assumed an umbrella shape below the waist.

Sound systems would often compete against each other in the same venue. Otherwise, one sound system would compete for the attendance of patrons with other sound systems playing different venues in the same vicinity on the same night. Most of these sound systems played regularly at dances in and around the working-class communities of Kingston, though they also entertained dance fans in rural communities. The competition between sound systems was so intense that the objective often became the ability to play at least one exclusive record at a particular point during the dance that would throw their patrons into a frenzy and drive the competing sound system to frantically seek out that hot musical shot.

At the end of the '50s, sound systems rocked dancehalls with mento-accented rhythm and blues such as Theophilus Beckford's "Easy Snappin'" in 1958 and Laurel Aitken's "Boogie in My Bones" in 1959. In 1960, the Folkes Brothers' "Oh Carolina" introduced Count Ossie's nyabinghi hand drumming to the popular domain. These recordings represented Jamaican popular music in embryo. In the year of Jamaica's independence from British colonial rule in 1962, there was a great sense of pride in the emergence of an indigenous popular music form that was as sophisticated and vibrant as Don Drummond's "Schooling the Duke," that year's popular ska hit. In 1963, the Maytals' "Six and Seven Books" introduced a Jamaican gospel sensibility laced with hints of poco-mania and kumina to the secular domain. The following year, Skatalites' recordings such as "Guns of Navarone" and their support of the Wailers' "Simmer Down" exploded sound-system dances throughout the island. Sound-system culture came of age as a conduit for locally produced recordings as ska captured the national consciousness.

The popularity of straight-ahead jazz may have been reduced but it was not completely absent from the scene. Sonny Bradshaw was the main individual from the jazz generation of the '40s who not only remained in Jamaica but also remained the chief proponent of Jamaican jazz. Throughout the periods of American rhythm and blues and Jamaican boogie blues in the '50s, ska and rocksteady in the '60s, and roots reggae in the '70s, Bradshaw continued to organize his big band to perform live jazz shows. Bradshaw ensured that straight-ahead jazz, though submerged and much less prominent, remained a permanent part of the fabric of Jamaican music culture. Jazz continued to live a vicarious popular existence as an integral element of the Skatalites' ska.

Eastern Standard Time

Don Drummond, the Skatalites, and the International Legacy of Ska and Jamaican Jazz

The official birthdate of the Skatalites band has been given as May 1964, even though the band's involvement in studio session work began before that date. The band's leading soloists were Don Drummond, Tommy McCook, and Roland Alphonso. Johnny Moore's contributions were also crucial. McCook and Alphonso both played tenor saxophone, and although there was always a competitive edge in their personal and professional relationship, each man's approach to the saxophone was quite different. Alphonso favoured an intuitive, bluesy, rhythm and blues attack that dispatched rambunctious notes reminiscent of his initial influences—American tenor players Tex Beneke, of the Glenn Miller Band, and Illinois Jacquet, who played with Count Bassie among others. Alphonso's solos on recordings like "Dick Tracy," "Ball of Fire," and "Phoenix City" are characteristic of that style. The influence of John Coltrane can be heard in McCook's esoteric, fluid, and lyrical tenor sax voice displayed on jazz tunes such as "The Answer" and on ska recordings like "Exodus," "Latin Goes Ska," and "Fidel Castro."

Drummond's moody, sometimes rebellious, sometimes sorrow-filled trombone playing, plus his deeply troubled state of mind made him the Skatalites' most famous musician and mythic personality. Drummond was a kind of Charlie Parker or Jimi Hendrix figure, a man with great talent who died much too young in tragic circumstances. Johnny "Dizzy" Moore—whose nickname reveals his Dizzy Gillespie influence—a skilled bebop stylist, acted as Drummond's main foil on the recordings of the trombonist's popular compositions like the classic "Man in the Street," and "Don D Lion." Alto saxophonist Lester Sterling was not one of the band's main soloists when it came to their recorded work, but his alto made its presence felt on tracks such as "Christine Keeler."

The Skatalites' rhythm section never failed to produce, on each tune, a bold rhythmic canvas on which the soloists could paint elaborate melodies. Brevette stroked the strings of his standing double bass with steady fingers, coaxing supple ska bass tones from his instrument. Brevette's fingers walked the bass strings like a rebel *rude bwoy* quickly skanking down Windward Road in East Kingston. Knibb sat around his drum set, moving arms and legs in coordination at the pace of a 400-metre runner as he used his drumsticks to create satisfying burru beats and intermittently fire off rounds of rim shots. The band's rhythm section included the vital piano phrases of ebullient teenager Jackie Mittoo and the indispensable rhythm guitar strums of "Jah Jerry" Haines. In addition to the core members of the band, guest musicians such as Ernest Ranglin, guitarist Lyn Taitt, saxophonists Dennis "Ska" Campbell and Bobby Gaynair, and trumpet players Rupert Dillon and Raymond Harper joined the Skatalites either in the studio or on the concert stage or both. On stage, the Skatalites sometimes featured vocalists Doreen Schaeffer and Lord Tanamo.

As session musicians for "Coxsone" Dodd's Studio One, the Skatalites' cutting-edge ska can be heard on the vast majority of ska vocal recordings including most of the ska songs recorded by Bob Marley, Bunny Wailer, and Peter Tosh as the Wailers. As an exciting live band, the Skatalites adopted much more of a jazz format on the bandstand, a format in which all the horn players were able to showcase their skills as soloists. The band had a regular gig at the Bournemouth Club in East Kingston. The club, located by Kingston Harbour at the foot of Sea Breeze Avenue, was not really a conventional nightclub, but rather a multi-purpose facility. The elegant facility featured a competition-size outdoor swimming pool backing out onto a stretch of beach fenced off to retain its exclusivity. Access to the swimming pool and beach was gained by entering the ground floor of a two-storey building that accommodated changing rooms and a bar. The upper-level space incorporated a large room used as a dancehall or concert venue and a deck offering a breathtaking view of the pool, beach, and sea. Bournemouth Baths officially opened in 1926 as an exclusive upper-class members' club for White people only. Public protest of the discrimination, in addition to the changing class and racial composition of the community surrounding the facility, led to its sale to the city of Kingston in 1937. By the '50s, Bournemouth was an important city landmark for all Kingston residents. Anyone who paid the admission fee could attend. During the day, the swimming pool was available to the public if it was not being used as the main venue for high-school swimming competitions. At night, Bournemouth transformed into a nightclub where patrons assembled on the hardwood floor of the dancehall to be entertained by recorded music from sound systems or by live jazz from bands such as those led by George Moxey, Eric Deans, and Carlos Malcolm.

One special night in the summer of 1964, the Skatalites were about to take the bandstand at Bournemouth Club. There was a collective sense of trepidation among the fans present about whether Don Drummond would walk onto the stage with the rest of the band. It was not unusual for Drummond to show up late for gigs or not at all. Drummond's unpredictable behaviour meant that there was always a question in the minds of the audience about whether they would be fortunate to experience Drummond's distinctive trombone that night. That question translated to a kind of anxious anticipation. When Knibb, Brevette, Jah Jerry, Mittoo, Moore, Sterling, Alphonso, bandleader McCook, and MC Lord Tanamo took their positions on the bandstand, Drummond stepped out with them. The collective buzz of anticipation in the room rose to a level that was palpable. The Skatalites proceeded to blaze a satisfying intense first set with blistering solos by McCook, Alphonso, Moore, and Sterling. Throughout the entire set of tunes the band played before taking their first break, Drummond just stood there without playing one note. The audience, though a little agitated, remained optimistic that Drummond would deliver after the break. When the band returned for their second appearance, Don was with them. Again, the band treated fans to another set of great Skatalites tunes, and, again, Don just stood there without placing the trombone to his lips for the entire second set. At this point, the audience began to display emotions of frustration, anger, and disappointment. It was about 2 a.m. While the band took their second break, Drummond walked out onto the bandstand as if he was ready and willing to play. The other band members were hurriedly encouraged to join him. Drummond then proceeded to satisfy his fans' heightened level of expectancy by playing for several hours.

The Skatalites also appeared at a number of other Kingston nightclubs and concert venues including the Students' Union at the University of the West Indies, the Sombrero Club on Molynes Road, and Silver Slipper Club in Cross Roads. Cross Roads was the dividing line between the more affluent uptown neighbourhoods to the north and the poor and working-class communities to the south.

Individual musicians in the Skatalites lived in working-class communities. In fact, most of them were residents of East Kingston. The band's fan base cut across Jamaica's class divide to include fans in the middle class, fans among high-school and university students, and admirers who were established writers, poets, and artists. The Skatalites, by virtue of their talent, musical sophistication, and humble origins were perceived as the people's band.

There were ska bands other than the Skatalites, such as Carlos Malcolm and the Afro-Jamaican Rhythms and the uptown band of Byron Lee and the Dragonnaires. The Skatalites, however, were clearly identified with the movement of Rastafari, particularly because of their association with Count Ossie. Band members Drummond and McCook, for example, possessed a Black consciousness, while Moore actually immersed himself in the Rasta faith and way of life.

The Skatalites' persona as a working-class band with connections to the Rasta movement negatively affected their ability to achieve any kind of international presence. When the Jamaican government decided to promote the island using its new form of popular music by sending a ska band, ska vocalists, and ska dancers to the 1964 World's Fair in New York City, the band they chose to send was Byron Lee and the Dragonnaires rather than the superior Skatalites. Despite losing the opportunity to represent Jamaican ska in the United States, their "Guns of Navarone" recording hit the #36 spot on the U.K. pop charts in 1967. "Guns of Navarone" was one of only three Jamaican records to break into the British charts during the '60s. The other two were Prince Buster's "Al Capone" that charted as high as #18 and Millie Small's #1 hit "My Boy Lollipop."

Don Drummond was not only the Skatalites' star performer, he was also the first folk hero of the island's popular music. Drummond's folk hero status grew mainly out of two important achievements: his exceptional ability on the trombone, and the way he used his music to tap into the pain, suffering, joy, and aspirations of his fellow working-class African-Jamaicans.

Drummond was born on March 12, 1932. He entered Alpha Boys' School at nine years old, where he learned to read and write music, and developed his affinity for playing the trombone. Don D, as Drummond was called, not only mastered the instrument but also crafted his own unique trombone sound.

Tommy McCook.

Drummond's professional career began in his eighteenth year when he joined the Eric Deans swing band in 1950. Throughout the '50s, Drummond established himself as a talented jazz trombonist who, at times, together with other Jamaican jazz musicians, supported famous American jazz artists on tour in Jamaica. Carmen McRae, Woody Herman, and Louis Armstrong all gave performances in Kingston between 1956 and 1958. On one particular engagement, Drummond provided accompaniment for the great jazz singer Sarah Vaughan when she performed in Jamaica in the late '50s. Tommy McCook discusses Vaughan's reaction to Drummond's artistry: "(Drummond's) tone on the instrument was the outstanding part of it because when Sarah Vaughan came to Jamaica in the '50s ... she rated him (among) the ten best (trombonists) in the world."[1] Roland Alphonso, who also supported Vaughan at that concert, has been quoted as saying that Vaughan was so impressed with Drummond's playing, she commented that Drummond's unique tone defined the trombone as an instrument for mourning.

Drummond dominated the ska era as a prolific innovative composer. His music often featured disturbing melancholy blues and dissonant minor-key lyricism, provoking dark, menacing, and rebellious rhythms as can be heard on tracks such as "Johnny Dark" and "Smiling." These edgier examples of Drummond's instrumentals were an antidote to lighter, upbeat, pop-style ska recordings. Other inventive Drummond compositions, through their titles, remembered historic African-Jamaican heroes who struggled against slavery or race and class oppression. "Reincarnation of Marcus Garvey" tributed the Jamaican Black nationalist leader whose cause of Black liberation went beyond Jamaica to the United States, where Garvey had a huge following while living there during the '20s. "The Return of Paul Bogle" pointed at the contributions of the Baptist deacon who fought racism and inequities suffered by African-Jamaicans during the immediate post-slavery era of the mid-nineteenth century. The tune "Addis Ababa" was named after the capital city of Ethiopia, the spiritual homeland of Rastafari, and "Man in the Street" turned a spotlight on the ordinary Jamaican citizen.

Poet and '60s Rasta activist Robin "Bongo Jerry" Small delivered a touching tribute to Drummond on a 1970 Jamaican radio program commemorating Drummond's life and art. Bongo Jerry's poetic words attempt to describe the emotion and feeling that fuelled Drummond's music:

> Music like the "Reincarnation of Marcus Garvey" was not only entertaining but it was also educational. It insisted on our being attentive and it also made man maintain them folklore by being emotional.
>
> Listen to him in (the tune) "Don D Lion" come to agreement with the trumpet of Johnny Moore. The unity that prevail in that music is something savoured like sweets. They maintain attention with their horns that made the drummer alert.
>
> Listen again, listen to "Treasure Isle" and you will hear how man can make instrument suggest travelling and motion and floating to man.
>
> Listen to the tune "Scandal" and you will hear a man

Don Drummond.

suggest a certain (sense) of shock … just by the way that him introduce the tune. You listen and you listen and you hear Lester Sterling's (alto saxophone) take over the music and introduce improvisation. And by the time Don Drummond('s trombone) is ready to speak again is like this said scandal but a reverse of Sterling's improvisation. (It) is just like the different versions of these stories that these same people always had when the scandal was about.

In a different light also, slower, but behind vocalists backing up Dotty and Bunny on "Dearest," you hear (Drummond's trombone) submitting … to the will of the vocalists and helping those vocalists to express what that tune "Dearest" was trying to say. Like a man dealing with him Dearest or vice-versa. The feeling was there and the willingness to express the extent and the boundaries of that said love to a man Dearest.

Every tune, every piece of music, over five hundred of which, this man made, every piece of music Don Drummond (created) was like a theme for a very great movie or a very great Broadway show. Every one of them, like even "Street Corner" ... was an announcement of some sort. "Man in the Street," every one of these tunes sound like a very great theme song. And every one of them was. Don Drummond music have the effect of ganja.[2]

Drummond, a victim of schizophrenia, was a quiet, withdrawn, and introspective man, frequently in and out of mental care. The erratic behaviour he sometimes displayed may have been caused by his illness. As Tommy McCook suggests schizophrenia was unable to conceal or dilute Drummond's genius: "(Don was) unpredictable but great ... musically, you know...the sounds he produced ... and the way he played his horn ... it was so mournful, sometimes you could cry inside ... you would marvel to know that a man so great ... who is sick mentally could play so well."[3]

In the late '50s when "Coxsone" Dodd first met Drummond, he had just resurfaced from a period of institutional care. Coxsone remembers that he acquired a trombone for Drummond so that he could play at his first Studio One recording session. Drummond participated in several significant ska recording sessions at Coxsone's studio including one specific Wailers' recording session.

Imagine Don Drummond and Bob Marley in the recording studio in 1963. Don at age thirty-one and a youthful Bob are preparing for the session that will record "I Am Going Home." Don is in one corner of the room seated. His head bowed. The bell of his horn rests on his thigh. His right arm secures the instrument by sitting on the bar of the trombone's slide. He is wearing a roomy cotton turtleneck sweater and a fedora hat. He appears pensive. Bob is positioned behind a mike. He has a serious determined look in his eye suggesting that he is ready and eager to work.

Bob will sing lead on this one. The other Wailers—Bunny, Peter, Cherry, Beverly, and Junior will provide patois-tinged rhythm and blues harmony. Don's job is to inject the song with an animated solo that will add an edge to the Wailers' thin sweet voices and act as counterpoint to Bob's wailing scat lines. Don D's trombone wails harder than the Wailers. After all, he and his ska co-conspirators are experienced veterans. Although the young

Wailers have several hit tunes to their credit and are popular with their contemporaries, they are still teenagers. They represent the next wave just entering the scene. Without the Skatalites providing the musical muscle, it is doubtful that Wailers' ska hits like "Simmer Down" would have been able to flex so hard.

On that day in 1963, two spirits connect. Bob Marley—the rebel *rude bwoy*, before Rasta, before dreadlocks, and before superstardom—was a trying youth with *nuff* talent, and was already a folk hero among his contemporaries. Don D possessed a persona larger than life. Over the previous fifteen years, Don D attained legendary status. Respected by his own generation, he and the Skatalites boasted an adoring youth fan base of Bob's generation.

On New Year's Day 1965, Drummond committed a tragic act. In a rage possibly inspired by his mental illness, he fatally stabbed his companion and lover Anita "Marguerita" Mahfood.

In almost all the books about reggae history that mention Drummond, Mahfood is simply portrayed as a one-dimensional character who probably would not have been considered if she had not been murdered. Only minimal details of her life are revealed, such as the fact that she was a rhumba dancer. Some commentators do not even know that her real name was Anita, and that Marguerita was her stage name. In Jamaica, where we would expect more detail about Mahfood from analysts and music historians, she has been virtually ignored.

There appears to be a general assumption that the details of Mahfood's life story add nothing to the narrative of Drummond or the history of ska and Jamaican music. Nothing could be further from the truth. In addition to being a dancer, Mahfood was a singer/songwriter with a talent for writing poetic lyrics that reflected the consciousness of Rastafari.

Anita Mahfood was a young woman, about twenty-one years old, when she died. Mahfood is the name of a wealthy Jamaican family of Lebanese heritage who would be considered "White" by Jamaicans. Although the fair-skinned Anita may have been related to the rich Mahfoods, she grew up in a working-class community in East Kingston, which suggests that her immediate family was probably, at the most, lower middle-class. Anita did, however, attend Alpha Academy, a prestigious Catholic high school for girls. Having attended a high school like Alpha, Mahfood's decision to pursue a career as an exotic dancer could not have been what her family wished for her.

Anita Mahfood was drawn to the music, culture, and politics of African-Jamaicans. Her attraction to Black culture was one thing, but her deep involvement with the Rasta movement and her activities as a rhumba dancer exhibited a certain kind of rebellion. Mahfood's rebellion, in a way, worked against the upward social mobility that her race and education could potentially deliver. Anita Mahfood did not seem interested in a life of middle-class light-skinned privilege. Instead, she lived a bohemian existence of a rebel, free spirit, and independent woman at a time in Jamaica of the late '50s and early '60s when her behaviour would have been perceived as nonconformist to the extreme.

Mahfood was not just an average dancer. Jamaican writer Verena Reckord—one of the few researchers to reveal interesting information about Mahfood—describes her as Marguerita "the famous rhumba queen." The art of rhumba dancing involves smooth intricate steps that contribute to sensuous, yet graceful hip movements. These elements of the dance combine with sexually suggestive gestures that add to rhumba's identification as a kind of erotic pantomime.

Mahfood's importance as a talented dancer is also underscored by an incident that involved an impending dance performance on Vere Johns' Opportunity Knocks variety show held at the distinguished venue of downtown Kingston's Ward Theatre in the late '50s. Opportunity Knocks was a showcase for new talent, but also for established artists, that could provide a gateway to a broader Jamaican mainstream audience and possibly a recording contract for singers and musicians. Anita Mahfood demanded that Count Ossie's drum ensemble provide the music for her dance routine. In '50s Jamaica, Rastafari were seen as social outcasts and quite often considered outlaws, so Mahfood's demand met with some resistance. She was insistent. As a famous dancer, her appearance on the show was a bonus for Johns, so he eventually relented. Count Ossie's group captivated the audience with their drumming and became a regular on the show. This incident suggests that Anita must have had a significant reputation and popularity as a dancer to be able to convince Johns to include Count Ossie on the show. It also means that Anita has the distinction of successfully negotiating Count Ossie's first performance in front of a mainstream audience—a performance that signifies his breakthrough to the arena of Jamaican popular culture.

Anita Mahfood's song "Woman A Come" is one example of her talent at writing poetry in song form that was recorded, possibly in 1963 or 1964. The record features her vocals and the music of the Skatalites. The song is a love letter to Don Drummond and a meditation on Anita's relationship with Don that is couched in metaphors of a Rastafarianized African cosmology:

I-ah-ta
Jah Daughter
From Venturion border
a come ...

Jah Daughter
I-ah-ta
a come to sound
Oongoo Maloongoo Man

If you see him before I do
Please give him
My heart message so true
Tell him
I don't want to live without him
For I'll be lost and lonely and blue
He is my love, my life, my all

We speak the language of the breeze
And harmonize it with the symphonies of the trees
And when I am in my solitude
I can hear
I can hear the breeze singing to me
Not imaginary songs
but true melodies
Of my beautiful
Oongoo Maloongoo Man[4]

This excerpt shows why the recording is historically important for a variety of reasons. "Woman A Come" is important for that time because it is a recording of a song written and performed solo by a woman. In Jamaica during the '60s, women were usually singing songs written by men and usually as part of a duet with a

male singer. The song is also significant because a woman—
Marguerita as I-ah-ta Jah Daughter from Venturion Border—is the
subject of the song. Even though it is a love song, it is far from typical in the sense that the woman is not the victim of some doomed
romantic or sexual encounter. In fact, if sex or romance is a significant aspect of the love I-ah-ta Jah Daughter expresses for
Drummond portrayed as Oongoo Maloongoo Man, then we do
not hear about it in the song. Instead, I-ah-ta Jah Daughter and
Oongoo Maloongoo Man are cast as shaman-type characters that
relate on a spiritual and artistic level in which I-ah-ta Jah Daughter,
when she is alone, can hear Oongoo Maloongoo Man's songs in
the wind. The song's narrative is driven by I-ah-ta Jah Daughter's
journey to physically connect with her beloved Oongoo
Maloongoo Man because it seems she is always spiritually connected to him through the power of his music.

Mahfood sings "Woman A Come" in a dissonant voice that ten
or fifteen years later would have fit comfortably in the context of a
certain kind of rock or punk, but sounds incongruous in the context of the more melodious and sweeter sounding ska vocals of the
day. Drummer Lloyd Knibb's instincts are perfect on this track as
he serves up a brooding burru syncopation that is encouraged and
prodded by Baba Brooks' haunting trumpet riff. McCook's tenor
sax solo on the track is wisely understated, leaving Mahfood's
voice as the main attraction as it surfs Knibb's nyabinghi-style trap
drum sounds. "Woman A Come" can only be compared to Judy
Mowatt's work such as the tracks on the *Black Woman* album that
debuted at least fifteen years after Mahfood's recording.

Anita Mahfood was married to a boxer named Rudolph Bent
with whom she had two children, Suzanne and Christopher.
Mahfood divorced Bent before she began living with Drummond.
The dynamics of her relationship with Drummond are sketchy, but
it is safe to say that Anita and Don were ideological and artistic soul
mates—they shared a radical Black consciousness and they were
both artists. There is no question that their relationship was often
contentious and sometimes violent. Lloyd Knibb provides some
insight into their stormy relationship with the following anecdote:

Well it happened 'round the back of the studio. (Don) was
writing out a ... tune ... and Marguerita rush in. (She) both-
ered him with an argument and he just stick (stab on the
back of her hand) her with the pen. I have to (take) her to a

doctor nearby ... When we (got) back (Marguerita) and
Don just ... hug up like nothing happen.[5]

The abuse suffered by Mahfood at the hands of Drummond in
Knibb's anecdote cannot be excused. Drummond's actions, however, are complicated by his schizophrenia and by the couple's
affection for each other. As Tommy McCook commented:
"Marguerita and (Don) were sort of inseparable." According to
Knibb, the voice of Drummond's trombone solo on the tune
"Silver Dollar" sounds like Anita's singing voice. In a way,
Drummond channelling Anita's sensibility in his solo demonstrates her influence on his art. In some ways, Anita Mahfood's
relationship to Don Drummond can be compared to the tempestu-
ous relationships of other more internationally famous couples
with careers in the arts such as artists Frida Kahlo and Diego
Rivera, or musician Miles Davis and actor Cicely Tyson.

Drummond was convicted of Anita Mahfood's murder and
incarcerated in Kingston's Bellevue psychiatric hospital where he
died under questionable circumstances in May 1969 at the age of
thirty-seven. Jamaica's economic and social frame of mind was just
as erratic and lethal as Drummond. A class-induced schizophrenia
wracked the consciousness of '60s Jamaica. The beauty of the lush
Blue Mountain range, Negril's white-sand beaches and the scenic
Dunns River Falls offered picture-perfect tourist vistas that cast a
dark shadow across ghetto tenement yards. Shantytowns found in
the southern sections of Kingston and the adjacent parish of St.
Andrew were populated by a series of one-room shacks built out
of wood boards and zinc sheets.

Naked babies take tentative steps in a tenement yard as thick
yellow snot runs like a river from their noses, draining onto cute
separated lips. Men and women dressed in ragged clothes walk
around the yard this workday morning; the stylish "good" clothes
they wore at the sound-system dance the night before were hung
up neatly in a tiny one-room space that serves as bedroom, living
room, and dining area. They woke up that morning not quite
ready for a job that makes unemployment sound like an upward-
ly mobile career. What will the hustling be today? Sell pants length
material downtown? Buy fish at the seaside to sell at the market?
Sell peanuts and cashews to spectators at a soccer game inside the
National Stadium? Pick a pocket? Grab a senior woman's hand-
bag? These tenement residents think about these options as they

walk through the yard's dust bowl grounds, negotiating the fresh droppings of mangy mongrel dogs, skinny to the point of *mawga*. Survival, not crime, is the *sufferah's* objective.

The exclusive communities of northeast St. Andrew, the wealthy suburb of the capital, are where the homes of the upper-middle class are located. Hacienda-style bungalows built out of cinder blocks and steel give these houses the look of pastel-coloured low-rise concrete castles. These residences—of doctors, lawyers, university professors, the upper hierarchy of the army and police force, business owners, and other professionals—posed snobbishly on landscaped lawns carefully decorated with colourful flowers. Residents of zinc-sheet shacks were allowed entry to these castles as gardeners, maids, cooks, and live-in babysitters. Even though the communities of the impoverished and the rich sometimes existed adjacent to each other, they were like oil and water.

In a sense, the split personality of Jamaica's social class system mirrored Don Drummond's own state of mind. Drummond lived in a society that did not recognize African-Jamaican genius in the field of indigenous culture. He was considered a "raving mad man" rather than a gifted musician with a mental illness. The dark side of post-colonial Jamaica acted like a demon that could just as easily exacerbate existing turmoil in the minds of cultural heroes like Drummond in the same way it exploded the sanity, blew the mind of everyday *sufferahs*, condemning unsuspecting victims to mental illness and sometimes physical death.

Drummond's departure from Jamaica's popular music scene in 1965, as a result of his incarceration, left a huge void in the Skatalites and in the continued expression of ska. The Skatalites as a band did not survive the year and disbanded in August 1965. The band, perceived and maybe conceived by Dodd as a collection of mainly star musicians, suffered the tensions of having to share the spotlight with each other, or, rather, whatever spotlight remained that was not consumed by Drummond's folk-hero mythic status.

There were always personality clashes between individuals in the Skatalites. In particular, there was some rivalry between the band's two tenor sax players Alphonso and McCook. The fact that record producer Dodd was close friends with Alphonso and favoured him not only as a leading soloist on Skatalites recordings, but also as a leader on non-Skatalites recordings, certainly did not help the unity of the band. The dissolution and subsequent split was the result of the growing fissure in the band. Brevette, Moore, Sterling, and Mittoo remained as a studio session band for Dodd under the leadership of Alphonso. Knibb joined a new band led by McCook that became the studio session band for Dodd's main rival Duke Reid. Alphonso's band was alternatively called the Soul Vendors or the Soul Brothers. The name of McCook's aggregation was the Supersonics. The divisive personality issues among individuals in the Skatalites seemed to remain submerged while Drummond was still in circulation, but his death seemed to bring these issues to a boiling point.

Less than a year after the break-up of the Skatalites, the era of ska as the prominent popular music on the island came to an end. In the summer of 1966, a new generation of musicians and singers—some of whom began their careers with ska recordings—celebrated the arrival of a newer, slower, bass-dominant beat appropriately named rocksteady, which itself gave way to reggae only two years later in 1968. Drummond's impact on ska and on the Skatalites as the music's main exponent cannot be overstated.

Ten years after Drummond's death, ska re-emerged, not in Jamaica, but in the U.K. This ska revival occurred at a time when Bob Marley's Jamaican roots reggae had a secure mainstream presence and the U.K. reggae of Steel Pulse was featured in the national album charts. Ska's rebirth in the U.K. during the late '70s also coincided with the anti-racist alliance of certain progressive White punk-rock bands and some Black British-Caribbean roots reggae bands. The Specials, the Beat, Selector, and the all-female band Bodysnatchers went one step further by integrating Black and White musicians into one unit that served up high-energy ska marinated in the attitude and rebellious lyrics of punk.

These U.K. ska bands, and others such as Madness and Bad Manners, were inspired by the music of Don Drummond and the Skatalites. But since they were far more interested in ska songs with lyrics—as opposed to instrumentals—their main inspiration was the recordings of Jamaican singer Prince Buster. These bands recorded cover versions of more Prince Buster '60s ska and rocksteady songs than of any other Jamaican ska band or vocalist. Interpretations of Roland Alphonso's "El Pussy Cat Ska" by Bad Manners and the Skatalites' "Guns of Navarone" by Special AKA—a group spawned by the Specials—confirm that the Skatalites' music was an important part of the U.K. ska revival. In fact, the Specials' debut album featured a contemporary of Don Drummond at Alpha Boys' School, Jamaican trombonist Rico Rodrigues. Rodrigues is a seminal figure in ska, who contributed to several Coxsone-produced ska records and was sometimes a guest player with the Skatalites before migrating to the U.K. in the early '60s. His presence on the Specials' first album added substance to the link between Jamaican ska and the U.K. ska revival—a link already established through band names: the Specials was taken from the Jamaican term *special*, meaning a limited edition pre-release recording or a dub plate—an exclusive mix of a recording manufactured specially for a particular dancehall sound system; Madness was taken from the title of a Prince Buster song; and Selector was the term for a deejay, the individual selecting and spinning the discs on the sound system.

The *mods* of '60s Britain were also an important influence on the U.K. ska movement. In the *mod* scene in London, it was cool to attend West End nightclubs such as the Roaring Twenties, to hear resident Jamaican DJ Count Suckle spin the latest Jamaican ska discs while emulating the *rude-bwoy* fashion sense of Jamaican immigrants. John Paul Jones, yet to become Led Zeppelin's bass player, was one of those English youths who hung out at the Roaring Twenties where he heard "Guns of Navarone" and Alphonso's "Phoenix City" for the first time.

The Specials' Jerry Dammers, a central force behind the U.K. ska revival as a movement, understood that even though ska was a Jamaican music, it had insinuated itself into the fabric of U.K. pop music during the '60s. It did so through prominent West End nightclubs, through hits on the British charts, through the U.K. record label Blue Beat, and through the limited mainstream presence of Prince Buster. Buster's U.K. television appearance on the program *Ready Steady Go* was a defining moment for many young fans at the time. Dammers—who in the '80s was a key figure in Britain's Free Nelson Mandela movement—not only brought back *rude-bwoy* fashions as a uniform for ska bands and their fans, but also constructed an infrastructure for the music by creating the Specials' own 2-Tone label. The label—with its distinctive black and white checkerboard logo and its simulation of a photo-negative image of pre-dreadlocks '60s ska era Peter Tosh in "stingy brim" hat, loafers, suit, and tie—wasted no time in signing several other bands such as the Beat, Madness, Selector, and Bodysnatchers. Dammers' 2-Tone label, in some ways, was like a late '70s, early '80s version of Emil Shallit's successful '60s Blue Beat label that recorded and distributed the work of a variety of Jamaican ska vocalists in the U.K.

2-Tone ska instantly breached the mainstream via the Specials' debut album, *Specials*, with the single "Gangsters" climbing quickly up the British pop charts to #6 in September 1979. The popularity of U.K. ska, however, peaked in the early '80s after only a few years.

As 2-Tone began its decline in the U.K., its new ska-oriented punk sound invaded the United States and Canada, generating a fresh fan base and inspiring a new generation of alternative bands in an underground, rather than a mainstream context. In 1982, New York resident Robert "Bucket" Hingley, a U.K. ska fan and British immigrant, formed the Toasters, the seminal American ska band. The following year, Hingley, using the 2-Tone template, established his own Moon Ska record label that served as a springboard for the Toasters and eventually for a number of emerging American ska bands.

In the mid-'80s, American ska received a significant boost from Fishbone, an all-Black band, originally from Los Angeles. As junior high-school students, the individuals who were to come together as Fishbone were transported from the predominantly African-American community of Watts to a school in a mainly White suburb of San Fernando Valley. Living in Watts and educated in the San Fernando Valley provided Fishbone with a mix of diverse musical influences. Fishbone shaped these influences into a gritty edgy musical attack of feverish funk, raw soul, kinetic punk, and erratic ska. Fishbone, then, was not simply a punk-ska band; the influence of 2-Tone formed only one aspect of the band's inventive sound.

Like so many gifted Black rock outfits, Fishbone never truly achieved a sustained mainstream breakthrough in terms of record sales. Their 1988 album *Truth and Soul* with its incendiary version of Curtis Mayfield's "Freddie's Dead" (including an exhilarating music video for that tune) and the energetic ska song "Ma and Pa" pushed the band as far into the mainstream spotlight as they would go. Fishbone's explosive concerts gave them a legendary reputation as incredible live performers. As a result, they were well known by a legion of ska, punk, and Black rock fans on both sides of the Atlantic. As an important punk band, Fishbone had the biggest profile of any American band playing ska during the '80s.

If the Toasters remained underground, and if Fishbone occasionally appeared visible on the mainstream radar, then the '90s wave of American ska with bands like the Mighty Mighty Bosstones and No Doubt exceeded expectations. The Bosstones' punk-oriented ska gave them two radio hits with "The Impression That I Get" in 1997 and "So Sad to Say" in 2000. No Doubt's pop-influenced ska finally hit big in 1996 with the *Tragic Kingdom* album and several singles from that work. Ska had not exactly conquered America or even come close to the successes of Bob Marley, but it came of age in the United States during the '90s.

The U.K.'s 2-Tone ska soaked into the fabric of Canada's pop-music culture for a decade before a substantial Canadian ska scene established firm roots in the early '90s. The Canadian scene has produced a large number of ska bands over the past fifteen years including some of the earlier contenders like King Apparatus, One, the Arsenals, the Hopping Penguins, Skaface, and Bim Ska la Bim. Canadian ska has remained an underground music operating well outside the mainstream consciousness. King Apparatus and One, however, were able to build a fairly visible profile just below the Canadian mainstream. King Apparatus had some success with their single "Made for TV," and One's singles such as "Madeline" and "Wideload" gained some notice beyond the ska scene.

The Arsenals' distinction is that they were a Black band—whose members had roots in Jamaica and the English-speaking Caribbean—that stood out in a scene that did not really emulate the racial diversity of the U.K. or even the American ska bands. Initially, the Arsenals, under the leadership of the late drummer Crash Morgan, were inspired by 2-Tone. But with the addition of trombonist Dizzy D, who became the Arsenals' linchpin after Morgan passed away, the band took their cue from Jamaican ska. Hingley's Moon Ska Records released the Arsenals' only album *Stomp* in 1995. Ska as played by Canadian bands has not had any success in sustaining a breakthrough into the mainstream. There are no Canadian ska bands that can be compared with, for example, the Specials and the Beat in the U.K., or Fishbone, No Doubt, and the Mighty Mighty Bosstones in America in terms of mainstream profile.

As punk began looking at 2-Tone ska for inspiration in the early '80s, the Skatalites re-entered the scene eighteen years after their departure. The idea to attempt reuniting the Skatalites came out of a discussion between Herbie Miller—the Jamaican manager of reggae star Peter Tosh at the peak of his career between 1976 and

Ska group Selector performs at the Palais Royale, Toronto, May 1980.
Photograph by Isobel Harry.

1981—and the principals of Synergy, Tony Johnson, Ronnie Burke, Don Green, and John Wakeling, the Jamaican company that originated and produced the annual Reggae Sunsplash Festival in Jamaica beginning in 1978. Sunsplash was the first major, international, week-long, outdoor reggae festival staged each year in Montego Bay. The festival secured the services of Jimmy Cliff as headliner in its inaugural year, Bob Marley as the marquee draw in 1979, and Peter Tosh as the star of Sunsplash 1980. The festival featured the cream of Jamaican reggae talent including Burning Spear, Third World, Dennis Brown, Marcia Griffiths, and Judy Mowatt. In those years, Sunsplash had a visionary approach and presented the best reggae bands in the Caribbean diaspora including Steel Pulse and Aswad from the U.K., Truths and Rights and Messenjah from Canada, and later Shinehead from the United States. Synergy was never narrow in their selection process for Sunsplash and also booked acts from beyond the Caribbean diaspora such as Stevie Wonder, Gil Scott-Heron, 2-Tone ska band the Beat, and South African reggae artist Lucky Dube.

The Skatalites were scheduled to appear on the night reserved to showcase "vintage" acts from the eras of ska and rocksteady on the 1983 edition of Sunsplash. All the original members of the band were brought together. Roland Alphonso, Johnny Moore, and Lester Sterling came back to the island from various locations in the United States. Jackie Mittoo, a long-time resident of Canada, returned from Toronto. Lloyd Knibb made the short trip to Kingston from Jamaica's north-coast tourist area, while Tommy McCook, Lloyd Brevette, and Jah Jerry were already in Kingston. Don Drummond, of course, was present only in spirit.

The Skatalites' performance at Sunsplash in June 1983 was well received by old fans reliving their experiences of twenty years before and by new converts hearing the band's excellent musicianship and great tunes live in concert for the first time. The Sunsplash concert was the first of three significant 1983 appearances for the band. Later in the year, the Skatalites appeared at the Reggae Superjam festival on a roster that included Peter Tosh. Superjam—the brainchild of Kingsley Cooper, a principal of Pulse, a Jamaican modelling agency—was held every year at various venues in Kingston. The 1983 version of Superjam was probably the best lineup of the festival's short but important tenure. The lineup included Dennis Brown, Beres Hammond, and Steel Pulse on the first night; Leroy Sibbles, Chalice, and Black Uhuru—the recipients of the first reggae Grammy award in 1985—on the second night; and, on the headlining third night, Gregory Isaacs, Skatalites, and Peter Tosh. The other important concert appearance by the reunited Skatalites was quite different from the large reggae festivals where they were among a number of internationally acclaimed reggae acts. The Skatalites' second concert of 1983 took place in July in the intimate setting of a new jazz club, Herbie Miller's Blue Monk Jazz Gallery on Constant Spring Road, an uptown commercial district.

Herbie Miller is a unique figure in music as someone who has been a manager and producer of major critically acclaimed reggae, ska, and jazz artists. Miller has not only worked with Peter Tosh, but also the great African-American jazz tenor sax player David Murray, and the reunited Skatalites. In recent years, Miller has decided to use his vast knowledge of jazz, ska, and reggae as a historian making a different contribution by documenting the accomplishments of Caribbean jazz musicians, ska innovators, and reggae artists.

The opening of Miller's Blue Monk jazz club in 1982 was much less strange at the time than it must seem today in hindsight. Today, looking back over twenty years ago, Jamaica, in terms of popular music culture, was dominated by roots reggae, while dancehall reggae enjoyed supremacy in the underground sound-system culture of the early '80s. The dancehall reggae avalanche of the mid-'80s—that would sweep aside roots reggae even on the international scene before the end of the decade—had not yet started its full assault. It is ironic that it was precisely during this interim period, when Jamaican popular music was, over the next few years, about to experience a momentous shift—that jazz and ska were actively conspiring to at least carve out a niche for themselves in the island's music landscape.

Local jazz had taken a back seat in the island's music culture since the breakup of the Skatalites, and since ska was displaced by rocksteady in the mid-'60s. Sonny Bradshaw's unwavering determination to keep jazz alive in Jamaica received an injection of renewed interest when young American trumpet titan Wynton Marsalis and other young American jazz talent placed classic bebop front and centre as the international mainstream focus of '80s jazz. Jamaican radio, through certain disc jockeys who promoted jazz as a youth music, presented the brilliant Marsalis as its pied piper.

A flurry of jazz activity buzzed around Kingston. Bradshaw's Big Band began getting regular gigs. Bradshaw was also invited to bring a small combo to the Surrey Tavern of Kingston's Pegasus Hotel three days a week. Tenor sax artist Cedric Brooks convened jazz sessions on the last Wednesday of every month at an art gallery housed in the building owned by the Mutual Life Insurance Company in New Kingston, the city's uptown financial district. Bradshaw organized several jazz concerts at the Little Theatre on Tom Redcam Avenue, featuring local jazz talent as part of his Big Band and American jazz musicians such as Byard Lancaster and Donald Byrd. At times, Bradshaw's bands, whether in small combo or orchestra format, would feature successful reggae musicians like Desi Jones, the drummer for Chalice; Michael "Ibo" Cooper, pianist and keyboard player for Third World; and flautist Egbert Evans, who had worked as session musician for Bob Marley and other reggae artists.

Herbie Miller introduced the Blue Monk to a Jamaican jazz scene that was vibrant and healthy in small, measured, but quality portions. Despite the increased interest in jazz, even a small club dedicated to nothing but jazz was an adventurous step. The Blue Monk lasted for about eighteen months. Miller's club, however, was historic in its very existence and for the artists he enlisted to perform there.

The quality of talent Miller booked for the Blue Monk sounded like an ad for upcoming events at any one of New York's prominent jazz venues. Max Roach, Dexter Gordon, Kenny Burrell, Johnny Griffin, and Andrew Cyrille all played the Blue Monk. Miller, however, did not make the mistake of only featuring American musicians. Important Jamaican jazz artists also performed at the club. Monty Alexander travelled from America to perform on opening night and Coleridge Goode made the journey from the U.K. to appear on a subsequent date. Tenor saxophonist Cedric Brooks—a leading figure in the Mystic Revelation of Rastafari, a super group of the '70s that combined Count Ossie's drummers and Brooks' band the Mystics—and Ernest Ranglin appeared at the Blue Monk on separate occasions.

The Skatalites, then, were one of several Jamaican jazz acts to play at Miller's club. The Blue Monk was actually the band's rehearsal venue for their Sunsplash gig. A month after Sunsplash, during the week of July 17, 1983, the Skatalites performed a series of concerts at the club. Free from the limitations of a reggae festival where the performance of their tunes was tailored to ensure a tight compact set in terms of time, the band—in an environment where they were the main and only attraction—were able to stretch out, to indulge the full energy of their creative improvisation. In this setting, they displayed the jazzier side of ska in a small room where an appreciative audience of various classes, a range of age groups, and politicians such as future Prime Minister P. J. Patterson were close enough to savour every expressive note. For the older fans, it must have brought to mind memories of twenty years earlier at the Bournemouth Club.

Fortunately, Miller had the foresight to record the Skatalites' June 27 Sunsplash rehearsals and the band's July 17 concert performance at the Blue Monk. Miller's reel tapes were first converted to cassette and released in 1986. The two-disc recording of the concert arrived in 1998. Miller produced the live recording, appropriately titled *Stretching Out*, which stands as the only album recorded in the reunification period to feature all of the original band members (with the exception of Don Drummond). *Stretching Out* is the only testament to the power and quality of a Skatalites concert experience in which the largest number of original members were present.

The following year, the Skatalites performed in the land of 2-Tone ska, courtesy of the touring Sunsplash package that played

London's Crystal Palace soccer stadium in the summer of 1984. The band gave another impressive performance. Shortly afterward, Island Records released *Return of the Big Guns* the first album of new material by the band in twenty years. It contained the partially written compositions of Don Drummond that were completed by Tommy McCook. The tunes were mainly sad, moody, and indulgent efforts tinged with the Drummond's ever-present melancholy tone. The album, in a way, represented the band's touching tribute to Drummond.

The Crystal Palace concert—captured on film as *Splash in the Palace*—and the international release of albums such as *Big Guns*, *Scattered Lights*, and later *Stretching Out* provided the Skatalites with an opportunity to kick-start the international career that eluded them in the '60s. The problems and personality conflicts that plagued the band twenty years before had not been resolved by time. Dizzy Moore, Jackie Mittoo, and Jah Jerry only appeared with the reunited Skatalites sporadically and were never really an essential and ongoing part of the rejuvenated band. Eventually, Moore, Mittoo, and Jah Jerry stopped recording and touring with the Skatalites. McCook, Alphonso, Knibb, Brevette, and Sterling became the consistent backbone of the band and—with Herbie Miller as their manager—took the plunge into the second phase of their career.

Fans of 2-Tone–inspired ska flocked to Skatalites concerts in the U.K., Canada, or the United States. They would attend the band's performances even if the venue was a jazz club. The punk-ska audience enjoyed the Skatalites' music despite the fact that it was played without punk attitude and with a greater sense of sophistication and jazz improvisation than 2-Tone and its derivatives. This appreciation from the fans of second wave ska led to tours in America pairing the band with American ska bands including the Toasters. The Skatalites in performance were not completely restricted to the punk-ska context; they were, at times, booked into venues attracting a Jamaican and Caribbean audience.

During Miller's tenure as Skatalites' manager, he was able to book them into clubs that featured jazz bands—clubs such as the Knitting Factory, a venue that catered to avant-garde jazz, alternative rock, and other types of cutting-edge music, and the Village Gate. In these venues, they had the opportunity of performing to a different audience. In the liner notes of *Stretching Out*, Miller discusses the band's series of gigs at the Village Gate:

... it was a month of Sundays at the world famous and now defunct (New York City venue) Village Gate that exposed the band to a wider audience and opened the gate to making contacts. ... They were joined by a different guest each week, among them Charley Palmieri, Arthur Blythe, and Monty Alexander. In the audience were other musicians such as Lester Bowie, Steve Turre, and David Murray.[6]

For band members Alphonso and particularly McCook, that kind of environment and audience must have been especially satisfying, although they appreciated the consistent support of the punk-ska audience.

Over a decade and a half, from 1984 to 1998, the Skatalites released more than a dozen new recordings and at least five compilations of reissued singles from the '60s. The outstanding compilations include *Foundation Ska* and *Ska Boo-Da-Ba*. *Foundation Ska* contains a decent cross-section of the band's '60s output—recorded for Coxsone's Studio One—that does not heavily rely on tracks featuring Drummond as lead soloist. The inclusion of Marguerita Mahfood's "Woman A Come" on the album is also an important bonus. *Foundation Ska* contains decent liner notes and interesting annotation by Brian Keyo. *Ska Boo-Da-Ba* is significant because of the sonic quality of the recordings collected on it. The sound quality is possibly the finest of any reissue package. Many of the Skatalites' "new" recordings reworked old classics, but only three of the tracks—"Guns of Navarone," "Man in Street," and "You're Wondering Now"—on their 1994 album *Hi-Bop Ska* were re-recorded instrumentals from the '60s.

Hi-Bop Ska has the distinction of being the most jazz-influenced of any Skatalites recording. The album features original Skatalites McCook, Alphonso, Brevette, and Knibb. Young American jazzmen Nathan Breedlove on trumpet and Will Clark on trombone appear as part of the new core of the group. Devon James played guitar on this session with Bill Smith on keyboards. Tommy McCook is named as co-producer on an album whose arrangements and solos offer ska with a pronounced jazz emphasis. McCook's intention, it seems, was to promote his aspirations as a jazz musician through the *Hi-Bop Ska* project that celebrated a collaboration of the worlds of ska and jazz.

Herbie Miller's role in assisting the achievement of this collaboration was indispensable. He used his connections and friendships in the jazz scene to secure the inclusion on the *Hi-Bop* sessions of several high-profile jazz musicians, many of whom were present at the Village Gate gig. The late Art Ensemble of Chicago front man Lester Bowie contributed the composition of the title track and his crucial trumpet sound to the session. David Murray brought his muscular tenor sax attack and his previously recorded tune "Flowers for Albert" recast as a ska workout. Steve Turre delivered intricate trombone notes. In a way, the *Hi-Bop* session was a perfect fit for Monty Alexander as a Jamaican jazz pianist appearing as a guest on a Skatalites recording because his career is filled with experiments fusing jazz with mento, ska, and reggae textures. Alexander's main contribution to the album is his composition "Renewal." The impressive list of guests appearing on *Hi Bop* also featured the skills of Jamaican celebrity vocalists Prince Buster, Toots Hibbert, Doreen Schaeffer, talented reggae bass player Val Douglas, and conga drummer Larry McDonald, whose career involved stints with poet Gil Scott-Heron and bluesman Taj Mahal.

Despite the guest contributions, *Hi-Bop Ska* clearly remains a Skatalites recording and, in particular, an album that reflects the personality and artistry of Tommy McCook. McCook is not only a producer of the album but he also wrote three compositions—"African Freedom," "Nelson's Song," and "Burru Style"—for the project. In addition, his tenor sax is heard soloing on almost every track.

If *Hi-Bop Ska* was McCook's project, then the Skatalites' 1998 album *Ball of Fire* served as Roland Alphonso's statement. The title track, although written by "Coxsone" Dodd, was, in its original '60s incarnation, an instrumental closely associated with Alphonso as chief soloist. *Ball of Fire* as an album fits neatly into the category of reinterpretations of popular Skatalites' tunes from the '60s. The ten-track work features "Rockfort Rock" and "Swing Easy," two superb reggae instrumentals originally recorded by the Soul Vendors, the band composed of ex-Skatalites that formed under Alphonso's leadership in the aftermath of the band's mid-'60s disintegration.

After triple-bypass heart surgery, McCook was unable to record or tour with the band and therefore was not part of the *Ball of Fire* project or any subsequent reunited Skatalites recordings. Ironically, *Ball of Fire* became Alphonso's final recording for the band. In 1998, the band's leading soloists died—Tommy McCook on May 5 and Roland Alphonso on November 17.

The Skatalites are still active today with Knibb and Brevette as the foundation members keeping the spirit of the band alive, but without either of their main soloists it is not quite the same sound. Their international legacy began with 2-Tone ska six years before the band's reunification. This legacy continued in the successful fusions of jazz, ska, and reggae with an emphasis on jazz improvisation that surfaced in Jamaica, the U.S., and the U.K. beginning in the '90s. These fusions had more in common with the improvisation and musicianship of the Skatalites—and in most cases, were inspired by them—than the 2-Tone, punk, or pop ska that generated a parallel Skatalites' international legacy focusing mainly on ska's rhythmic sensibility and its support of song lyrics.

Ernest Ranglin's *Below the Bassline*, an extraordinary reggae-jazz fusion album, hit the streets in 1996 using a similar approach to the Skatalites' *Hi-Bop Ska* project. Ranglin, a Jamaican jazz guitarist with impeccable ska and reggae credentials, is joined on this session by American jazz musicians Ira Coleman on bass, Idris Muhammad on drums, keyboard player-percussionist Gary Mayone, together with Monty Alexander and special guest Roland Alphonso. *Below the Bassline* features Coleman plucking out thick reggae bass lines from an acoustic upright with Muhammad locking in a roots groove that swings in '70s Jamaican style. Gary Mayone provides the bubbling reggae keyboard stew, leaving room for Alexander to improvise solos and creatively support Ranglin's exciting guitar work.

Ranglin is nothing short of brilliant on this session, strumming and picking out clear jazz tones, sometimes delivering rapid-fire solos that are safely cushioned by the deadly slow-burning roots reggae dub supplied by the rhythm section. Ernest's guitar and Monty's piano play off each other so well throughout the disc, but especially on their version of the late Augustus Pablo's "King Tubby's Meets Rockers Uptown." On that track, Ranglin and Alexander use their instruments to simulate the echo and reverb sounds of a reggae dub mix produced by electronic equipment.

Below the Bassline presents more covers of '70s reggae classics immersed in jagged jazz improvisation; these interpretations include: Frederick "Toots" Hibbert's "54-46," Burning Spear's "Black Disciples," and the Abyssinians' "Satta Massagana." Four of Ranglin's own compositions are also featured, among them are the ruminations of "Surfin'" and Nana's "Chalk Pipe." Roland

Alphonso appears as a guest, supplying a fine tenor sax solo on his tune "Ball of Fire."

The special chemistry between the guitar and piano displayed on *Below the Bassline* developed through several collaborations between Ranglin and Alexander over several decades. One reason they work together so well is their shared passion for combining Jamaican rhythms and jazz. Alexander's jazz artistry has allowed him to grow a substantial career in the United States over the last forty years.

Jamaican musicians on the whole have had a difficult time making a serious impact in the American marketplace. Even Bob Marley did not crack the U.S. in a big way until after his death. In jazz, however, there is a double dilemma because unfortunately pedigree and commercial viability in jazz are sometimes measured not just by talent but also by whether the artist is an American. Monty Alexander seems to have avoided these obstacles.

Unlike Harriott, Reece, and Burrowes, Alexander is a contemporary of Bob Marley; he was born in Jamaica eight months before the late reggae superstar on June 6, 1944. The music of his youth on the island was mento and ska. Alexander became an integral part of the island's emerging music scene in the late '50s and early '60s. Like Marley, the Wailers, and the other young talent of the time, Alexander participated with Don Drummond, Roland Alphonso, Ernest Ranglin, and producer Dodd on various recording sessions. Alexander was even leader of a band called Monty and the Cyclones.

Like most of Jamaica's jazz musicians, Alexander benefited from a formal music education. In his case, this training began when he was thirteen, but he had been developing skills as a piano player since the age of four. Pianist Aubrey Adams and Ranglin were influential to the young Alexander as talented Jamaican musicians. As Alexander testifies, he was also keenly listening to American jazz: "Of course, I also soaked up a lot of jazz while I was in Jamaica: Louis Armstrong, Nat 'King' Cole, Errol Garner ..."[7]

Outstanding Jamaican musicians and artists in Alexander's age group became internationally known reggae stars. The courageous Alexander, however, decided to begin the process of carving out a niche for himself in jazz during the early '60s, a time when the music, although moving from strength to strength creatively, was suffering from a sort of mid-life crisis commercially.

In 1961, when Alexander was seventeen, he moved with his

family to Florida in the United States. Alexander, like Dizzy Reece, was placed in the forefront of the jazz scene by an American icon. While he played piano in a Miami nightclub, Alexander was spotted by Frank Sinatra and his friend Jilly Rizzo. After a second chance encounter at a gig Alexander played in Las Vegas, Rizzo invited him to perform at the jazz club Jilly's in New York. That Jilly's performance led to collaborations with Cannonball Adderley, Milt Jackson, Sonny Rollins, Ray Brown, bassist Sam Jones, Dizzy Gillespie, and Miles Davis.

Throughout the remainder of the '60s, Alexander recorded for reputable jazz labels RCA and Verve. In the mid-'70s, the deep international impression made by Bob Marley's roots reggae gave Monty Alexander the permission to attempt a fusion of jazz with mento and reggae, a direction he had always wanted to take.

Earlier in his career, Alexander was constantly compared to Oscar Peterson and Nat "King" Cole; now he was charting his own distinct jazz territory. His catalogue of recordings now included jazz-calypso tunes such as "Sly Mongoose" and a version of "Hold 'Em Joe," which was first popularized by tenor sax great Sonny Rollins. Alexander also recorded interesting and innovative jazz interpretations of Bob Marley songs "Lively Up Yourself" and "Jammin'."

The musicians Alexander worked with reflected his eclecticism. African-American artists such as drummer Idris Muhammad, bassist Ira Coleman, and especially steel drums player Othello Molineaux were very open to Alexander's island-flavoured jazz ideas. The inclusion in his recording projects of Ranglin, percussionist Marjorie Whylie, and conga man Larry McDonald added the Jamaican jazz styling he required.

During the '80s, Alexander continued to experiment with his particular blend of jazz, indigenous Jamaican, and Caribbean rhythms without totally abandoning live or recorded straight-ahead jazz performances. In the '90s, Alexander engaged in bolder experiments working in ensembles that contain both reggae and jazz musicians. One such project was recorded live at the 1995 Montreaux Jazz Festival in Switzerland and, with the addition of recorded studio sessions, became the album *Yard Movement* released a year later.

Below the Bassline is a good example of the creative possibilities that can be achieved through this harmonious marriage of jazz and reggae. Ernest Ranglin is leader on this session, but Monty

Alexander and executive producer Trevor Wyatt conceived the idea of the project. In fact, *Bassline* is really a continuation of the approach previously put on display at live performances in London, England where Alexander got together with his old friends Ira Coleman and Idris Muhammad to phase together a creative mix of roots reggae and jazz. *Bassline*'s reggae-jazz version of Alphonso's classic "Ball of Fire," deploying Alphonso as guest soloist, is a solid connection to the Skatalites' ska-jazz.

When the Skatalites were on the road with the Toasters in the early '90s, certain individuals in the Toasters were convinced by the insistence of certain Skatalites members that their ska breathed an important jazz aesthetic. Toasters saxophone player Freddie Reiter, trombonist Rick Faulkner, and drummer/lead vocalist Jonathan McCain were so convinced that this was the right approach that they formed a new racially diverse band called the New York Ska Jazz Ensemble in the early '90s. This new band incorporated guitarist Devon James, a young American who had played with the reunited Skatalites, plus bassist Victor Rice and keyboard player Cary Brown from another American ska band the Scofflaws. The New York Ska Jazz Ensemble brought together the energy of the ska beat, the dread of roots reggae dub rhythms, with jazzy horn solos. The band's sound provided them with a very distinct character in the landscape of American ska that was mainly focused on channelling different permutations of the 2-Tone ska sound.

On the other side of the Atlantic in the U.K., where 2-Tone had become a pleasant memory, new ska developments stirred in 1991. Gary Crosby—a gifted bassist with a substantial jazz resume beginning with the early '80s jazz revival in Britain—became the key figure in reintroducing ska to the U.K. in the tradition of the Skatalites. The year 1991 was when Crosby's concept of creating a new sound, blending reggae and ska with innovative jazz improvisation took shape. In January 1992, he formed a new band Jazz Jamaica to express this concept.

Gary Crosby is a musician with a history that placed him in a perfect position to make this concept meaningful and successful. As someone born in January 1955, growing up in London as a young boy of Jamaican parents, Gary is old enough to have heard stories of Joe Harriott's exploits, and to have heard Jamaican ska in its heyday of the '60s. As a young man in the '70s, Crosby fell under the influence of roots reggae and American soul music. In the '80s, Crosby became a talented jazz bassist who worked with important American jazz musicians on tour in the U.K. that include Art Farmer, Gary Bartz, Sonny Fortune, and Larry Coryell. Crosby was an integral figure in the Jazz Warriors collective, which produced rich gems of U.K. jazz talent—such as tenor sax man Courtney Pine, alto saxophonist Steve Williamson, vibraphonist Orphy Robinson, vocalist Cleveland Watkiss, pianist Julian Joseph, and trombonist Dennis Rollins—that were at the heart of the U.K. jazz resurgence in the mid-'80s. As Williamson and Pine emerged as the future of British jazz in the late '80s and early '90s, Crosby worked with both of them in the recording studio and in concert.

Courtney Pine is probably the U.K.'s most famous jazz star, certainly since the '80s, and his success has extended to America. Delfeayo Marsalis—the younger brother of Wynton—produced Pine's 1988 album, *Destiny's Song*, while Pine's 1989 album, *Vision's Tale*, featured Ellis Marsalis, father of the Marsalis clan. As a British-Jamaican jazz artist, Pine—who started his music career playing saxophone in reggae bands—has been vocal in various interviews about his kinship to Joe Harriott, a fellow British-Jamaican innovator. From very early in his jazz career, Pine's music reflected a fusion of influences combining Sonny Rollins and John Coltrane with the sensibilities of Don Drummond and Bob Marley. Pine's 1992 album *To the Eyes of Creation* delivers a very interesting cover version of Don Drummond's "Eastern Standard Time," featuring Dennis Rollins' brilliant interpretation of Drummond's trombone solo with Crosby laying down inventive ska bass lines. On *Creation*, Pine also tributes Marley with a cover of "Redemption Song." On another album *Closer to Home*, Pine delivers work that is less a fusion and more his playing jazz phrases over reggae rhythm tracks that is, in the end, satisfying mainly because of his outstanding artistry.

Crosby's Jazz Jamaica project has found the correct proportions of reggae, jazz, ska, and rhythm and blues to create a fusion that succeeds on many levels. The Jazz Jamaica material works as danceable ska music, but also showcases various kinds of jazz improvisation, skillfully bringing these elements together into a seamless whole. The music of Jazz Jamaica reflects Crosby's diverse inspirations such as Jackie Jackson, Robbie Shakespeare, and Charles Mingus as bass players; Coltrane, McCook, and Cedric Brooks as saxophonists; as well as Count Ossie, Augustus

Pablo, and Crosby's uncle, Ernest Ranglin. Ranglin played with Jazz Jamaica in 1992 when they were just beginning their journey as a band with a different perspective on how to present ska. The concept behind the genesis of the group evolved out of Crosby's desire to highlight the jazz aesthetic in ska and to present ska as Jamaican jazz. Crosby suggests, "In some ways the punk-ska approach trivialized the depth of the music."[8]

Crosby's own playing on Jazz Jamaica's recordings illustrates his intentions to go beyond the perceived limits of how bass should sound in ska and reggae. On *Skaravan*, the band's 1993 album, Crosby's inventive jazz solo at the centre of roots reggae track "Africa" works because it is executed with the appropriate pauses or reggae spaces and is therefore completely compatible with Kenrick Rowe's *rockers'*-style reggae trap drumming. On tracks such as Herbie Hancock's "Butterfly" and Wayne Shorter's "Night Dreamer" from Jazz Jamaica's 1998 album *Double Barrel*, Crosby's bass cooks an earthy resonant groove that phases together rhythm and blues, jazz, and reggae in an unassuming way. On the Motown cover "I Heard It Through the Grapevine," Crosby's bass dispatches decidedly non-reggae chords that are drawn into a reggae orbit by Rowe's drumming and Clifton Morrison's bubbling reggae keyboard. "Footprints"—a track from the band's 2001 album *Massive* featuring a Jazz Jamaica all-star unit expanded to a core of twenty musicians and a pool of thirty—is introduced by Crosby's creative solo that eases its way into a swinging roots reggae interpretation of Wayne Shorter's composition.

Instrumental ska is celebrated for its exciting horn solos and harmonies maybe more than it is for its rhythm. More than any other ska outfit, with the possible exception of the original Skatalites, Jazz Jamaica has included some extraordinary talents. For the *Skaravan* debut album, Jazz Jamaica features Eddie "Tan Tan" Thornton on trumpet, Michael "Bammie" Rose on tenor saxophone, and guest contributor Rico Rodrigues on trombone. Thornton, an Alpha Boys' School graduate who emigrated to the U.K. in the '50s, found a niche in various pop, rock, and reggae formats working with Georgie Fame, Rod Stewart, and successful U.K. roots reggae band Aswad. Rose, also a Jamaican who moved to the U.K., achieved international acclaim as part of Cymande, a Caribbean diasporic band that played a mixture of rock, funk, and nyabinghi.

Cymande's 1972 debut album produced "The Message," a hit

on both sides of the Atlantic. "Zion I" and "Rastafarian Folk Song," both co-authored by Rose, are the nyabinghi tracks on that debut. "Zion I," in particular, features undiluted Rastafari hand drumming on an international release two years before the Wailers' "Rastaman Chant." Cymande's music has been revived by hip-hop groups such as the Fugees and De La Soul in the '90s. Spike Lee's film 25th Hour features Cymande songs "Bra," "Dove," and "The Message." Michael "Bammie" Rose was also a member of the Aswad horn section during the '80s.

Rico Rodrigues, an Alpha graduate and 2-Tone co-conspirator, blows his Drummond-influenced solos on his own compositions "Ramblin'" and "Africa." Courtney Pine contributes his considerable skills to *Jamaican Beat–Blue Note Blue Beat*, Jazz Jamaica's second album. A featured soloist on *Double Barrel* is outstanding jazz trombonist Dennis Rollins, whose playing on tracks such as "Confucius" and "Marcus Junior" wisely do not attempt to emulate Drummond's melancholy tone, but instead issues an energetic wailing lyricism. On "Butterfly," Rollins delivers an exciting funky solo that is the high point of the tune.

Massive deploys a host of U.K. jazz talent including tenor sax player Denys Baptiste, alto saxophonist Jason Yarde, trombonist Annie Whitehead, vibraphonist Orphy Robinson, and the assured articulation of young alto saxophonist Soweto Kinch, who could well be his generation's Joe Harriott. Kinch—an Oxford University graduate whose solo 2004 debut, *Conversations with the Unseen*, is critically acclaimed—contributes a sizzling solo on a cover of "My Boy Lollipop." This mature sophisticated version of "Lollipop" stars Juliet Roberts' expressive mellifluous singing that provides the song with a touch of elegance. In addition, her vocal performance is irresistible on an inspired reggae arrangement of "Again." Two of the most exciting tracks on *Massive* that feature inventive jazz improvisation are "Ball of Fire" and "Vitamin A," two brilliantly interpreted '60s Skatalites classics.

Jazz Jamaica has succeeded admirably in taking the Skatalites ska and Jamaican jazz legacy into the twenty-first century with a confidence and artistry that suggests the future of ska and Jamaican jazz is assured.

One-Drop Dubs the Maple Leaf

The Story of Reggae in Canada

It is a cool Sunday evening in Toronto in the fall of 1979. A modest cultural program hosted by the Rastafarian Cultural Workshop is in progress. Lillian Allen, a petite reggae poet with caramel skin and an infectious smile, reads for an audience of about thirty. Without the assistance of a microphone, Allen's rhythmic Jamaican patois energizes the cramped performance space situated above a store on Eglinton Avenue near Oakwood. Her dramatic vocal inflections invigorate verse with cadences of reggae as she stands in a building that huddles with a vibrant spectrum of Caribbean shops. One shop sells beef patties, coco bread, and chicken rotis. Another offers mangoes, yellow yams, green bananas, and a variety of fruits and ground provisions. This section of Eglinton Avenue is populated with too many Black barber shops and an overdose of stores trading in reggae music on vinyl. It is Sunday and all the shops are closed, but they still ooze a thick island presence that eases its way into the room where Allen reads, mingles with the Caribbean-Canadian audience, and assists Allen's dub poetry performance.

Dub poetry usually refers to verse crafted from Jamaican language that flows to the rhythm of reggae. Dub poetry can be engaged on the page but communicates with more power when it is read in performance with or without music. The dub poet differs from the deejay (as rappers are called in the reggae world) in that the rhythm of the deejay's spoken words is primarily shaped by an existing reggae beat, while the metre of the dub poet's verse usually influences and shapes the music created specifically to accompany the poem.

At the same time in different countries, a number of individuals nurtured dub poetry during its gestation phase, which began in the early '70s and concluded in the early '80s when dub poetry evolved into a full-fledged citizen of the roots reggae landscape. Pioneer dub poets include Linton Kwesi Johnson and Benjamin Zephaniah in England; Oku Onuora, Mutabaruka, Jean Breeze, Mikey Smith, Afua Cooper, and Poets in Unity in Jamaica; and Clifton Joseph, I-Shaka, Devon Haughton, Ahdri Zhina Mandiela, and Lillian Allen in Canada.

Allen relocated to Canada from Jamaica in the early '70s as a young adult of the roots reggae generation. Thematically, Allen's poetry drew inspiration from the justice and equity sentiments expressed in the lyrics of artists such as Bob Marley. Rhythmically, her verse took its cue from roots reggae's fat bass lines and one-drop drum syncopation. Allen's poetry spoke in the language of the grassroots Jamaican and was inspired by the dialect poetry of Louise Bennett.

That grey Sunday evening in Toronto, in the fall of 1979, Allen revived Bennett's animated patois missives, recited the poetry of Oku Onuora, and introduced her own verse. Allen's reading touched a receptive chord with an audience that shared her culture and heritage and were familiar with Louise Bennett, but were probably learning about dub poetry for the first time. Many in the audience recognized in Allen's reading a modernized update of Bennett's approach that found an edgier voice through the tempo of reggae's militant rhythms as opposed to the lilting metre of mento— a Jamaican form of calypso—favoured by the gifted Bennett.

Less than a decade after the Rastafarian Cultural Workshop reading, Allen stood on a stage at the O'Keefe Centre in downtown Toronto. Here, she confronted an audience that extended beyond the back rows of the auditorium into living rooms across Canada through the magic of CBC television cameras. Anyone tuned to the CBC broadcast of the 1987 Juno Awards would have been a witness to Allen's acceptance of an award for her debut album, *Revolutionary Tea Party*.

Just a few weeks before Allen's poetry reading on Eglinton Avenue, the rebel music of Bob Marley and the Wailers captivated a packed Maple Leaf Gardens in a concert that was a milestone of Jamaican reggae's journey in Canada. Nineteen seventy-nine was also the year that Bruce Cockburn's album *Dancing in the Dragon's Jaws* was released. The album produced a hit reggae track "Wondering Where the Lions Are." The musicians who gave that recording its reggae "feel" were bass player Larry Silvera and drummer Benbow, the rhythm section of Ishan People, one of the first Jamaican-Canadian reggae bands.

These events in 1979 involving Lillian Allen and Bruce Cockburn shared an odd connection. Marley was an important influence for Allen, who several years later performed onstage with Cockburn in Toronto's Diamond nightclub (now the

Lillian Allen at the Diamond Club, Toronto, December 1984.
Photograph by Isobel Harry.

Phoenix). The most interesting correlation of these events, however, is that they were a reflection of how reggae began the process of sinking deep roots into Canadian culture.

Reggae's insinuation into the culture of nations such as Britain, the United States, and Canada occurred in different ways through various types of facilitators. Before Allen, before Cockburn's reggae adventures, and before Bob Marley's first concert in Canada, reggae's initial imprint in the land of the maple leaf occurred as a result of a migration wave from Jamaica during the late '60s and early '70s. Stranger Cole, Jo Jo Bennett, Nana McLean, Leroy

Sibbles, and Jackie Mittoo were reggae artists with credible careers in Jamaica before migrating to Canada. Carlene Davis, although born in Jamaica, grew up in England and started her career as a reggae performer and recording artist in Canada. Leroy Sibbles and Jackie Mittoo, however, were more than just credible recording artists; they were important innovators of Jamaican popular music before they arrived in Canada.

In Jamaica during the '60s, Jackie Mittoo as keyboard player and Leroy Sibbles as bass guitarist were both house musicians at the recording studio of Clement "Coxsone" Dodd. Dodd's recording facility Studio One, in its heyday, was like the reggae combination of Motown and Stax. If that sounds like an exaggeration, consider just a few examples from a seemingly endless list of high-calibre talent that appeared on Dodd's Studio One, Coxsone, and Supreme labels at that time: Bob Marley and Peter Tosh, the two most famous personalities of the roots reggae era together with the talented Bunny Wailer, recorded for Dodd as the Wailers; Don Drummond and the Skatalites, the leading-edge band in its day acted as Dodd's studio session band during the ska era; Dodd was the first to record Burning Spear, the singer with the unique earth-tone voice and unorthodox phrasing; and the story of Marcia Griffiths' eventual international success began when she signed to Studio One.

When Mittoo and Sibbles worked at Studio One, it was a prolific hit factory. In addition to Sibbles' bass playing on Jamaican reggae classics such as the Abyssinians' "Satta Massa Gana," he was the capable lead singer of a popular Studio One harmony trio called the Heptones. Sibbles and Mittoo together were responsible for the "Full Up" rhythm, which was sampled in British reggae band Musical Youth's 1983 international hit "Pass the Dutchie."

As residents of Canada, Mittoo, and Sibbles were unable to translate their considerable talents into the kind of success they enjoyed in Jamaica. In the case of Sibbles, respect for his gifts as a vocalist eventually led to an opportunity for him to launch a kind of pop career in Canada through a recording project featuring Canadian folk-rock heavyweights Bruce Cockburn, Murray McLauchlan, and Hugh Marsh. Unfortunately, that project resulted in the flawed 1982 *Evidence* album.

Sibbles was respected as a seminal figure of the Canadian scene whose work was honoured with Juno and Canadian reggae awards. But he remained an important element of the Jamaican music indus-

Dub poets Mutabaruka and Oku Onuora.

try by frequently travelling back to the island to record and perform. The lyrics and music of Mittoo and Sibbles, however, did not really convey a sense of the social conditions and experiences of Caribbean residents in Canada. A generation of Caribbean-Canadian reggae performers with a different mentality embraced the approach of adapting reggae's lyrical and rhythmic framework so that it took into account the musical environment and social issues confronting Blacks in Canada. These young Caribbean-Canadian reggae artists emerged during the late '70s and early '80s as one faction of a new Caribbean diasporic generation.

The Caribbean diaspora can be described, in part, as significant populations of Caribbean heritage in cities like London and Birmingham in the U.K., New York and Miami in the U.S., and Toronto and Montreal in Canada—populations of Caribbean heritage that have had a significant impact on the national culture of the countries in which they live. A new generation of the Caribbean diaspora, born in the '50s and '60s, with a strong dose of Caribbean heritage pumping through their veins, grew up British, American, and Canadian. Although living outside of the Caribbean, many of them maintained an umbilical-cord connection to Caribbean culture and in particular to the music of reggae and calypso. As young adults during the '70s and '80s, some became the reggae artists responsible for a deeper immersion of reggae into the cultural fabric of Britain and North America. The substance of this impact was not the imitation of Jamaican reggae, but the innovation of a different kind of reggae—a reggae that drew inspiration from a Jamaican framework, but whose music and lyrics found its distinct character in the musical environment and social conditions of the country in which the diasporic reggae artist lived.

When Caribbean diasporic reggae first surfaced, it had to contend with the international profile of Jamaican reggae; the reggae adventures of mainstream rock, pop, and rhythm and blues artists; and the reggae musicians of Caribbean heritage who imitated Jamaican reggae. Diasporic reggae justified its existence and produced its own major artists partly because it spoke to the everyday experiences, struggles, hopes, and aspirations of young people of Caribbean heritage in cities like London (U.K.), Toronto, or New York.

The penetration of diasporic reggae into America's music culture began in the early '80s through Jamaican-American dancehall deejays such as Shinehead and Sister Carol. In the U.K. during the late '70s and early '80s, roots reggae bands Steel Pulse and Aswad, dub poet Linton Kwesi Johnson supported by Dennis Bovell's Dub Band, and singer Maxi Priest were the international face of U.K. diasporic reggae.

Canada's tradition of diasporic reggae bands began to surface in the early '70s. Ishan People represented the initial promise of reggae created in Canada. Band members such as bass guitarist Larry Silvera, guitarist Michael Murray, and vocalist Johnny Osbourne were musicians in Jamaica before their arrival in Canada. Unlike Sibbles and Mittoo, they were not major names in the music industry there. Osbourne, however, was the exception. His recordings "Come Back Darling" and "Warrior" provided him with a reputation that assisted in enhancing the band's profile among fans in Canada who were familiar with the Jamaican scene.

Two years before Ishan People recorded "Wondering Where the Lions Are" with Bruce Cockburn, they collaborated with another icon of Canadian music: David Clayton-Thomas, the soulful lead voice of Blood, Sweat, and Tears. Clayton-Thomas produced their 1977 album *Ishan People*.

Ishan People were a band attempting to grow a career as reggae artists in Canada, but not necessarily as a band rooted in the Caribbean-Canadian experience. The lyrics and music of Ishan People seemed to be inspired more by the international reggae of Bob Marley and Third World than it was about speaking to the

Leroy Sibbles at the Palais Royale, Toronto, May 1980.
Photograph by Isobel Harry.

concerns of Caribbean-Canadians. Despite that, Ishan People must
be recognized as a talented band and a pioneer of the early
Canadian reggae scene.

The next phase of Canadian reggae evolved in the '80s when
reggae musicians, singers, and poets began to distinguish their work
from the sound and lyrical themes of reggae from Jamaica. The '80s
were a fertile period for Canada's roots reggae bands. A new wave
of artists included bands Earth, Roots, and Water, 20th Century
Rebels, Messenjah, the Sattalites, Errol Blackwood, Culture Shock,
and Truths and Rights, and singers such as Chester Miller, Adrian
"Sheriff" Miller, and Lazo. These very talented reggae acts represented a wide variety of approaches: the Sattalites were like a
Canadian UB40, Messenjah was constantly compared to Steel Pulse,
and Chester Miller was Canada's version of influential Jamaican
roots reggae vocalist Dennis Brown.

Although the quality of music produced by Canadian reggae
artists was impressive, their success in terms of popularity, mainstream profile, and international currency was not comparable to
their counterparts in the U.K. In the U.K., an infrastructure existed
that allowed reggae as an industry to grow and develop. Record
companies such as Lee Gopthal's Trojan and Chris Blackwell's

Island, both owned by British-Jamaicans, formed the backbone of that infrastructure. Island Records, in particular, provided the marketing and promotion required to assist Steel Pulse and Linton Kwesi Johnson to achieve mainstream profiles in the U.K. and international reputations in various parts of the world including Canada. No such infrastructure existed in Canada. There were no record companies, independent or otherwise, that believed in the music enough to consistently and aggressively promote Canadian reggae. Ishan People secured a two-album deal with GRT of Canada that achieved very little in advancing the popularity of the band. The Sattalites and Messenjah were both briefly signed to WEA Canada. The albums WEA released for these bands were promoted by issuing singles from those albums that featured mild reggae cover versions of American rhythms and blues tunes. If WEA thought that the cover of a previously recorded hit was the road to perceived success of finding an international market for the recordings of these reggae bands, then maybe a wiser move might have been to release a single covering a popular Bob Marley song. After all, a Bob Marley reggae song has already proven it has the potential to cross over to a rock and/or pop market. As an added bonus, a Marley cover would probably not alienate these bands from their core fan base.

Despite the lack of record company interest and very little, if any, support from mainstream radio, Canadian reggae bands still managed to establish a national profile on the underground scene or as bands percolating just below the mainstream. These bands and artists achieved this first and foremost by independently releasing singles and albums and through club gigs and concert tours across Canada. Airplay on college and alternative radio stations, rotation of independently produced videos or concert clips on Citytv and MuchMusic, and favourable reviews and assessments in the alternative weekly *Now* magazine, *Fuse* magazine, the *Toronto Star* and sometimes the *Globe and Mail* provided critical support and promotion for Canadian reggae artists in sustaining a national profile. A significant international reputation remained elusive.

If one of the defining characteristics of diasporic reggae is its ability to convey the struggles and aspirations of Caribbean people in their specific diasporic environments, then two good examples of artists expressing diasporic reggae in Canada are dub poet Lillian Allen and the band Truths and Rights. Allen and Truths and Rights

Mohjah (left), Ovid (centre), and Qwammie (seated on right) perform as Truths & Rights at the Horseshoe Tavern, Toronto. Undated.
Photograph by Isobel Harry.

as performers and recording artists were important in establishing a distinct Caribbean-Canadian sound combined with lyrics focusing directly on the social issues facing African-Canadians.

Lillian Allen's poetry introduced a fresh feminist viewpoint to the existing themes of roots reggae lyrics that were already rich with topics about equity, justice, and liberation. In true diasporic fashion, the poems on Allen's debut album, *Revolutionary Tea Party*—released in 1986—travel from Jamaica to the Caribbean communities of Toronto. In "Nelly Belly Swelly," a poem about rape and child abuse of a teenage girl by a mature man, she tackles a vital issue affecting women in Jamaica. In the poem "I Fight Back," Allen exposes the oppressive conditions of Caribbean women who work as nannies and domestics in the homes of wealthy Canadians in a defiant voice that sounds like anguish comforted by resolve: "I scrub floors / serve backra's meal on time ... Here I am in Canada / bringing up someone else's child / while someone else and me in absentee / bring up my own."[1]

Allen's feminism is packaged in a Caribbean-Canadian context. The themes of her poems were not restricted to a single issue. In the poem "Riddim and Hard Times," Allen mentions the 1978 killing of Albert Johnson, a Jamaican-Canadian shot to death by police in Toronto under questionable circumstances. The African-Canadian community was so outraged by the manner in which Johnson died that several large demonstrations were staged to protest what was viewed as an extreme form of police brutality.

Another poem, "Rub A Dub Style Inna Regent Park," conjures images of life in Toronto's low-income community of Regent Park: "... Monday morning broke news of a robbery / Pam mind went / couldn't hold the load / dem took her to the station / in a paddy wagon / screaming ... / her Johnny got a gun from an ex-police-man."[2] This poem conveys the emotional stress of African-Canadians living in society's crevices whose "dreams (gather) dust on the shelf / ... every time you slam the door sey: no job." "Rub A Dub Style" really set the tone for talking about the issues of specific African-Canadian communities in Toronto. The *Revolutionary Tea Party* album is now nineteen years old, but it is only in fairly recent times that artists have been comfortable about mentioning the names of Canada's Black communities in their songs. Today, giving recognition to specific neighbourhoods in Toronto with sizable Caribbean-Canadian populations, such as Jane and Finch, Scarborough, Malvern, or Regent Park, is almost a given in Toronto hip-hop. "Rub A Dub Style" represents an early example of reggae and reggae-related Black music forms recognizing specific communities of African-Canadians.

Conditions Critical, Allen's second album, hit the streets in 1987 and earned the dub poet a second Juno. This album has more of an international perspective, tackling apartheid in South Africa on the track "Freedom Is Azania," world peace and the environment on "Dis Ya Mumma Earth," political and economic crisis in Jamaica on the title track, and a vivid poignant portrait of a homeless woman using a bus shelter as protection from the deep freeze of a Toronto winter in "Unnatural Causes." Although "Unnatural Causes" certainly qualifies as a diasporic poem, reggae is not used to underscore this track. The lack of reggae on the recording is not an issue because guest guitarist Elaine Stef's jangling guitar chords sound like the gust of an icy wind in sympathy with the poem's winter scenes. Stef's instrument, alone in its support of Allen's vocal, provides a tender folk-like soundtrack that is ideal for Allen's subtle delivery of the poem.

The music providing fuel to the flames of Allen's verse did not fit any typical reggae formula. Diasporic musicians—hand drum-

Carlene Davis in Toronto, March 1980. Photograph by Isobel Harry.

mer Quammie Williams and bass guitarist Terry Lewis—were joined on the recording sessions by keyboard player Laurie Conger, trap drummer Billy Bryans, and guitarist Dave Gray, who were members of alternative pop band Parachute Club. This interracial Canadian session band delivered reggae on *Revolutionary Tea Party* and *Conditions Critical* that did not attempt to imitate its Jamaican cousin, instead offering a unique Canadian blend.

Allen's "spoken-word" voice gives her recordings its substantial character as an instrument in its own right, and is immediately distinctive in its use of improvised sounds that emerge from her throat as police sirens, echo, or drumbeats. The sense of drama in Allen's enunciation of her verse allows for the modulation of tone from a high-pitched frenzy to a calm confident rebellion. Allen sustained a prominent profile as an alternative artist despite the fact that she never signed to a major or mid-level independent record company. Both of Allen's albums mentioned here were released by her Verse to Vinyl label.

Lillian Allen began nurturing her reggae poetry before she was aware that seminal dub poets such as Linton Kwesi Johnson or Oku Onuora were charting a similar poetic course. A version of Allen's poem "I Fight Back" appeared in a 1970 edition of a New York publication *Caribbean Daily*. Her introduction to the work of Onuora strengthened her resolve in advancing the art of dub poetry. Allen first met Oku Onuora in Cuba at the eleventh World Festival of Youth in 1978, where both performed their work. The festival was programmed in a way that made it impossible for Allen to attend Onuora's presentation. When they did connect to exchange ideas about their craft, Onuora treated Allen and two other individuals to his entire forty-five minute festival performance while standing in front of the broken-down wall guarding Havana's Jose Marti School. As Allen listened to Onuora use his voice to energize a creative aesthetic through his poetry, she realized that she was witnessing the crystallization of a new art form. She recognized that a fresh aesthetic was coalescing into definite shape, an aesthetic that she herself had been developing independent of Onuora. Onuora had brought this new form to life by crystallizing it, giving it a name and, in Allen's words: "Pressed the name dub poetry on to the consciousness of practitioners and supporters."[3]

In 1971, seven years before that meeting, Oku Onuora was still known as Orlando Wong. He was a rebellious teenager living in Jamaica's East Kingston neighbourhood of Franklin Town near the Dunkirk area when he was arrested, endured a trial, and was sentenced for the armed robbery of a post office. The young Rasta revolutionary committed the crime in order to finance the operations of his neighbourhood community group—a collective whose purpose as outlined by its leader Ras Negus was "liberation through education." Teaching the Dunkirk community youth about Black consciousness and Black empowerment assumed the form of an after-school program called Tafari that also provided a modest meal for its students. The proceeds from the post-office robbery—and similar incidents in which "money was liberated" from certain institutions—purchased books and assisted families in the community.

Orlando Wong spent seven years subsisting under the hideous conditions of the Fort Augusta prison, an old colonial British fort situated on a beach at Port Henderson in the parish of St. Catherine. Wong's skills as a writer, which emerged while he was a student at Camperdown High School, matured inside these

Lorraine Segato with Mohjah in the V band. June 1982.
Photograph by Isobel Harry.

walls. His artistic talent rallied a number of individuals, journalist Barbara Gloudon in particular, to negotiate his early release. By the time Wong's freedom from jail was secured, several of his poems had been published in both of the major Jamaican newspapers, the *Daily Gleaner* and the *Jamaica Daily News*, and in various magazines and journals. Three of his poems received awards in the 1976 Literary Competition of the Jamaica Festival. *Echo*, Wong's first book of poetry, became available only months before he walked out of Fort Augusta for the last time.

Now known as Oku Onuora, his poetry offers a range of themes. From a description of how the music in a roots reggae dance temporarily massages away the pain of ghetto living in "Escaping the Blues" to the romantic verse of "Soul Flower." From the detailed definition of Jamaican poverty and how it affects the mentality of its victims in "Dread Times" to the introspective "Last Nite" in which the moon does not suggest the thought of lovers, but instead the reality of seeing a man with a load on his back that moves the narrator to tears. Onuora's poems, whether written in Jamaican language or not, are built on a rhythm that is often reggae, but sometimes inspired by nyabinghi, rhythm and blues, or jazz. While his work is not limited to reggae, that music has been his chief muse, and the original Wailers his main influence.

Four years after the Youth Festival in Cuba, Lillian Allen published two poetry collections: *Rhythm An' Hardtimes* and one written specifically for children *If You See Truth*. In 1983, Allen issued a recording together with Clifton Joseph (who is now a writer and reporter with CBC television) and Devon Haughton (who is currently a writer/director of plays and films) as De Dub Poets, a coalition that promoted the trio's individual work and issued a recording. The EP cassette featured Allen's "Riddim an' Hardtimes," Joseph's "Chuckie Prophesy," Haughton's "Mi Cyaan Believe It" (a poem that only reprised the title of Mikey Smith's work of the same name), and "Unity Song," a poem showcasing the three of them. Allen's 1986 debut album, *Revolutionary Tea Party*, aside from being awarded a Juno, in many ways is a marker that identifies the blossoming of dub poetry as a prominent component of the '80s reggae scene in Canada.

The Canadian dub poetry scene developed in very innovative ways. Clifton Joseph's poetry took its rhythmic cue from the calypso of Short Shirt and the rock-influenced eclectic funk of George Clinton. Joseph's verse drew inspiration from the musicality of Amiri Baraka's African-American jazz poetry and the work of Edward Kamau Brathwaite. His first recording "Chuckie Prophesy," although voiced to the backdrop of solid roots reggae, offers verse built on a rhythmic metre of Eastern-Caribbean calypso. Much of Joseph's verse gyrates to an innate beat that interlocks calypso and funk. Creative eclecticism is the kind of phrase that may come close to describing the span of his work, which ranges from the avant-garde approach of using wordless sounds in a tribute to jazz icon John Coltrane to the energetic funk workouts of "Lookin' for a Job" and "(Political) Pimps." Joseph's devotion to funk is rivalled only by his interest in jazz. One of his strongest poems is the extraordinary "Chant for Monk," a séance in verse that virtually resurrects the enigmatic figure of Thelonious Monk and his piano genius.

Joseph's poetry showcases important thematic elements. In the poem "Caribana '84 / Smash Apartheid Dead!" he uses the partying at Toronto's annual Caribana calypso carnival as a vehicle to discuss some very serious social concerns: "dance in wild block-oramas of rage / dance in Ontario housing Bantustans / dance down (Toronto) Don jail's shudder of steel ... rub a dub dub on fine bottoms of radical culture / erupt in spear chants against blood sucker oppression ... play mas like rass in dem ass."[4] As a diasporic narrative, this poem suggests that Caribbean-Canadians in Toronto enlist the energy of their culture in the struggle to address crucial social and political issues that confront racial minorities in the city. Joseph underlines the gravity of these issues by comparing Ontario housing to the Bantustans where Blacks were segregated when apartheid existed in South Africa.

As a performer, recorded or live, Joseph's voice suggests a saxophone that honks, squeals, squawks, or rings out orthodox melodic sentiments in a fusion of reggae-tinged "funkaiso" accents. As a rebel-word artist, his verse boogies to the syncopated beat of rich metaphors and a sharp wit.

Allen and Joseph are joined by a variety of Canadian-based dub poets who have been vital contributors in expanding the form's thematic scope. In her collection of work appropriately titled *Memories Have Tongue,* historian Afua Cooper uses some of her poems to uncover interesting aspects about Jamaican and African-Canadian history. Theatre and film director Ahdri Zhina Mandiela is an important poet on the Toronto dub scene who writes plays such as *Dark Diaspora in Dub* in dub verse.

Toronto's dub poets were closely connected with the city's roots reggae musicians. Truths and Rights was one of the main Toronto reggae bands that recorded with dub poets. They supply the reggae heard on the *De Dub Poets* recording. When that cassette surfaced in 1983, Truths and Rights were already at the peak of critical acclaim and popularity as a quality live band with only four recordings to their credit. Peter Goddard, then the pop music scene writer for the *Toronto Star,* praised Truths and Rights as Toronto's "Band of the Year" in the newspaper's December 28, 1983 edition.

Truths and Rights began to take shape several years earlier as one of the artistic elements of Immi-Can, a Black community cooperative association based in Regent Park. Truths and Rights, a group of Toronto residents with roots in Trinidad, Guyana, the Eastern Caribbean, and Nova Scotia, poured its frustrations, ambitions, and talents into a positive, message-driven, and distinct reggae sound. If the band had a leading personality, it was the charismatic lead guitarist, lead vocalist, and songwriter Mohjah. Truths and Rights' interpretation of reggae was creatively nurtured by the Latin-African flavour of conga drummer Rudi Quammie Williams and the jazzy rhythm and blues seasoning of skilled keyboard player Iauwata. Deliciously ominous reggae grooves sculptured by trap drummer Abnadengel and bass guitarist Xola expertly anchored the music's rhythmic foundation. Percussionist Ahmid, lead guitarist Vance Tynes, and another lead vocalist Ovid Reid also made valuable contributions.

Immi-Can provided the band with a support network of socially conscious management, advisory, and publicity personnel. Jamaican-Canadian Ato Seitu, a community worker at Immi-Can, assisted in focusing the efforts of the band and became the key management and advisory figure with Truths and Rights during its post–Immi-Can phase. A Toronto visual artist, Seitu's unique images decorated the sleeves of Truths and Rights' recordings and the stage backdrop for the band's live shows. Lillian Allen, in a different role as community legal worker at Immi-Can, was also closely linked to the band. Quammie Williams describes Allen's relationship to Truths and Rights, in the post–Immi-Can period, as that of an intellectual resource. The collaboration between the band and its artistic advisors spilled over into the songwriting process. Truths and Rights' debut recording, "Acid Rain," was co-written by Mohjah, Allen, and Seitu.

The band's publicist and official photographer was Canadian photojournalist and writer Isobel Harry whose camera captured the historic performances of Bob Marley and Peter Tosh at the April 1978 One Love Peace Concert in Jamaica for *Maclean's* magazine. She was not only Truths and Rights' photographer, she also shared publicist and administrative management duties with Seitu. An artist, a photographer, a poet, and engineer Jeff Holdip, the band's sound mixer for live performances (who now works with Nelly Furtado) were all part of the total Truths and Rights experience.

The band's songs reflect the concerns of racial minorities in Canada and the concerns of all Canadians. Truths and Rights' 1980 single "Acid Rain" tackles a Canadian environmental issue at a time when the environment was not a theme discussed in reggae. The music underpinning the track is also far from derivative reggae. Mohjah's rough-edged vocal tone marinated in a Trinidadian accent, his guitar crying the gloomy blues, underscores Iauwata's

Stranger Cole outside a Kensington Avenue record store, Toronto, March 1980. Photograph by Isobel Harry.

church-organ keyboard sound that floats above Xola's implosive robust bass and Quammie's subtle percussive flourishes. If the music was inventive, the lyrics were groundbreaking for reggae: "Acid rain / falling from our skies / it would fall down on I ... / what are they doing to man, woman, and child / Messing with our lives and the environment."[5]

The words of Truths and Right's second recording, "Metro's No.1 Problem," also investigates a contentious Canadian social problem: "Racial violence explodes in anger ... Trouble down in Rexdale / Pakistani family battered ... Metro's No.1 problem / Racial tension / Metro's No.1 problem / Racial violence ..."[6] This song broadened the scope of the discussion about racism in Toronto so that it went beyond African-Canadians and was inclusive of the South Asian community. The lyrics flow from Mohjah's voice in a non-confrontational tone energized by a whining harmonica and dark-blue piano phrases that ease the tune into a full-blown blues groove. From there, the track segues to a jerky ska beat alternating with rhythm and blues keyboard vamps. Musically and lyrically, Truths and Rights was a band on the creative edge of Canadian reggae.

The fact that most members of Truths and Rights were not of Jamaican heritage is a particular feature of diasporic roots reggae bands in the U.K. as well. Two of the main personalities in Aswad have Guyanese heritage. Steel Pulse's drummer Steve Nesbitt is originally from St. Kitts, and gifted bass player Dennis Bovell is Anglo-Bajan. For Truths and Rights, their Caribbean diasporic diversity meant that they could credibly represent two music cultures, one from the Eastern Caribbean and the other from Jamaica, both of which remain a profound influence on the overall music scene in Canada. Calypso was the cultural breast milk that suckled the talents of some band members. Quammie Williams' introduction to music came through his association with Cavaliers, a famous steel band based in the South Trinidad town of San Fernando, where he spent his early childhood. Mohjah's grounding in Trinidad's popular music came partly as a result of his uncle, calypsonian Lord Nelson. A Truths and Rights concert often included the performance of several soca and calypso tunes. Truths and Rights was an important agent in spreading the "gospel" of reggae and especially soca to certain alternative pop-rock bands of Queen Street West during the early '80s.

In those days, downtown Toronto's Queen Street West strip did not accommodate chain stores like the Gap, Roots, and HMV. That section of Queen West displayed offbeat boutiques and alternative nightclubs as it flowed eastward to University Avenue where it stopped to confront the staid grey buildings of Canadian business. As the strip ran in the opposite direction of suits, bow ties, and oxford shoes, it passed the ubiquitous Citytv studios, independent bookstore Pages, and Steve's Music Store posing on the strip's Rasta-hippie-punk environment of nose rings, Doc Martens, and dreadlocks to cross Spadina and collide with Chinatown. The drastic change in the look of the buildings and people seemed surreal. When flickering neon signs and beaming streetlights replaced the fading daylight, the strip's live-music nightclubs assumed prominence. The Rivoli, the Black Bull, the Horseshoe, the Bamboo all vibrated to a broad spectrum of music from blues, jazz, punk, and alt-rock to world beat, ska, reggae, and soca—the soca popularized by Truths and Rights. Liam Lacey, then a music journalist with the *Globe and Mail*, documents the impact of the band's leading figure in an October 1983 edition of the newspaper: "Mohjah ... has been an important figure in Toronto music in general, creating the strong Caribbean influence of so many Queen St. Bands."[7] Mohjah, for example, was crucial to the Parachute Club's integration of a calypso aesthetic into its specific pop stylings.

Before the birth of Parachute Club, three of its founding members Billy Bryans, Lorraine Segato, and Terry Wilkins were part of a band with a one letter name—V—that also included Mohjah and Quammie. When Parachute Club was at its peak of popularity the following comment in a *Globe and Mail* article written by Alan Neister was attributed to lead vocalist Lorraine Segato: "Truths and Rights have inspired us." Parachute Club's signature hit "Rise Up" exhibits that inspiration.

Until late 2004, Mohjah was vocalist and rhythm guitarist with Big Sugar, a popular Canadian band that spiced its blues-rock repertoire with reggae. Mohjah and bass player Gary Lowe, another important figure from the Canadian reggae scene of the '80s, were crucial to Big Sugar's ability to inhabit authentic reggae groove territory. The reggae song "Turn the Lights On" was one of the band's most popular tunes. Big Sugar is one example of how roots-reggae continued to operate within Canadian rock much as it did over twenty-five years before in the music of Bruce Cockburn and others.

The legacy of Mojah, Truths and Rights, and Lillian Allen is evident in the music of artists from a new generation of the Caribbean diaspora making their presence felt in the new millennium. Rap artists such as Toronto's Kardinal Offishal and MC Collizhun (formerly of Nefarious) and Vancouver's Rascalz fuse heavy doses of reggae and reggae vocal style into hip-hop laced with lyrics that sometimes offer incisive social commentary about the Caribbean diaspora in Canada.

Kardinal Offishal's hip-hop shifts from the funk of "Powerfull" to the roots reggae of "Maxine." On "Husslin'," hip-hop and dancehall reggae beats coalesce into one groove. Kardinal's lyrics work Caribbean diasporic thematic territory without apology. In the tune "BaKardi Slang" he raps: "You all think we're all

Jamaicans / But nuff man a Trinis, Bajans, Grenadians, whole heap a Haitians, Guyanese / The whole West Indies combined / To make the T-dot O-dot one of a kind."[8] With these words Kardinal makes a clear statement that his generation of Caribbean-Canadians sees itself as being united by Caribbean-Canadian culture and social reality regardless of any specific island of heritage. Kardinal's "Powerfull" is much more pointed in its view of how sections of the Caribbean diaspora respond to racism and unfair treatment from certain institutions in the land of their birth or citizenship. The lyrics comment on some sensitive and controversial issues including mistrust between Black youth and the police, pride in Black unity—which he insists is misunderstood as reverse racism—and the ever-present issue of the threat to Canadian identity from the spectre of American domination.

MC Collizhun also throws down creative hip-hop with reggae attitude. His flow, although steeped in Jamaican patois, is delivered in rap style as opposed to traditional Jamaican deejay phrasing. On his debut album as part of the rap group Nefarious, he works exclusively with grungy hip-hop beats, but his edgy jerk-spiced patois rap provides all the reggae vibes necessary. On the track "Toe to Toe," Collizhun's words convey a different side of the Caribbean diasporic experience in Canada:

Well a di bwoy from Jamaica, Duhaney Park, Kingston / Welcome to foreign where Nefarious got MCs on the run / … You know what's funny when you go a Jamaica and say yu from foreign / Dem think you have money / But mi bruk y'know / Dem wan mi fi send down a barrel an a telegram / Mi look in a mi wallet and say weh di raas mi fi get it from / …[9]

Collizhun's rap describes the tension between recent Jamaican immigrants and those of Jamaican heritage who were born or grew up in Canada. He also assesses the thoughts of Jamaican-Canadians on visits to Jamaica in the face of the sometimes-unreasonable demands from relatives and friends.

Canadian hip-hop and Toronto hip-hop specifically has always incorporated a distinctive reggae, ska, or Caribbean flavour in its rhythmic structure, and its lyrics have always used the cadences and speech of the diaspora to discuss the situation of Caribbean diasporic youth. The early work of seminal Canadian hip-hop acts like Michi Mee, Dream Warriors, and Maestro underscores that fact. Collizhun, Kardinal, and others—such as skilled rap artist and poet Motion—whose hip-hop is immersed in reggae references, not only maintain but advance the tradition of diasporic reggae by being musically creative and lyrically expressive about the current condition of Caribbean-Canadians.

Reggae continues to exist as an independent genre in Canada. Talented roots reggae bands and singers such as Lazo, Jah Beng, Blessed, Len Hammond, Leejahn, Ibadan, Sonia Collymore, Kareem Green, and Belinda Brady still toil below the mainstream, while the creativity of Michael St. George and d'bi young keep the flames of progressive dub poetry burning.

The diverse lyrical flavour of the Toronto dub environment is a fertile nurturing ground for Michael St. George, a second-wave dub poet influenced by post-1985 dancehall reggae as well as Bob Marley and Dennis Brown. St. George delivers his unique thematic contribution to reggae through his discourse on the discrimination and challenges faced by seniors in recorded poems that appear on his second album *Root 2 Fruit*. Poems on this album such as "Anti-Ageist Rage," "Grandma Ideology," and "Elder Abuse" reveal St. George's messages about the importance of seniors in the context of his upbringing in Jamaica and his experiences as a gerontologist and caregiver in Toronto.

Set It Off, an album released in 2002 by alternative pop artist and Jamaican-Canadian Jarvis Church, formerly of the Philosopher Kings, achieved mainstream success with two very popular reggae tracks. The hit single "Run for Your Life" is a proto-dancehall tune that in its remixed state incorporates a more pronounced dancehall feel featuring Jamaican deejay Elephant Man. Two versions of the album's title track were included on the CD, a rhythm and blues take and a roots track sounding like vintage reggae lovers' rock of the '70s. The reggae version, although hidden on track seventy-one of the disc, was given decent rotation on mainstream urban music radio stations in Toronto. Jeff Holdip, mentioned earlier as Truths and Rights sound mixer for their live shows, crafted an innovative and exciting reggae dub album fused with jungle called *Hard End: The Luge Sessions*. On this 1999 release, Holdip skillfully samples songs by U-Roy, Gregory Isaacs, English folk-rocker Billy Bragg, and loops a contentious and provocative

Peter Tosh interview. One of the best tunes on the album is "Six Love," which showcases the lush voice of Dahlia Anderson singing a lovers' rock melody in French to the rugged, sensuous, rub-a-dub bass lines of ex-Messenjah bassist Charles "Tower" Sinclair. *Hard End*, like Patrick Andrade's *Dancing on John Wayne's Head*, is a great example of a Canadian dub album.

While the diasporic reggae of the U.K. and the U.S. has been recognized by writers assessing the history of reggae's impact beyond Jamaica (read, for example, *Reggae : The Rough Guide* by English reggae enthusiasts Steve Barrow and Peter Dalton), until now, diasporic reggae in Canada has not enjoyed the kind of profile it deserves. In a variety of different forms, reggae—particularly, Canadian diasporic reggae—has become a permanent and vital feature of Canadian culture that, in part, expresses the experience of Caribbean-Canadians.

Dub Fire

Reggae in the Caribbean Diaspora

In the U.K. during the early '70s, the lives of three young Black men—David Hinds, Linton Kwesi Johnson, and Brinsley Forde—were connected only by their passion for reggae, their relationship to the art of Bob Marley, and their desire to rebel against racism and injustice.

Bob Marley's distinct tenor floated through speaker boxes of different sound systems across the Midlands city of Birmingham. Marley's wailing vocal invaded the consciousness of a teenager named David, who did not know the owner of the voice with the unique texture that held such a seductive appeal.

David lived in the Handsworth neighbourhood of Birmingham with his Jamaican parents. Handsworth exhaled the rhythms, food aroma, and fashion of hard-working Jamaican immigrants, an environment that instilled in David a strong bond with the culture of his parent's homeland. Like a growing number of Black youth at the time, David looked to the liberation theology of Rastafari and the solutions of African-American Black Power advocates to understand and contend with the issues of racism and discrimination in the U.K.

David decided on a career in reggae to complement his rebel perspective—a career like the musicians' and singers', whose ominous rhythms and anti-oppression lyrics echoed out of speaker boxes at the sound-system dances he attended. He partied at one reggae-blues dance or another, certain that he would eventually hear that elusive seductive vocal on at least one record, chanting that specific style of rebellious words wrapped in the loving embrace of a certain kind of riveting syncopation that was so attractive to him. The identity of the man behind the voice finally revealed itself when David first heard the entire collection of songs on the Wailers' *Catch A Fire* album.

David was so taken with Bob Marley's vocal style that he exercised his own vocal abilities by singing along with Marley's music. Marley's songs encouraged David's existing intentions about how he should express his own messages of social protest and Rasta spirituality. In a sense, the Wailers' music gave him permission to proceed on the journey of musical creativity that he had already initiated. David Hinds became chief songwriter, lead vocalist, and foundation member of Steel Pulse, the first British roots reggae band to establish a mainstream presence in the U.K.

Linton, a twenty-year-old student majoring in sociology at the University of London, began a study of reggae as a hobby in 1972, the year of *Catch A Fire*'s U.K. release. He set out to investigate a music that originated in Jamaica, the land of his birth. Linton left Jamaica at age eleven to join his mother in South London. He and his mother lived in Brixton, a community populated with enough Jamaican and other Caribbean immigrants that, despite the architecture of the houses and England's damp miserable weather, could have passed for a low-income neighbourhood in Jamaica's capital city.

Linton was an activist and member of the Black Panther movement, a radical organization that shared the name but had no affiliation with its U.S. counterpart. Linton decided to express his thoughts about racial discrimination and its effect on British residents of Caribbean, African, and South Asian heritage through poetry. His literary influences included Caribbean poets Edward Kamau Brathwaite and Robin "Bongo Jerry" Small, and W.E.B. Dubois' book *The Souls of Black Folk*. Linton's community activism and his poetry fuelled each other. As a British-Jamaican poet and student of reggae, he was intrigued by the way that roots deejays such as U-Roy, I-Roy, and Big Youth, using Jamaican language, weaved their spoken-word rhymes and catchphrases around menacing roots reggae rhythms. Linton was so impressed with the skills of these deejays or reggae rappers that he named their craft dub poetry.

Linton realized that in order to properly discuss the Caribbean experience in Britain through his poetry, he would have to use Jamaican language rather than conventional English. He realized that his words would have to dance to the precise rhythmic timing of reggae. Eventually, Linton's verse would be set to innovative dub rhythms to be recorded like the work of other reggae artists and the deejays that he admired. The name he designed for the deejays came to describe his own work and the work of other reggae poets.

Linton soon became a member of an independent Black Marxist collective of community activists. The group was based in

Brixton and published a periodical *Race Today*, in which Linton's poetry was first published (it also published Johnson's first poetry collection *Voices of the Living and the Dead*). Linton's poetry was often distinguished by a critical class analysis devoid of the theological elements that often fuelled the work of poets and reggae musicians inspired by the Rasta movement. Linton's reggae studies eventually found an outlet in a 1982 BBC radio documentary series where he suggested that *Catch A Fire* was the first example of roots reggae offering a new international sound. Linton Kwesi Johnson became the first British dub poet to register an impact on the international music scene.

Brinsley, a young man born in the U.K. of parents from the South-American nation of Guyana, worked in a fruit and vegetable store in West London's Neasden area. Brinsley's work history began years earlier as a successful child actor in British television appearing on ITV's *The Magnificent Six and 1/2* and the BBC's *The Double Deckers*. His tenure at the greengrocer was simply a temporary diversion before reigniting a new career in the arts. This time it would be music. Brinsley's singing voice and the guitar that he was in the process of mastering were the tools he would employ as a reggae artist. Brinsley was, at the time, between artistic occupations; his only fans were fruits and vegetables.

One day, while he was outside the shop, he looked up to see the slender six-foot frame of Peter Tosh bouncing towards him on the sidewalk. The Wailers were staying only a short distance away. After Brinsley introduced himself as an aspiring reggae musician, Peter invited him to meet the other Wailers. Brinsley, accompanied by his instruments, visited the Wailers' apartment several times where he practiced mainly with bass player Family Man.

By the mid-'70s, Brinsley became foundation member, guitarist, and lead vocalist of roots reggae band Aswad. In 1980, he starred in an important U.K film *Babylon*, for which Aswad provided the soundtrack. *Babylon* cinematically embodied the themes of British diasporic reggae. Aswad eventually became Britain's premier reggae outfit.

The Wailers and the new international sound of reggae typified by *Catch A Fire* were a pivotal influence on the reggae careers of David, Linton, and Brinsley. Eventually, Steel Pulse became one of Bob Marley's favourite bands, Bunny Wailer referred to Aswad as the young Wailers, and Marley liked Linton Kwesi Johnson's reggae poetry recordings enough to agree to distribute them in Jamaica through his Tuff Gong Records.

Before the release of the Wailers' *Catch A Fire* album in 1972, reggae had already begun to exert what became a pervasive influence on U.K. popular-music culture. Over the three-year period prior to the arrival of the album, Jamaican reggae was regularly making an appearance in the top ten of the U.K. pop charts with records such as the Upsetters' *Return of Django* (#5 in 1969), Desmond Dekker's *Israelites* (#1 in 1969), Jimmy Cliff's *Wonderful World, Beautiful People* (#6 in 1969), and *Young, Gifted, and Black* by Bob Andy and Marcia Griffiths (#5 in 1970).

The Jamaican film *The Harder They Come* with its exciting soundtrack of reggae recordings by Jimmy Cliff and a variety of Jamaican artists represented the music's initial breakthrough to a sustained mainstream presence in the U.K. The film is a cinematic dub plate whose every frame drips with the sweat of a rude reggae aesthetic. Its narrative—co-written by its Jamaican director Perry Henzell and one of the island's outstanding playwrights Trevor Rhone—unravels the life of the story's main character Ivan played by Jimmy Cliff.

The Harder They Come traces Ivan's transformation from country *bwoy* to reggae recording artist and finally to flawed tragic folk hero as gunman. The thoroughly Jamaican, yet universal story treats us to a humane and dignified portrayal of Rastafari that was rare or non-existent in the local or international media of the day. The film bravely exposes the exploitative aspect of the island's recording industry. *The Harder They Come* is a *rude-bwoy* reggae musical—a roots rebel film equivalent to the rebel reggae music from which it draws its strength. It still stands as the most outstanding piece of Jamaican reggae cinema. No other theatrical film has provided that particular glimpse, that particular *prips* below the surface of Jamaican society to reveal the island's nagging problems of race and class and certainly not with the ambitions of artistry to which it aspires. The movie debuted in Kingston in early 1972, and was emotionally embraced by the downtown audience whose experiences it reflected.

The Harder They Come was released internationally later in 1972, and it developed a cult following in the U.K. and America. The film's popularity provided roots reggae with a new vehicle for promotion. Island Records released the soundtrack album to coincide

Aswad. From the left Tony 'Gad' Robinson, Angus 'Drummie Zeb' Gaye and Brinsley Forde. Undated.

with the film's arrival in the international marketplace. Unlike some of the previous reggae hits in the U.K., the soundtrack to *The Harder They Come* is not a diluted version of the music, but instead contains reggae with passion, grit, and, most important, a beat that is as legitimate to the music as ackee and salt fish is to Jamaican cuisine.

The soundtrack is a compilation of ten songs by various artists that are crucial to the film's narrative flow. Cliff contributed four songs: the title track, "You Can Get It If You Really Want," "Many Rivers to Cross," and "Sitting in Limbo." The Maytals' "Sweet and Dandy" and "Pressure Drop," Desmond Dekker's "007 (Shanty Town)," the Melodians' "Rivers of Babylon," the Slickers' "Johnny Too Bad," and Scotty's deejay track "Draw Your Brakes" were singles previously released in Jamaica, many of them popular hits on the island.

The Harder They Come as a reggae album found new converts for reggae in the U.K. to the extent that in order to be current and "hip," London's West End nightclubs were encouraged to spin the "tighten-up" sound of reggae on their turntables.

The Harder They Come as a film crafting a sympathetic portrayal of Rastafari character Pedro and the rebel reggae singer Ivan, in a sense, was the perfect introduction to the Wailers' Rasta rebel reggae of Catch A Fire. The Wailers, however, were not the first choice to capitalize on the film's success. Jimmy Cliff, with his 1969 top-ten hit, his starring role in The Harder They Come, and as the artist with the most recordings on the film's soundtrack, had become the voice and face of reggae in the U.K. and America.

Cliff's career outside of Jamaica began when he joined Prince Buster, Eric "Monty" Morris, and Millie Small as a prominent singer performing in Jamaica's ska showcase at the World's Fair in New York. Cliff then signed to Chris Blackwell's U.K.-based Island Records in 1965. Island Records' success with #1 U.K. hit "My Boy Lollipop" and Island's links to Jamaica's incipient recording industry gave Chris Blackwell's record company the distinction of being part British/part Jamaican with international ambitions. In some ways, that is an appropriate description of Chris Blackwell himself.

Blackwell, an astute White British-Jamaican businessman, who now has financial interests in music, film, and hotel properties, was born in England, but grew up in an affluent suburb of Jamaica's capital city. He arrived in Jamaica six months after his birthdate of June 22, 1937. Although in the early '50s he briefly attended Harrow, a prestigious English private school, his formative years were mainly spent in Jamaica.

Blackwell's family background has deep roots in Jamaica's elite upper classes. His Irish-Jamaican father, Middleton Blackwell, possessed a removed kinship to the fortunes of the Crosse and Blackwell canned food business. The family of Blackwell's mother, Blanche Lindo, were invested in Appleton, Jamaica's internationally famous brand of rum. As a young man in his early twenties during the late '50s, Blackwell took his first tentative steps toward carving out his own independent path in business while still relying on his family connections. Initially, he attempted a variety of disciplines including accounting, real estate, as well as teaching water skiing and renting motor scooters at the Half Moon Hotel in Montego Bay. Ian Fleming—author of the James Bond novels, resident of Jamaica, and a friend of Blanche Lindo—recommended Blackwell for first job in film production as a gofer for Canadian producer Harry Saltzman on the set of the first James Bond movie, *Dr. No.*

Music always played a prominent role in Blackwell's life, and like many Jamaicans of his generation, he enjoyed jazz and was a fan of Miles Davis. Blackwell's relationship with the embryonic Jamaican popular music industry began in 1959, and his first success in the business came with his production of Laurel Aitken's "Little Sheila" in 1960. As a White upper-class Jamaican, his involvement in the music culture of African-Jamaicans was, to say the least, unusual. For the most part, rich White Jamaicans either despised the culture of Black Jamaicans or, if they found it quaint, did not view it as a worthy investment or a legitimate business venture. Blackwell's positive view of African-Jamaican culture was instilled through his relationship with the staff of maids and gardeners who worked in the Terra Nova mansion where he lived as a boy. As a boy, he suffered from bronchial asthma forcing him to spend a lot of time at the Terra Nova in the care of the mansion's African-Jamaican staff, who provided the young Blackwell with an insider's sense of African-Jamaican culture and folklore.

In 1962, Blackwell relocated his modest recording and distribution operation, which he named Island Records, to London, England. The focus of the company's business—until the success of "My Boy Lollipop"—remained the distribution of Jamaican ska to Caribbean immigrants.

Jimmy Cliff's connection to Island proved to be a mixed blessing because Blackwell's focus became transforming the record company from a company mainly interested in producing and distributing ska into a company that became home to British rock bands such as the Spencer Davis Group, Traffic, Jethro Tull, Free, and singer/songwriter Cat Stevens. The label experienced significant success in album sales.

Blackwell's continuing involvement in Jamaican music during the rocksteady and early reggae periods came through his 1968 partnership with South Asian-Jamaican Lee Gopthal's Trojan Records. Trojan and Island eventually parted ways in 1972, but for four years Trojan, in a sense, became the reggae label of Island. By 1967, Island stopped releasing any Cliff recordings and he eventually became a Trojan artist. Cliff represented Jamaica in the 1968 International Song Festival held in Brazil. Brazilians responded positively to his entry "Waterfall," which established a profile for him in South America, a presence that has endured throughout the years. The journey to South America seems to have been a turning point in his career. A few months later in 1969, Cliff's Trojan release "Wonderful World, Beautiful People" went to #6 on the U.K. chart. The record is a pretty pop-reggae song with socially relevant lyrics, whose music was softened by syrupy strings.

"Wonderful World, Beautiful People" fell squarely into the category of recordings by Jamaican reggae singers produced for a foreign mainstream audience. The formula sometimes failed because attempts to force reggae into a pop mould resulted in something too innocuous even for non-discriminating pop music fans. "Wonderful World" worked well, incorporating Cliff's sincere vocal, a catchy melody, and his capable songwriting. The floodgates were now wide open, and Cliff's objective of firmly establishing himself on the international music scene seemed visible on the horizon. A year later his version of Cat Stevens' "Wild World" settled at #8 in the British top ten. In 1970, Cliff's protest single "Vietnam" was also released, announcing that reggae was concerned with serious social and political issues of global significance.

Cliff's "Vietnam" told the story of an American GI victim of the war. The tune's steady reggae beat is peppered with rapid-fire guitar licks, and a solemn saxophone riff creates the mood for the song's lyric that describes the message in a telegram an American mother receives from Vietnam informing her of her son's death. Cliff is precise about the song's purpose when in one anguished line of lyric he pleads for someone to end the war immediately. "Vietnam" peaked at #46 on the U.K. pop chart, but it represents an important social commentary reggae song that caused progressive American recording artists such as Paul Simon and Bob Dylan to start paying attention to reggae.

Eight years earlier, Jimmy Cliff was still James Chambers, just another teenager who arrived in Kingston from his hometown of Somerton, St. James, interested in initiating a profession as a singer. Cliff jump-started his career as a performer and recording artist with "Hurricane Hattie" and "Dearest Beverley," which earned him measured success on the local Jamaican scene during the early years of ska. Soon after the World's Fair gig, Jimmy Cliff relocated to England. His only connection to the island's rugged rocksteady beats produced for the dancehall was that he sometimes recorded in the same Jamaican studios in which these songs were created. Cliff's music was not really designed for a Jamaican audience. In fact, Trojan positioned Cliff as a kind of rock-reggae-pop crossover artist. Consequently, his presence in Jamaica was incidental with the possible exception of 1968's "Hard Road to Travel." The lack of a close relationship with the Jamaican scene was part of the price Cliff paid in his attempts to launch himself and Jamaican music far beyond the island's shores.

After the success of *The Harder They Come* as film and soundtrack album, Blackwell saw Cliff as the "next big thing," the man who could take reggae into the mainstream to enjoy more than a fleeting two-hit moment. Jimmy Cliff had other ideas. Cliff's view was that Island had not properly promoted him in the past, and that Blackwell was more serious about the rock artists on Island's roster. Cliff realized that he had a window of opportunity flowing from his profile as reggae's most prominent personality and opted to terminate his association with Island and ink a deal with EMI. Blackwell was devastated. In his view, the timing was right to move reggae to the next level and he believed he had the expertise to successfully achieve that move with Jimmy Cliff. Bob Marley was in the U.K. at that time struggling in the aftermath of a failed attempt to initiate a career outside Jamaica through the efforts of American pop singer Johnny Nash and American producer Danny Simms. When Marley visited Chris Blackwell at his Island offices in West London, both men were seeking to reposition themselves and start a fresh journey to launch reggae as an international genre of music.

The first time that Blackwell and Marley spoke to each other in person, two very different rebels came face to face. Blackwell saw in Marley the defiant reggae singer Ivan, the character played by Jimmy Cliff in the reggae film *The Harder They Come*. Blackwell found himself in the presence of a man whose music he admired. He knew that the Wailers' reggae was very popular in Jamaica. He would have also known about their reggae-funk single "Reggae on Broadway" produced by Danny Simms that received airplay on U.K. radio. Marley faced a fair-haired blue-eyed Jamaican who was owner of a maverick U.K. record company that experienced main-stream success with ska, reggae, and rock music. Marley met a White British-Jamaican who seemed prepared to produce an album of rebel reggae songs and market a Rasta band from Trench Town in the same way that he would promote an album-oriented rock act.

Blackwell's idea of packaging the first set of *Catch A Fire* vinyl

in an album jacket that looked like a Zippo cigarette lighter represented more than simply smart marketing. It signified the belief
that reggae, as a new type of roots music, could be marketed like
rock music and appeal to both reggae and rock fans. Unlike the
approach Trojan took with Jimmy Cliff, Island did not attempt to
dilute the Wailers' reggae in order to make obvious overtures to a
pop audience. The roots reggae rhythms of *Catch A Fire* were carefully seasoned with the psychedelic rock flavours of John "Rabbit"
Bundrick's keyboard sound and Wayne Perkins' wailing guitar
lines at the suggestion of Blackwell and with the blessing of Bob
Marley. Some purist critics consider the rock influence on the
album to be a dilution. The rock seasoning, however, does not
dilute or soften the Wailers' authentic roots reggae but instead
enhances its creativity.

The influence of Bob Marley and the Wailers on mainstream
British rock was immediate. Rock guitar "god" Eric Clapton wasted no time in recording a version of Marley's "I Shot the Sheriff"
only several months after its 1973 release on the Wailers' second
Island album *Burnin'*. Clapton's interpretation of the Marley composition—released in 1974 as a single from the *461 Ocean Boulevard*
album—went straight to #1 on both sides of the Atlantic, revived
Clapton's career, and became a high-water mark for reggae's
seduction of British rock. Clapton's success with "I Shot the
Sheriff" expanded Marley's resumé to include another achievement as an important songwriter on the international music scene.

When punk rock arrived on the scene in the mid-'70s, some
punk bands sourced reggae the way that '60s rock and roll cribbed
from African-American blues. Female punk band The Slits recorded a searing anarchic version of Jamaican reggae singer/song-
writer John Holt's "Man Next Door" that, true to punk's intentions, exploded the melodic flow of the reggae original. The Clash
recorded a decent version of Junior Murvin's "Police and Thieves"
and an original reggae song "Bank Robbers." The music of The
Police personified "white reggae" in the London pop-punk scene
of the late '70s. Police lead vocalist and bass player Sting admitted
at the time that Marley was a major influence on The Police. The
punk-reggae romance was not one-sided. In 1977, Bob Marley
released a 12" single in England called "Punky Reggae Party." The
lyrics of that 1977 tune salutes the unity of the two rebel music
forms and views both White and Black rebels as being treated

Steel Pulse (from left): Selwyn Brown, David Hinds, Phonzo Martin, and Steve Nesbitt. May 1991. Photograph by Peter Ashworth.

unfairly by society. The song identifies The Clash and the Wailers themselves as names on the punky reggae party guest list.

The term "British reggae" did not really apply to the reggae excursions of British rock or punk musicians; it described the innovative Caribbean diasporic reggae of bands like Steel Pulse and Aswad and the dub poetry of Linton Kwesi Johnson. The lyrics of British reggae documented the condition of Black people in England during the late '70s and throughout the '80s. Aswad's "African Children," for example, describes the circumstances of Black children living in low-income high-rise apartments (known as flats) of any English inner city. Conveying the dismal environment of how some people subsist, the band discusses rent increases, structural repairs, and stinky elevators that are too often non-operational. Steel Pulse, on the title track of their first album *Handsworth Revolution*, sing about the situation of Blacks in their hometown of Handsworth as a place where the innocent are convicted, where minimum wages are paid for hard labour, and people go hungry. "Handsworth

Revolution" went beyond simply stating the problems, it also suggested the possibility of revolt. Three years after the tune's release, riots shook Brixton and other minority neighbourhoods in London, and sent decisive political tremors throughout England.

One of the more serious issues for Black youth in Britain has been police harassment. Linton Kwesi Johnson, in his reggae recording of the poem "Sonny's Lettah," poignantly dramatizes an incident that gives substance to the suggestion that truth is sometimes better served by fictional accounts. The verse is related from Sonny's first-person viewpoint in the form of a letter to his mother from a prison cell. He recounts a violent saga of three policemen with batons who rush his brother Jim while they were both standing at a bus stop. For reasons known only to the policemen, they announce that they are going to take Jim in. They attempt to arrest him. Jim resists. He is punched in the stomach, back, and head, and kicked in the testicles. Sonny defends his younger brother by poking one policeman in the eye and punching another in the mouth. The policeman who receives a blow from Sonny on the chin, drops, hits his head on a bin, and dies. Jim and Sonny are eventually subdued. Jim is charged with suspicion; Sonny is charged with murder. One of the interesting aspects of the poem is that the victims of the harassment do not passively accept the unjust treatment. Resistance to injustice is an important theme of Johnson's reggae poetry. "African Children," "Handsworth Revolution," and "Sonny's Lettah" represent much more than a documentation of the condition of U.K. Blacks; they represent a voice for change.

If words and music could inflict pain, then every British fascist who ever thought about assaulting individuals of Caribbean, South Asian, or African descent would have died back in the early '80s. Those racists would have suffered a cruel death from exposure to Johnson's dub poems such as "Fite Dem Back," which prided itself in not being equivocal or diplomatic: "Smash their brains in / cause they aint got nofink in 'em ... / Some of dem say dem a nigger hater / some of dem say dem a Black stabber / and some of dem say dem a Paki basher / ... Fascists on the attack / we will fight dem back."[1]

The National Front—a political party that gained mainstream notoriety in the '70s as the economic crisis in the U.K. politically unhinged the country—represented the nasty face of British fascism. It started in 1967 as a unifying umbrella organization for several extreme right-wing groups. Predictably, it was anti-Semitic, praised Hitler, and advocated a "Keep Britain White" policy. The National Front became the fourth largest political party in Britain by 1976. A number of anti-fascist united fronts and coalitions emerged to oppose the National Front. The Rock Against Racism (RAR) movement was the alternative-rock community's contribution to the anti-racist offensive. RAR brought together Black bands such as Matumbi and Merger with White groups such as Tom Robinson Band and Stiff Little Fingers in order to combat the idea of racial segregation fostered by the National Front.

White musicians in the coalition were mainly progressive punk rockers. The Black bands represented the seminal cry of British roots reggae. Initially, there was an uneasy interaction between punk bands and reggae bands in RAR's anti-racist coalition stemming from the fact that the Black reggae bands saw themselves as being a more authentic voice of anti-racism for two main reasons. The most obvious reason was that as Black people, they were direct victims of racism and fascism. The second reason involved the idea that the struggle against racism was an integral and inseparable element of '70s reggae culture, a culture that had protested racism before punk was born, before punk became the "popular trend of the moment." Despite whatever issues may have occurred inside the Rock Against Racism coalition, it was an effective multiracial alliance in the fight against racism. RAR is historically important for that reason and also because it deployed the rebel music of punk and reggae as its main weapons of struggle. The Sex Pistols, possibly the most notorious band of '70s British punk, did not participate in RAR, though John Lydon (aka Johnny Rotten)—the Pistols' leading personality and ardent reggae fan—was quoted in the RAR coalition's magazine promoting an anti–National Front position.

On the way to becoming British reggae's first major success story, Steel Pulse participated in RAR events. The band was such an integral part of the uneasy marriage of reggae and punk during that time that they were nicknamed "Jah Punk." Steel Pulse's first club dates in London were at saliva-stained, beer-splattered punk venues where they appeared on the same stage as bands such as XTC, Generation X, and the Stranglers. Steel Pulse's appearances at punk-rock venues, particularly in London, were a breakthrough for the band since, at that time, it was difficult for a roots reggae band from Birmingham performing original material to get booked at reggae venues. At punk concerts, fans showed their appreciation for a performance by gobbing or spitting at band members. Although these performances provided Steel Pulse with a profile in London, they were wary of the gobbing and scuzzy venues; they wanted to appeal to a reggae audience that included fans from the Caribbean diasporic communities of the U.K. Steel Pulse satisfied their desire of performing in front of a reggae audience when they opened for Bob Marley and the Wailers on their European tour in the summer of 1978. Steel Pulse signed with Island Records in late 1977, and in February 1978, Island released the single "Ku Klux Klan" followed in July by the band's debut album, *Handsworth Revolution*.

Despite their advance in the reggae world, Steel Pulse remained committed to RAR. In April 1978, Steel Pulse, The Clash, X-Ray Spex, and Tom Robinson Band performed in front of eighty thousand people at Victoria Park, Hackney in East London. That same year, a line-up including Aswad, Elvis Costello, and Stiff Little Fingers played an RAR concert in Brixton. Steel Pulse featured "Jah Pickney–RAR" on their second Island album, 1979's *Tribute to the Martyrs*. The song, although rarely mentioned in connection to the RAR movement, skillfully uses reggae to record for posterity the struggle of rock musicians against the National Front: "Rock against Racism, smash it / Rock against Fascism, smash it / … We're gonna hunt … the National Front."[2]

The lyrics of British reggae set it apart from the Jamaican music that inspired it. The rhythms and melodies of reggae artists in Britain were also distinctive. The U.K. Caribbean diasporic interpretation of Jamaican reggae supplied the art form with creative innovations. Every track on Steel Pulse's debut album attempts to paint different rhythmic portraits than the ones framed by Jamaican reggae rhythms of that time.

"Prediction" is an outstanding track with a gorgeous rhythm construction initiated by a hollow drum roll, followed seamlessly by Ronnie "Stepper" McQueen's slow loping bass line that is then joined by the sound of clicking castanets. When the bass drops out of the mix, the castanets continue clicking to drummer Steve Nesbitt's nattering backbeat. The song moves easily into creative hyper-drive as an organ that sounds like a crisp cool wind blowing eerily through the rhythm complements Basil Gabbidon's cryptic flamenco guitar chords. As the lumbering stutter bass returns, it is accompanied by voices harmonizing a line of lyric and David Hinds' voice furiously rolling an "R" to inform the established Latin vibe. It is one of the best intros to a reggae tune. The Latin flavour that Steel Pulse brings to reggae on "Prediction" was pioneer work at the time.

"Soldiers" prominently features Nesbitt's distinctive hi-hat-tinged one-drop, which became a trademark of the early Steel Pulse sound that was almost as characteristic as David Hinds' wispy tenor.

The bass heard on "Sound System" from *Tribute to the Martyrs*, moves in and out of a mix seasoned with Gabbidon's crunchy lead guitar riffs and bawling rock-style solo all accented by intermittent waves of Phonso Martin's animated hand drum beats. The dissonant marriage of squealing rock guitar and nyabinghi percussion was hardly the language of reggae at the time.

"Unseen Guest," another track from this album, has an unusual but satisfying a-cappella introduction that features David's warm tenor interchanging with rhythm and blues–style harmony of Phonso Martin, keyboard player Selwyn Brown, Gabbidon, and percussionist Michael Riley. The voices echo and fade as if the band were singing inside a cave and the equipment recording the song was situated at the cave's entrance.

The tone of David Hind's fragile, yet supple singing voice is riveting, charismatic, and possibly the most important element of the Steel Pulse sound. His silky tenor is capable of producing the mournful tones heard in "Biko's Kindred Lament," a virtual eulogy in tribute to fallen South African leader Steve Biko, or the passionate romance of songs like "Throne of Gold," a Rasta love ballad. Like Marley, Hinds possesses the ability to scat in a style that reinterprets jazz vocal improvisation in a way that suits the melodic purposes of reggae. Hinds' voice combines a smooth Leroy Sibbles quality with the rebel wail of a Bob Marley.

Aswad, the first U.K. roots reggae band to sign with a major label began their relationship with Island Records in 1976, the year their debut album, *Aswad*, hit the streets. As a result of their excellent musicianship, the band was invited to act as backing musicians for Burning Spear on his U.K. tour of 1977. The concert album *Burning Spear Live* was produced from the performance at North London's Rainbow venue. The following year, members of the band participated in a studio session with Bob Marley to record a version of the Wailers' "Keep on Moving." Aswad's second album *Hulet* also appeared in 1978 on Grove, an independent label.

Aswad soon decided that instead of splitting their time between providing services for visiting Jamaican reggae acts and their own work, they should focus entirely on building the band's career. The initial fruit of that focus was 1980's "Warrior Charge," Aswad's contribution to the soundtrack of the film *Babylon*. "Warrior Charge" is a blistering sound-system-style roots reggae instrumental featuring, for the first time, Aswad's distinct use of jazzy trumpet, saxophone, and trombone solos and harmonies. The tune, however, was simply an introductory segue to their 1981 studio masterpiece *New Chapter*.

New Chapter—released by CBS Records U.K.—though poorly promoted and therefore experiencing moderate sales at the time, expressed a significant creativity. The reggae supporting each carefully crafted recording on *New Chapter* strikes the balance between the use of electronic studio-dub techniques and the earthy texture of real instruments. The balance—created through the skillful sound mix by drummer Angus "Drummie Zeb" Gaye and producer Michael "Rueben" Campbell—is slanted in favour of real instruments with dub techniques of delay, reverb, and echo deployed in a way that does not overwhelm the music but instead adds colour and character.

Tony "Gad" Robinson's bass lines for the album's opening track "African Children" talk in brash moody notes that drill down to "bassment" level. His low-down dub sounds are at the centre of a rhythm storm encouraged and faithfully supported by the menace of Angus Gaye's lively cacophonic one-drop that jumps to ticking hi-hat work. Robinson's playing leaves less space between notes than would a Jamaican roots bassist, but Gaye creates enough rhythmic tension to satisfy any examination of the music's reggae credentials. Clifton Morrison's crafty keyboard and piano flavours the rhythm with a dark attitude that complements the song's description of ghetto existence.

On "Natural Progression," hand drummer Levi introduces the tune by hammering out a flurry of percussive ripples. The harmony of Eddie "Tan-Tan" Thornton's trumpet and the alto sax of Michael "Bammie" Rose transport the intense jazzy soloing of Vin Gordon's sincere trombone voice. Drums and bass introduce their presence at the same time as the horns. The bass, though prominent, is mixed so that it is slightly less imposing than the rolling drum sounds. The saxophone, trumpet, and trombone are mixed upfront like vocals. That production decision, highly unusual for reggae, does not detract from the human voices but considerably increases the song's jazz quotient. Essentially, "Natural Progression" has two lead voices: Brinsley Forde's vocal and Gordon's trombone. Forde sings in a soulfully gruff timbre that is a contrast to the sweet, ethereal harmony of Robinson and Gaye. The tune's finale belongs to the horns. They hold court without the intrusion of drums, keyboards or vocals. Robinson's bass, mixed low in the background, is the finale's only rhythmic anchor. Sax and trumpet riff the same barrage of heralding notes while Gordon blows a satisfying, lyrical, and emotional solo that poignantly provides substance to the song's theme about the tragedy of colonialism.

Another *New Chapter* track "Love Fire" is a ballad coloured with sinister beats that spray plump implosive bass notes intent on penetrating the earth's core. These sombre beats accommodate keyboard growls with the swiftly skipping tick-tock of hi-hat figures and the creative harmonic intervention of the Aswad horn section. Brinsley's vocal strikes a softer soothing pose that is given an eerie quality by the echo-reverb sound effects used on his voice and on the vocal harmony. "Love Fire" is *New Chapter*'s most influential track. Dennis Brown—who sometimes performed in Europe with Aswad as his backing band—set his own lyrics and devised his own melody to the "Love Fire" rhythm on his recording of the song. Beyond the song's influence on major Jamaican reggae star Dennis Brown, Aswad's vocal version of the tune and its instrumental dub were even played in Jamaican dancehalls by popular early '80s sound systems like Jah Love Muzik International.

The innovative quality of *New Chapter*'s reggae gained the recognition it deserved in the U.K. when in 1982, Aswad re-signed with Island, who that year released an instrumental dub version of the album. The critically acclaimed album titled *A New Chapter of Dub*, considered one of the finest reggae dub albums, became more popular than the version with the complete songs and vocals. Aswad's outstanding musicianship was often matched by their tight three-part vocal harmony and distinct solo singers.

Notably, Aswad possessed two competent vocalists: rhythm guitarist Brinsley Forde and drummer Angus Gaye. Tony Robinson, the band's third voice and innovative bass guitarist, usually provided harmony with one of the other two. Forde's dramatic soul vocal, in some ways, was better suited to the dub-style rhythms that defined the band's work up to the early '80s. "African Children," "Love Fire," and "Natural Progression" all featured Forde as lead voice. Gaye's softer velvet voice informed *New Chapter*'s "Ways of the Lord" and "Didn't Know at the Time." It was often used on Aswad's sublime reggae ballads like "Roots Rockin'," which appeared on *Not Satisfied*, the album that followed *New Chapter*, and the exceptional lovers' rock ballad "Need Your Love," a cut from 1984's *Rebel Souls*.

After Virgin Records released Linton Kwesi Johnson's debut album, *Dread Beat an' Blood*, Johnson—like Aswad and Steel Pulse before him—signed with Island where he recorded four of his most acclaimed albums of reggae poetry. The poetry on 1979's *Forces of Victory*, which includes "Sonny's Lettah" and "Fite Dem Back," speaks to struggles of the Caribbean diasporic communities and the struggles of all racial minorities in the U.K. An important theme of 1980's *Bass Culture* is how the intense soul-searching impact of powerful reggae rhythms—flowing out of speaker boxes at U.K. sound-system dances—act as the therapeutic sounds of struggle and resistance. Through the verse of tracks such as "Bass Culture" and "Reggae Sounds," Johnson conveys how roots reggae rhythms are, in a sense, a balm that attempts to soothe the effects of the recurring nightmare of slavery and the continuing challenges of racism in the diaspora.

Johnson's fourth and last Island album, 1984's *Makin' History*, knits together a variety of important themes that in some ways summarize the political thought of Linton Kwesi Johnson. Two poems "Reggae fi Radni" and "Reggae fi Dada" are set in the English-speaking Caribbean. "Reggae fi Radni" eulogized Walter Rodney, a historian, scholar, and left revolutionary who was assassinated in his homeland of Guyana in 1980. Geographically, Guyana is a South American republic but culturally and politically Guyana is an integral member of the family of islands constituting the English-speaking Caribbean. "Reggae fi Dada," another poetic eulogy, relates Johnson's feelings about his father as a man who lived and died in Jamaica. The poem is skillful in the way it takes the very personal tragedy of the death of Johnson's father and places it in the context of Jamaica's poverty and social injustice without being dogmatic or sloganeering. "Reggae fi Dada" is also a good illustration of the umbilical-cord family connections between the English-speaking Caribbean and its diaspora.

The *Makin' History* tracks "Di Eagle and di Bear," "Wat About di Working Class," and the title track highlight Johnson's Marxist politics; and "New Craas Masahkah" and "Di Great Insohreckshan" fulfill the thematic requirements of Caribbean diasporic reggae by discussing tribulations and resistance of Blacks in Britain.

The music supporting Linton Kwesi Johnson's spoken-word poetry also seasoned reggae in a way that set it apart from the Jamaican sound. Barbados-born South London–bred Dennis "Blackbeard" Bovell and his Dub Band, in the recording studio and in concert, created fearless British reggae rhythms that propelled Johnson's militant poetry. Johnson's deep monotone spoken-word voice resonated like a reggae bass as it synchronized with Bovell's actual bass guitar lines. Bovell is a talented bassist who was leader of Matumbi, a U.K. roots reggae band that preceded Aswad and Steel Pulse and was therefore a pioneer band in terms of U.K. reggae history. Matumbi's theatrical stage presence was an important influence on Steel Pulse. Bovell was not only a gifted and creative bassist but he was also an outstanding producer. He produced Steel Pulse's first single "Nyah Luv" and was producer of *Cut*, the debut album of all-female punk band The Slits.

On Johnson's first two Island albums, *Forces of Victory* and *Bass Culture*, Bovell's bass is melodic, fat, and spacious. The Dub Band's bare-bones drum and bass, an approach that does not crowd the spoken-word performance, can be heard on *Bass Culture* tracks such as the title track, "Reggae Sounds," and "Street 66." "Fite Dem Back" presents reggae dipped in ska tones with horns feeding sympathetic harmony to Johnson's split-personality vocal that mutates from cockney to Jamaican patois.

A number of dub poems on *Makin' History* find more creative avenues to assist Johnson in sketching poetic portraits of rebellion. The title poem and "Di Great Insohreckshan" both express themselves with rapid reggae bass notes, energetic trap drumming, horns that seem to wail at will, and keyboards that bubble over with excitement. The music of "Reggae fi Radni" creates a sense of melancholy with a trap drum shuffle rhythm underscoring a light Latin keyboard melody that makes room for extraordinary Spanish guitar work by the gifted John Kpiaye.

196 — Klive Walker

Aswad, Steel Pulse, and Dennis Bovell's Dub Band were not necessarily more creative or more musically adventurous than producers and musicians in Jamaica. Jamaican producers such as "Coxsone" Dodd, Lee Perry, and King Tubby and musicians such as Don Drummond, drummer Sly Dunbar, and bass guitarists Leroy Sibbles and Robbie Shakespeare all advanced Jamaican reggae in ways that set the tone for the music's creative evolution. Aswad, Steel Pulse, Dennis Bovell, and other U.K. reggae artists introduced an innovative diasporic sensibility to reggae.

The dread rhythms of Aswad, the Steel Pulse sound, and Linton Kwesi Johnson's dubbed-out poetry recordings captured the attention of a certain type of audience that were not dogmatic about how reggae should sound—an international audience including fans in Jamaica that did not measure diasporic reggae purely on the basis of how it compared with Jamaican reggae. During the immediate post–Bob Marley era of the early '80s, the triple threat of British reggae gained significant popularity in reggae markets around the world initially secured by Burning Spear, Peter Tosh, Third World, and particularly Bob Marley. Steel Pulse, Aswad, and Linton Kwesi Johnson joined Jamaican reggae acts such as Dennis Brown, Black Uhuru (with Sly and Robbie), and Judy Mowatt as important elements of reggae's second wave. Aswad and Steel Pulse both played various reggae festivals in Jamaica on several occasions, and both bands at different times in their career recorded in Jamaica. Throughout the '80s and '90s, Aswad and Steel Pulse appeared separately and sometimes together in festivals and multi-reggae act tours—incorporating Jamaican and U.K. reggae bands—in various cities in Europe, the United States, Canada, and elsewhere. In a post–Bob Marley era, the divide between the architects of diasporic U.K. reggae and the artists of Jamaican reggae became virtually nonexistent and the two merged together to form a kind of international roots reggae movement.

Diasporic reggae bands were not the only major players in the arena of British reggae. In terms of mainstream profile in the U.K. during the '80s and '90s, UB40 is without question the U.K. reggae band that has had the biggest success. UB40 was a permanent fixture in the top ten U.K. singles and album charts during the '80s with #1 hits such as "Red, Red Wine," "I've Got You Babe," and "Can't Help Falling In Love." Like Steel Pulse, UB40 originated in Birmingham, but the similarities end there. As a multiracial band singing lyrics with progressive politics, UB40 was associated with the 2-Tone ska movement at the time of their arrival on the scene, despite the fact that they played reggae rather than ska. The lyrics of UB40 songs have, at times, been pointed in their criticism of power: the early single "One in Ten" blasted Thatcher for Britain's unemployment rate and "Sing Our Own Song" is the band's anti-apartheid anthem.

The bulk of UB40's popular songs, however, have been cover versions of reggae classics such as "Breakfast in Bed," rhythm and blues standards such as Al Green's "Here I am Baby," pop evergreens such as Sonny and Cher's "I've Got You Babe," or original reggae material designed to appeal to a pop audience. In other words, UB40 is not really a diasporic reggae band since their themes do not attempt to discuss the specific social issues and concerns of communities in the English-speaking Caribbean diaspora as it exists in the U.K. Musically, UB40's earlier albums *One in Ten*, *Present Arms*, *Present Arms in Dub*, and *Geffery Morgan*—which surprisingly arrived after the band discovered their initial success with cover versions on 1983's *Labour of Love*—are creative enough to suggest that they could have been more of an innovative band in the vein of their diasporic reggae counterparts. The cover-version pop-reggae route chosen by the band was financially lucrative and gave them immense popularity as an admittedly talented band, but they cannot be assessed as producing U.K. reggae at its most creative and cutting edge.

Although Maxi Priest began recording in 1985 when Steel Pulse, Aswad, and UB40 were already mature in their careers, he must be included in an assessment of U.K. reggae's significant artists during the '80s. Priest's emergence on the London reggae scene came through his association with the Saxon sound system as a vocalist who sometimes sang live to a recorded backing rhythm in the city's dancehall parties. Priest has always favoured the reggae ballad for which his soulful melodic voice is well suited. His debut album, *You're Safe*, paid homage to his roots in U.K. reggae dancehall with a gritty exciting sound. The followup album, *Intentions*, released by Virgin in 1986, was produced by Aswad and featured the cutting-edge musicianship of Aswad members Gaye and Robinson.

You're Safe and *Intentions* are clearly Priest's most diasporic reggae releases, at least from a musical standpoint. His relationship to the lyrics of diasporic reggae on these two albums is not as obvious. The roots reggae love ballad performed by female reggae singers in the U.K. became known as lovers' rock, a reggae genre that established itself as a staple at U.K. sound-system dances from the late '70s. Priest was not the first male singer to indulge in lovers' rock, but he was probably the most successful. The idea, true or not, that lovers' rock was a unique creation of the Caribbean diaspora in the U.K., places Maxi Priest's first two albums squarely in diasporic reggae territory. Priest achieved his desired mainstream breakthrough in 1988 with the singles "Wild World" and "Some Guys Have All the Luck" from the self-titled *Maxi Priest* album produced by Sly and Robbie. Although the album was not an example of obviously diluted reggae crudely pitched at a pop audience, the album was slickly produced, smooth, lovers' rock reggae that avoided any kind of raw roots edge. The arrival of *Maxi Priest* signalled the shift of the singer's music toward a more commercial direction in a search for a crossover pop appeal, consistent access to pop charts, and mainstream success. Subsequent releases, including 1990's *Bonafide*, which contained Priest's next hit single "Close to You," attempt to strike a balance between crossover songs and lovers' rock reggae.

Aswad's relationship to mainstream success has been tortuous. The band's first national chart showing came with the 1984 single "Chasing the Breeze" from *Rebel Souls*, which was Aswad's second studio album upon returning to Island Records. The track is a social-commentary ballad about life after school, and proved Aswad could write a substantial pop song. The melodic flow of the song had a Beatles-style pop sensibility, but the tune's rhythm reflected a laid-back roots feel that remained characteristic of the Aswad sound.

In the spring of 1988, the "Don't Turn Around" single taken from the Island release *Distant Thunder* hit the #1 position on the U.K. chart. Although the track was a lovers' rock ballad rather than a song about the plight of Blacks in the U.K., the success the song brought to the band after twelve years in the business was long overdue. Six years later, "Shine," a fast-paced proto-dancehall reggae track laced with Aswad's trademark three-part harmony vocals, went as high as #5 on the U.K. singles chart.

Comparatively, Linton Kwesi Johnson saw himself as a literary poet and community activist with no ambitions to be a success in the

Maxi Priest (Max Elliott). Undated. Photograph by Sheila Rock.

world of popular music. He therefore felt no pressure to dilute or alter his work for commercial reasons. Despite this attitude towards mainstream success, Johnson began a parallel career as a producer of documentaries and as a commentator/analyst on British radio and television during his time as a reggae recording artist. His significant profile in the worlds of reggae and poetry continues.

The chart success of Steel Pulse's first album *Handsworth Revolution* featuring strictly diasporic reggae remained the only mainstream recognition of the band's work in the U.K. despite the quality of their subsequent Island albums *Tribute to the Martyrs* and 1980's *Caught You*. After the release of *Caught You*, Steel Pulse terminated its association with Island and eventually relocated to the U.S. to seek their fortunes in that notoriously tough market for reggae.

The relationship between reggae and the popular music culture in the United States has been tentative, like an illicit love affair that is sometimes passionate, often contentious, and mainly kept in the backroom away from the spotlight of constant scrutiny. Bob Marley has become the icon of reggae in America, where his stature is usually measured by posthumous record sales. America's recognition of Marley's legacy through the Grammy Lifetime Achievement Award and induction into the Rock and Roll Hall of Fame is flattering but has not been illuminated by the details of his influence on rock, punk, pop, world beat, rhythm and blues, and jazz. In fact, there has been very little discussion about the impact of reggae in America—one exception is Patty Smith Group band member Lenny Kaye's essay "White Reggae" in the anthology *Reggae International*.

If Jamaican music's first intrusion on American soil was the island's ska entourage at the World's Fair in New York in 1964, then the music's first major triumph in America was Millie Small's huge hit "My Boy Lollipop," which settled at #2 on the U.S. pop charts in the same year. Five years later, Desmond Dekker's Jamaican reggae hit "Israelites" used its infiltration of American radio as a springboard to leap into the top ten of the U.S. pop charts in the spring of 1969 and signified reggae's initial mainstream connection in America. That year, prominent American pop singer Paul Simon was sufficiently impressed by Jimmy Cliff's anti-war reggae song "Vietnam," that he began to investigate the island's music. The result of Simon's research was America's reintroduction to ska through his successful 1972 single and album track "Mother and Child Reunion" recorded in Jamaica, utilizing mainly Jamaican musicians.

Five years earlier in 1967, African-American pop star Johnny Nash, in an effort to revitalize his career, relocated to Jamaica where he recorded the album *Hold Me Tight*. Byron Lee and the Dragonnaires supplied the music for the album's title track and Nash's remake of Sam Cooke's "Cupid." "Hold Me Tight" peaked at #3 on the U.S. chart in 1968. Nash also initiated a business relationship with Bob Marley in 1967 that did not bear fruit until the release of Nash's *I Can See Clearly Now* in 1972. The album, a clear success in America, included Marley's "Comma Comma," "Guava Jelly," and "Stir It Up," a tune that joined the title track as a hit single. Two American pop singers Johnny Nash and Paul Simon, who both recorded in Jamaica, were the initial American conduits of reggae into mainstream America.

When the Wailers' *Catch A Fire* quietly debuted in America in January 1973, it attracted critical praise from important publications including *Rolling Stone* and *Time* magazines, but it received cool public response and modest album sales. Jamaican reggae, with its raw bass lines and percussive trap drumming by Jamaican musicians who represented the music's true rebellious spirit, had finally commanded some measure of critical attention in America. If the American public were not yet attuned to reggae, certain superstar artists were drawn to the power of the exotic "inside-out" beat and the sexy romantic lyrics of Marley's love songs. In 1974, Bob Marley's "Guava Jelly" appeared on Barbra Streisand's *Butterfly* album. A movie star, recording artist, and exceptionally gifted vocalist, Streisand, like Nash, seemed mainly interested in decorating her songs with a fresh "tropical" beat.

A number of U.S. rock singers began to pay attention to the social-commentary themes that were an integral aspect of roots reggae. They began to see reggae as a new vehicle for expressing their own protest. Bob Dylan—the quintessential voice of folk-rock protest during the '60s and '70s—waded into the "uncharted" river of reggae with his 1977 recording "Don't Think Twice." Two years earlier, New York rock vocalist Martha Velez travelled to Jamaica to collaborate with Bob Marley on an album that was eventually titled *Escape from Babylon*. Marley songs such as "Get Up, Stand Up" and "Bend Down Low" joined the Velez compositions "Wild Bird" and "Living Outside the Law" in creating a firm foundation for the project. Lee Perry and Marley acted as producers for the album, while the insistent reggae of the Wailers band informed the rhythm track of each recording.

When *Escape from Babylon* was released in 1976, the alternative rock scene in America was in the process of unleashing their brand of punk as a challenge to the prevailing "corporate" and "glam" rock and the impending volcanic eruption of discomania. American punk and new-wave bands found a home in New York clubs such as CBGB's and Max's Kansas City, a venue where Bob Marley and the Wailers appeared as opening act for Bruce Springsteen in 1973. American ears initially received the rebellious Jamaican-accented delivery of reggae's lyrics underscored by rugged, yet unusual rhythms as an alternative sound. The emerging American punk movement, like their U.K. counterparts, viewed reggae as a kindred spirit and ally. The Patti Smith Group, one of the leading American punk bands, included a reggae track "Ain't It Strange" on their 1976 *Radio Ethiopia* album. The album's title announced the band's attraction to reggae and Rasta. A notable American new-wave intersection with reggae surfaced in 1980 when Blondie featuring Debbie Harry ruled the American pop charts with their cover of John Holt's "Tide is High."

Rock and pop acts were not the only American musicians incorporating reggae into their music. The influence of Jamaican music on rhythm and blues, soul, and blues dates back to the early '70s. The Staple Singers' 1972 recording "I'll Take You There" was energized by a funky interpretation of a reggae rhythm borrowed from the 1969 Jamaican instrumental "The Liquidator." The bumpety-bump reggaefied funk of "I'll Take You There" complemented the endearing raspy soul of Staple Singers' lead vocalist Mavis Staples. Two years later, Taj Mahal, a significant blues singer and guitarist, released interesting versions of *Catch A Fire*'s "Slave Driver" and *Harder They Come*'s "Johnny Too Bad" for an album titled *Mo' Roots*. The most popular reggae-inspired track by an African-American in 1974, however, was Stevie Wonder's rumpled offbeat funk "Boogie on Reggae Woman" from *Fulfillingness' First Finale*. Wonder's initial attempt at releasing a record with a more accurate interpretation of a reggae beat emerged six years later in the form of a well-received tribute to Bob Marley called "Master Blaster (Jammin')." The song quotes *Exodus*' track "Jammin'," name-checks Marley and the band Third World, speaks of unity in Jah, and mentions the independence struggle that had just been victorious in Zimbabwe. "Master Blaster" breathes the rhythmic framework and the lyrical essence of roots reggae. Wonder's interest in reggae and its Jamaican creators led to collaborations on the recordings of Third World and Steel Pulse, and an appearance at the 1981 Reggae Sunsplash festival in Montego Bay, Jamaica where he shared the concert stage with Third World and Rita Marley.

When jazz great Miles Davis discovered Bob Marley's Natty Dread album, he was intrigued by the rhythmic possibilities that Marley's reggae presented. Davis subsequently recorded several reggae-influenced tunes during the '80s. "Don't Lose Your Mind" on his 1986 album *Tutu*, for example, deploys a menacing reggae bass to construct a moody atmospheric sound-canvas on which Davis' trumpet and Michael Urbaniak's wired violin paint electrifying jazz portraits.

Reggae's influence on American music continues in the new millennium. Folk-rock singer Ben Harper successfully channels the Wailer's one-drop reggae rhythm on 2003's "With My Own Two Hands," while rhythm and blues vocalist Lauryn Hill's cover of Bob Marley's "Turn the Lights Down Low" appeared on the soundtrack of the popular film *Best Man* at the turn of the century. Reggae in America was not limited to the fusion experiments of pop, rock, punk, soul, blues, or jazz artists. Eventually, American ska and reggae bands began to flex their muscles in the alternative underground scene. American reggae bands Inner Circle and Big Mountain have experienced mainstream success, but, like the reggae that was successful in the U.K., the lyrics and music of these recordings are infused with a pop sensibility and have no connection with diasporic reggae.

The Florida-based Inner Circle band—anchored by Jamaican brothers Ian and Roger Lewis—enjoyed a top ten hit with "Bad Boys" in 1993, a song that achieved popularity when it was selected as the theme song for Fox television's reality show *Cops*, which premiered in 1989. Inner Circle had previously recorded the song for *One Way*, an obscure 1987 album released on American independent reggae label RAS Records. As the television show began attracting increased viewership, the song evolved into an American pop-culture reference. "Bad Boys" was eventually reissued as a single in 1991 and charted in several European countries before it was re-released in the United States in 1993. The longevity of the recording seems endless as evidenced in the song's appearance in the Will Smith action film *Bad Boys* in 1995 and in the 2003 sequel *Bad Boys 2*.

Since its birth in Jamaica in 1968, Inner Circle developed as a pop-funk–rhythm and blues cover group. That '60s configuration of Inner Circle included keyboard player Michael "Ibo" Cooper, guitarist Stephen "Cat" Coore, and vocalist William "Bunny Rugs" Clarke, a trio that became the backbone of the internationally prominent band Third World. Formed in 1973, Third World took the approach of combining roots reggae with rock, funk, and rhythm and blues to new creative heights within the framework of their own original material. The band began an association with Island Records in 1976. Their second release, the exceptional album *96° in the Shade*, was issued in 1997 to critical acclaim. Third World is possibly the most successful Jamaican roots reggae band, if success is measured in terms of chart position in America. Over a period of fourteen years, from their third Island album *Journey to Addis* in 1978 to the *Committed* album issued by Mercury in 1992, Third World experienced a variety of U.S. top-twenty rhythm and blues hits in both the album and singles charts. The most significant chart accomplishments include the single "Now That We Found Love" from *Journey to Addis*, which itself eased into the top twenty-five U.S. rhythm and blues album charts in 1979, and the 1982 *You've Got the Power* album and its single, the Stevie Wonder composition "Try Jah Love."

Third World has endured the criticism that classifies them as an uptown or upper-class band playing a "sophisticated" crossover brand of reggae that lacked solid roots reggae credentials. Their remarkable musicianship, however, is beyond reproach as Cooper, Coore, and Clarke represent three of roots reggae's most gifted musicians. Coore and Cooper started their careers with Inner Circle, but departed to craft a more original sound.

Inner Circle eventually attempted original material that often reflected a fusion of roots reggae with funk and rhythm and blues that did not always work. Before "Bad Boys," the high point of Inner Circle's career was their association with popular Jamaican singer Jacob Miller prior to the band's relocation to America. A series of attempts to be the next Jamaican roots reggae band to break internationally were made through Trojan and U.S. label Capitol Records, but proved premature. In 1979, however, with an assured roots reggae sound and with Miller—their charismatic and talented lead singer as the band's main attraction—Inner Circle signed with Island Records. They were generally considered to be poised as the next big thing in reggae on the international scene, but Miller died in a car crash in 1980 and the tragedy destroyed their ambitions and tore the band apart. Since their 1986 re-formation in Florida, Inner Circle as a Jamaican-American band—with the Lewis brothers still at its centre—has not really explored any kind of diasporic reggae approach.

California band Big Mountain's moment of mainstream prominence began when they were asked to record a reggae version of Peter Frampton's "Baby, I Love Your Way" for the Ben Stiller film *Reality Bites*. The movie's soundtrack album was released in February 1994, and the single "Baby, I Love Your Way" climbed into the top ten of the U.S. charts. Big Mountain works a smooth lovers' rock groove that faithfully encourages love ballads and social-commentary songs. The band's central figure and lead vocalist Jimmy "Quino" McWhinney, an American of Irish and Mexican heritage, was inspired to pursue a career as a reggae musician after watching a *60 Minutes* segment on Bob Marley, reggae, and Rasta in 1980 when he was fourteen years old. Quino's approach to singing, however, is clearly influenced by the vocal style of Steel Pulse lead singer David Hinds.

The year after Quino watched that *60 Minutes* episode, Steel Pulse began its first tour of the United States, performed at Reggae Sunsplash in Jamaica for the first time, and secured a new recording contract with major U.S. label Elektra. In 1982, Elektra released *True Democracy*, possibly Steel Pulse's best album of that period. The album represented a critical breakthrough for Steel Pulse, and established the band as an important player on the American music scene. In some ways, *True Democracy* was a departure from their work on *Handsworth Revolution* and *Tribute to Martyrs*. The rock guitar licks were gone and their roots reggae became more influenced by rhythm and blues. The band's lyrics were vintage Steel Pulse with the diasporic spice of "Blues Dance Raid," the Marcus Garvey tribute "Worth His Weight in Gold," the social commentary of "A Who Responsible," and the ode to Rasta theology "Chant a Psalm." Hinds' distinctive voice is smooth and militant at the same time, supported by crisp vocal harmonies of Selwyn Brown and Phonso Martin that floated above Stepper McQueen's skanking bass lines and Grizzly Nesbitt's crashing cymbals and busy hi-hat work.

Steel Pulse's second Elektra album, 1983's *Earth Crisis*, maintained their profile in America. At this point in their career, their popularity in the U.K. was negligible, and the bandmates, for all intents and purposes, were now residents of the United States. In 1984, the inaugural year of the reggae category at the American Grammy Awards, *Earth Crisis* was nominated in that category. African-American director Spike Lee included the specially commissioned Steel Pulse song "Can't Stand It" in his 1989 film *Do the Right Thing*. By the early '90s, Steel Pulse was appearing on popular television talk shows including the *Tonight Show with Jay Leno* and the *Arsenio Hall Show*. In January 1993, the band's significance in the American music landscape was confirmed by their invitation to perform at Bill Clinton's presidential inauguration celebrations. Although Steel Pulse never really achieved national chart success in America, they were very popular in select markets including New York, Miami, and the U.S. West Coast where *Earth Crisis* tracks "Steppin' Out" and "Roller Skates" made a huge impact. It is not surprising that Steel Pulse would have been an influence on Quino of Big Mountain. Although Quino's progressive Chicano perspective is sometimes reflected in his lyrics, Big Mountain does not really represent a diasporic reggae approach.

Unlike Canada or the U.K., diasporic reggae in America was not found in the music of American roots reggae bands. In America, diasporic reggae percolated in the work of certain Jamaican dancehall deejays. Two good examples of American diasporic reggae artists with significant profiles during the '80s and early '90s include New York–based deejays Sister Carol and Shinehead.

Carol East left her humble community of Denham Town in Jamaica's West Kingston for New York City in the late '70s. She graduated from college as a teacher, but went to work with sound systems in Brooklyn as a dancehall spoken-word deejay known as Sister Carol. Carol did her teaching through her rhymes and chants as a recording artist and performer. As a Rasta woman, her words of conscience imparted her views concerning women's independence, praise for Jah, and the consistent Rasta theme of Black liberation.

Sister Carol represents the female deejay with a substantial profile who, in the late '80s, stood at the middle of the crossroads where the once highly travelled road of Rasta roots reggae crossed paths with the new easy-access highway of dancehall with its mainly synthesized "computer" beats and racy lyrics. Sister Carol stood at the middle of the crossroads watching her progressive Rasta-conscious sisters Judy, Rita, and Marcia walk quietly away from the spotlight. In the meantime, a different set of rambunctious independent sister deejays trading in words of sex and "slackness" runs toward her from the opposite direction—looking brazen, strong-willed, and, in their own way, rebelling against reggae's male-dominated perspective—ready to capture and dominate the spotlight.

Sister Carol consciously placed herself in the roots tradition associating with deejay icon Brigadier Jerry, who was a kind of mentor for her during her formative phase as an artist. Judy Mowatt—an important influence as a female Rasta reggae artist—recorded a cover of Bob Marley's "Screwface" that featured Sister

Carol's deejaying skills. Carol marked her initial solo success in 1984 with the *Black Cinderella* album, which included solid work like the title cut and "International Style," an important diasporic reggae track.

Sister Carol's photogenic persona and charismatic stage presence attracted American film director Jonathan Demme—a fan of reggae and Haitian music—when he saw her perform at S.O.B.'s in Manhattan. Demme included Sister Carol in two of his offbeat comedic dramas, *Something Wild* with Melanie Griffith, Ray Liotta, and Jeff Daniels in 1986 and *Married to the Mob* with Michelle Pfeiffer and Alec Baldwin in 1988. Her role as a restaurant owner in *Something Wild* was a cameo-type appearance without any dialogue. In the *Married to the Mob* role, in which she played a hairdresser styling the Pfeiffer character's hair, Sister Carol's character spoke. Carol's contribution to the *Something Wild* soundtrack—also containing reggae by UB40 and Jimmy Cliff—is a reggae interpretation of "Wild Thing" that skillfully combines hip-hop-style rap and Jamaican deejay talk.

In terms of Sister Carol's persona as a Jamaican-American diasporic reggae artist, "International Style" is her most important recording. On that track, she confidently deejays that she must use different "styles" or ways of expressing her lyrics. The song's implicit unspoken conceit is that Carol, as a New Yorker of Caribbean heritage, must express her lyrics in a way that can be clearly understood by her fellow brothers and sisters of the Caribbean diaspora. Her diaspora is not limited to the English-speaking Caribbean, so she not only deejays a verse in English with a Trinidad accent, she also deejays verses in Spanish and French to ensure that she includes New Yorkers of Puerto Rican and Haitian heritage. "International Style," although pitched as a kind of Caribbean diasporic anthem, does not ignore Sister Carol's Afrocentric Rasta sentiments as she demonstrates with a verse in Swahili. She begins the song with a verse in American rap, which in a way can be seen as "International Style" acknowledging its New York context. The separate verses are linked by her natural Jamaican-accented deejay voice explaining that she cannot deejay in one style, implicitly suggesting that her intention is to entertain more than just a Jamaican audience.

Back in the early '80s, Sister Carol sometimes shared the microphone on Brooklyn's Downbeat sound system with Shinehead, another significant New York deejay. Shinehead's music really defined American diasporic reggae during the late '80s and early '90s. His initial album for Elektra, 1988's *Unity*, featuring several tracks from his independent debut, *Rough and Rugged*, fused hip-hop and roots reggae dancehall so creatively that it produced a new diasporic innovation called raggamuffin rap. In Shinehead's music, dancehall reggae and hip-hop were able to engage in conversation at the rhythmic level, and in the way African-American rap and Jamaican patois deejaying collided and intersected.

Three of the tracks on *Unity*—the title tune, "Chain Gang–Rap," and "The Truth" are built around hip-hop beats produced by the late Jam Master Jay of Run-DMC. "Unity" savours an erratic flow alternating quasi–New York–accented rap and Jamaican patois-powered deejay style. "Chain Gang–Rap" is basically a straight rap, flavoured with one Jamaican phrase. On "The Truth," the approach is reversed as Shinehead negotiates crashing waves of dancehall-seasoned hip-hop beats using a verbose deejay flow in thick Jamaican language. The Jam Master Jay–produced recordings are interesting and in the case of *Unity*, a groundbreaking example of dancehall/rap fusion.

Claude Evans, the Jamaican New Yorker whose African Love label issued Shinehead's debut album, produced the recordings lifted from *Rough and Rugged*. These tracks offer a different level of intensity and excitement. "Hello Y'All," for example, is anchored by a buoyant '70s-style roots reggae rhythm. Acting like the initial drum roll of an early reggae recording, Shinehead's introductory chatter riffs in Jamaican the stylish part-singing, part-deejay talk known as singjay before heading into a well-paced American-accented rap he employs to vividly describe the history of reggae and dancehall.

"Know How Fe Chat," one of the album's gems, strikes a rebellious pose dressed in a rough clatter of hip-hop drum patterns stitched together by spurts of nattering, programmed, dancehall organ sounds. Shinehead deejays with a steady constant flow that expresses a *rude-bwoy* attitude and is executed like an unscripted freestyle that hugs the rhythm the way a man embraces a woman who is his long lost lover. "Know How Fe Chat"'s beats seem intent on urging Shinehead's creative deejaying to continue to gush until the rhythm itself echoes its final satisfying gasp.

Shinehead is a skilled impressionist who can impersonate the style of a variety of well-known Jamaican deejays. He sometimes uses that skill to sample his favourites into a particular tune, and his own unique approach sometimes gets lost in the mix. His craft as a rap artist is commendable but is most effective when it is fused with elements of Jamaican deejaying.

The themes of Shinehead's lyrics on *Unity* pinpoint issues including disunity among rap artists, drug abuse, and criticism of war and strife across the globe. These social-commentary themes directly connect Shinehead with the tradition of Marley, Tosh, and his roots reggae deejay predecessors U-Roy, Big Youth, and Brigadier Jerry.

Shinehead was born in Kent, England to Jamaican parents who named him Edmund Carl Aitken. The Aitkens moved back to Jamaica in the mid-'60s when Shinehead was still a toddler, which means that he acquired his grade school and some secondary education on the island. In 1976, he moved yet again to New York City. The young Aitken arrived from Jamaica with a love of roots reggae that served as a solid base for an eclectic taste that included pop music, rhythm and blues, country and western, and gospel. He plugged into the Bronx underground music scene with his ears primed to indulge new sounds. In 1976, hip-hop was an embryo, nourished by the womb of the Bronx. As a teenager, Shinehead would go to neighbourhood parks, soak in the seminal MC competitions, and observe the growth of rap as a new art form. Five years later, Shinehead, as a college student studying computer science, was deejaying on Downbeat International sound system, crafting a fresh spoken word permutation that phased together the reggae of his roots with the hip-hop from the city where he lived.

In 1983, Shinehead joined forces with Claude Evans' sound system African Love. The following year, his first single, a version of Michael Jackson's "Billie Jean," hit the streets. The record did not feature any deejaying, just the sweet strains of Shinehead's singing voice rippled with a dead-on tongue-in-cheek impersonation of the Michael Jackson hiccup. A cover version of arguably the most popular Jackson song could have been disastrous, but Shinehead's whistling of *The Good, the Bad, and the Ugly* movie theme as the tune's intro, his semi-comic interpretation of the lyrics, and his sincere vocal tone underlined by one of the most nastily insidious roots reggae rhythms imaginable make this tune a triumph. Shinehead's "Billie Jean" was an overwhelming *boom-*

shot that reverberated sound-system dancehalls in London, New York, Toronto, and Kingston. The tune was included on 1986's *Rough and Rugged*, which introduced "Who the Cap Fits," "Know How Fe Chat," and "Hello Y'All" for the first time.

On the basis of his growing reputation as an outstanding reggae/hip-hop artist, Shinehead was approached to work on the crucial Sly and Robbie Island Records project *Rhythm Killers* released in 1987. The album reworked funk classics like Ohio Players' "Fire" and the Pointer Sisters' "Yes We Can Can," and a funked-up version of Super Cat's then-contemporary dancehall favourite "Boops." The reggae-tinged funk of "Boops" was tailor-made for Shinehead's mutant vocals. Anyone not familiar with his spoken-word skills would have thought that there were two vocalists on the track—a rapper and a reggae deejay.

After *Unity*, Shinehead's next two Elektra albums were an attempt to seek acceptance in the pop marketplace, an approach that resulted in compromising his instincts for a more cutting-edge style. Despite these considerations, *The Real Rock*, his second album for Elektra, included "Strive," a big hit in reggae circles worldwide. "Strive" is a quality roots track that mainly showcases Shinehead's attractive singing.

A cover of a Sting reggae song retitled "Jamaican in New York" became the focus of the 1992 release *Sidewalk University* when that single entered America's Billboard charts. "Jamaican in New York" retains the rhythm and melodic arc of Sting's "Englishman in New York," but revises the lyrics to discuss in very diasporic tones the journey of a variety of Jamaicans living in New York City. Shinehead's version of the song references honest ambitious New York Jamaicans as well as the *rude-bwoy* and *bad-man* elements. He mostly sings on this track, although it is emphatically interspersed with Jamaican deejay talk.

Troddin', Shinehead's final album for Elektra, in some ways signified a return to rugged dancehall and hip-hop beats and an edgier spoken-word posture. The title track, "Boom Bangin'," "Good Girls-Bad Boys" (which reprises the Billie Jean rhythm), "Keep On," and the exceptional "Me and Them" (with its shot-gun marriage of a bumpin' hip-hop backbeat and a dangerous hardcore '90s dancehall rhythm) are some of the toughest tunes from Shinehead since *Unity*.

Shinehead is a seminal figure of reggae deejay/rap fusion. The foundation of his music is reggae, but it is shaped by his interaction with African-American culture. In this way, his work is comparable to U.K.'s Steel Pulse and Canada's Truths and Rights because it has drawn from a cultural environment beyond Jamaica's borders and contributed fresh creative elements to reggae as an art form.

Visions

Dennis Brown, the Most Influential Voice in Reggae

The '70s roots reggae era in Jamaica opened the gates to an array of vocal tones and singing styles, possibly more varied than any other time in the music's existence. For example, Culture and the Mighty Diamonds, two important harmony trios from that time, possessed completely different vocal approaches. The voice of Culture's lead singer Joseph Hill resonates a rugged grainy tone that owes more to the influence of indigenous African-Jamaican music forms than it does to American rhythm and blues singing. The lead voices of the Diamonds use a rhythm and blues template that inspires Tabby's smooth timbre and Judge's thin falsetto. Dennis Brown's singing, however, owes a debt to American soul, but his voice also represents the unique capabilities of a fluid reggae vocalist.

Brown's career began as a pre-teen in the late '60s during reggae's seminal phase. When he started recording at "Coxsone" Dodd's Studio One, he served an informal apprenticeship with Ken Boothe, Alton Ellis, Delroy Wilson, and Leroy Sibbles, some of the best rocksteady vocalists of that time. These singers shaped their singing style from '60s American rhythm and blues singing. Although they were influenced by the vocal style of African-American singers they admired, there was a definite Jamaican quality to their phrasing. As a young boy observing and learning from these skilled Studio One vocalists, Brown's natural gifts as a singer developed in the direction of innovation.

At the earliest stage of his career, Brown's adolescent voice possessed a maturity and inventiveness that posed a serious challenge to established singers much older than him. His warm silky vocal tone created instant fans of anyone who had the vaguest idea of great soul singing, of great reggae singing. His soothing voice travelled smoothly over mean, clean, or in-between reggae grooves. The magnetic personality and charismatic charm of his singing inspired fans who never met Brown to refer to him as simply Dennis—to speak of him not as a reggae superstar but as if he were a close personal friend. Brown's rich voice sounded like he gargled with cool molten gold. When roots reggae arrived at a certain level of maturity by the mid-'70s, his fully realized singing style arrived with it. If reggae singing is like the seed at the centre of a Julie mango, then the beautiful tone of Dennis Brown's singing voice is like the mango's sweet succulent flesh.

Brown's unique voice immediately placed him at the forefront of the early reggae scene. "No Man Is an Island," his first popular recording, was released in 1969 by "Coxsone" Dodd when Brown was only a twelve-year-old boy. A decade later, Brown tasted international success with a British top-ten hit "Money In My Pocket," an appearance at the Montreaux Jazz Festival, and a subsequent three-album deal with U.S. label A&M Records.

Dennis Brown's body of work is difficult to categorize. He was like an actor who evaded typecasting by playing a variety of roles. He sang romantic ballads such as "Love Has Found Its Way," incisive social commentary in "Handwriting on the Wall," adopted a militant persona for "Revolution," and praised Jah Rastafari on "Ababa Janhoi." The diversity of Brown's work was overshadowed only by his voice's ability to shape any lyric with a sincere touch.

Using an international measure, Dennis Brown, in terms of vocal texture, range, and the ability to vocally adjust to various types of songs, shares the stylistic intentions of someone like Luther Vandross. Initially, however, it was the stellar vocal of Delroy Wilson that had a profound influence on Brown. Wilson and Brown possessed different tones, but Brown adopted Wilson's idiosyncratic improvisation flourishes. He put a fresh spin on these flourishes and neatly fit them into his own distinctive flow. New York–based Jamaican journalist Stan E. Smith writes about Brown's admiration for Wilson's abilities as a singer: "… I asked (Dennis Brown) to name the single greatest influence on his style of singing. (Dennis answered) 'Delroy Wilson.' (He continued to) speak of (how) as a youngster he had a fascination with Wilson's phrasing and slurring … how he practiced to sound like (Wilson)."[1] The connection between Wilson and Brown goes beyond their shared affinity for vocal phrasing. Both singers began their musical careers as pre-adolescents, both began recording with "Coxsone" Dodd, and they both shared the tragedy of dying before their fiftieth birthday.

As a tenacious and influential Jamaican soul singer, Delroy Wilson was a unique vocalist of the rocksteady period. His full-bodied voice was a master at interpreting the lyrics of romantic

Leroy Sibbles with Terry Wilkins and Fergus Hambleton at Ontario Place Forum.
Photograph by Isobel Harry.

love ballads. Wilson shared with Stevie Wonder the ability to season a lyric with gospel accents, to ease in a slurred line—sometimes subtle, sometimes vocally acrobatic. He also shared with Wonder a recording career that started as a pre-teen. Wilson, however, was an influential original in his own right. As a boy, he recorded the ska tunes "Joe Liges," "Spit in the Sky," and "I Shall Not Remove." Before he was twenty, his maturing bluesy voice testified on classic rocksteady diamonds "Dancing Mood," "Conquer Me," "Once Upon a Time," and "I'm Not a King." In 1971, at a youthful twenty-three years of age, Wilson hit big in Jamaica and Caribbean diaspora communities in the U.S., Canada, and the U.K. with "Better Must Come." His expressive singing on that recording dramatizes biographical lyrics about his arduous uphill journey in the music business, his efforts to make it as a singer, and his optimism that "better must come" one day.

"I'm Still Waiting," one of Wilson's best vocal performances on a recording, arrived five years later. The Wailers originally recorded the song, a Bob Marley composition, in 1965 as a smouldering Impressions-like ballad. The lush harmonies of Bunny, Peter, and Beverly Kelso surrounded the twenty-year-old Marley's thin vocal.

Wilson uses his voice to re-sculpt the song with a raw anguished edge. His gritty slur of lyrics merges with bittersweet harmonies as he pleads with the song's female character—who is testing his patience by making him wait for her—to have mercy on him. Wilson's "I'm Still Waiting" is a far more urgent and desperate read of the lyrics. Every moan, every vocal inflection reflects an anguished impatience, reflects a plea to bring the waiting to an end. Delroy Wilson's "I'm Still Waiting" was very popular in England in 1976 and became a staple on the U.K. sound-system circuit.

Wilson died in 1995 at forty-seven, leaving the artistic aspects of the music with the important legacy of his rich tone, inventive phrasing, and unique improvisation. Unfortunately, he did not achieve the kind of international recognition that his contemporaries accomplished. Wilson was a singer's vocalist, respected and admired by other top-quality artists. His contemporary Ken Boothe—himself an exceptional talent with a deep soul voice, whose outstanding reggae single "Everything I Own" topped the U.K. pop chart in 1974—enthusiastically offers the following observation about Wilson and the Jamaican music scene of the early '60s: "When I see him (Delroy Wilson) on the street, I see a lot of people gather around him. He was Jamaica's first baby star. He inspire Bob Marley; he inspire me; he inspire a lot of us …"[2] Wilson also inspired Dennis Brown.

Following the popularity of Dennis Brown's outstanding debut with the Curtis Mayfield–penned "No Man Is an Island," he recorded an album with the same name in 1970. At the tender age of twelve, Brown's singing on this album is stunning in the way it presented a maturity and confidence in his phrasing and assured voice control. "Coxsone" Dodd mirrored that approach the next year by releasing the reggae classic "If I Follow My Heart" as a single and album.

After recording two albums for Dodd, Brown moved on. His initial post-Coxsone hit, 1972's "Baby Don't Do It," launched his first phase of freelancing with various producers in the same way that a freelance journalist contributes articles to a variety of newspapers and magazines. In the early '70s, Brown recorded with Randy's Studio, Herman Chin-Loy, and Alvin "GG" Ranglin, among other producers—a common practice among singers in Jamaica attempting to maximize payment for their work, rather than remain in a long-term arrangement with one producer that may be less lucrative. Brown, however, chiselled a fine art out of freelance recording that rivalled his skills as a vocalist. During the '80s and '90s, the simultaneous release of Dennis Brown recordings by various producers eventually hurt his career by saturating the marketplace and leaving him overexposed.

A handful of producers were instrumental in advancing his career in an artistic sense. "Coxsone" Dodd provided the first nurturing artistic environment for Brown, as did his collaboration with Derrick Harriott. Harriott started in the music business as a singer in the vocal group the Jiving Juniors during the pre-ska period of the late '50s. As a solo artist, he loved interpreting romantic rhythm and blues ballads, although he also recorded popular original material. As a producer, his work includes Keith & Tex's "Stop That Train," which formed the basis of another significant Harriott recording: Scotty's deejay version "Draw Your Brakes" featured on the *Harder They Come* soundtrack. Harriott also produced notable efforts by the Chosen Few, the rustic Kingstonians, and the uptown sound of Rudy Mills. In terms of consistent quality recordings, Dennis Brown was probably the most important artist on Harriott's roster at that time.

The songs Harriott produced for Brown, such as "What About the Half" and "Concentration," both Brown compositions, remain an essential part of Brown's vast volume of recorded work. On "Concentration," Brown advises certain ghetto youth to focus on obtaining a weekly paying job rather than panhandling. The Now Generation band, led by keyboardist Geoffrey Chung, took care of those recording sessions anchored by the rhythm section of Val Douglas and Mikey "Boo" Richards, guitarist Mikey "Mao" Chung, and Robbie Lyn (also on keyboards). "Concentration" is underscored by Douglas' chunky bass riffs carefully embroidered with extra rhythm and blues–derived notes that surround Richards' cantankerous drumming as both indulge in empathetic dialogue with Brown's stern warnings. Brown issues his advice with singing that surfaces in between a steady flow of flute notes that exude an air of mystery.

Brown's Derrick Harriott productions also include some really creative cover versions. Dennis Brown never engaged in crass imitation, he always found a way to breathe new life into covers by reinventing the way a lyric was originally phrased, the way a lyric was originally dramatized. Glen Campbell's popular recording "Wichita

Lineman" and Herman's Hermits' bubble-gum pop hit "Silhouettes" were imaginatively converted into Dennis Brown reggae-soul songs. Harriott's intelligent production decisions gave Brown's extraordinary interpretive skills the required encouragement.

If Dennis' tenure with Coxsone was like elementary school and the time with Derrick Harriott like high school, then university was his association with Winston "Niney the Observer" Holness at the height of the roots reggae era during the mid to late '70s. Niney's hardcore production values provoked the Soul Syndicate band's sometimes busy, sometimes sparse roots dancehall beats to create the right atmosphere for Brown's ripe Black-consciousness lyrics, commentary about ghetto life, and, of course, relationship ballads. Niney, a key roots reggae producer, did for Dennis Brown what Lee Perry did for the Wailers: assist in moving Brown to that next level of creative expression. Niney's production signatures were his accentuation of drummer Carlton "Santa" Davis' flying cymbals technique, and especially highlighting the guitar work of Earl "Chinna" Smith as an indispensable aspect of the Observer sound. Bassist George "Fully" Fullwood, rhythm guitarist Tony Chin, and Bernard "Touter" Harvey on keyboard were the other members of Soul Syndicate, who were the authors of an eclectic selection of backing rhythms that worked hard to serve Brown's voice.

The fact that "Westbound Train" became a classic track must be credited equally to Brown's sincere vocal and Niney's creative production decisions. Led by repetitive guitar chords, punctuating horn honks, and a steady bouncing bass, Niney shapes a rhythm that sounds like a railway train heading west in a hurry. The release of the follow-up "Cassandra" was clearly designed to cash-in on the success of "Westbound Train." The new record was not a rip-off of "Train" but a crafty reworking that sped up the bass line and shifted the emphasis in the mix from the guitar to the pump of bubbling keyboards while maintaining the crucial saxophone bleats and solos in different pose.

Niney produced a number of Afrocentric and socially relevant Dennis Brown records including *So Long Rastafari*, *Africa*—both adapted from traditional Rastafari chants—*Tribulation*, *Tenement Yard*, and the inspired *Wolf and Leopards*, whose title track is driven by a sensual lumbering bass. Brown's voice is more than capable of surfing the languorous bass lines of that track as it launches into a lyric laced with Biblical metaphors that compare informers and

Dennis Brown.

gossipmongers to wolves and leopards trying to kill the sheep and the shepherds.

Dennis Brown's voice is so outstanding that his more than capable writing talent is usually discounted. His output, recorded in collaboration with producer Joe Gibbs and his engineer Errol "E.T." Thompson, displayed the work of a singer/songwriter at the peak of his career. *Visions*, a significant album of the Brown/Gibbs association, behaved more like a genuine album as opposed to a collection of previously released hit singles. "Deliverance Will Come," "Concrete Castle King," and "Malcolm X," the album's three tracks never released as singles, were rich in roots reggae dancehall rhythms, passionate vocals, and well-crafted poetic lyrics.

"Deliverance Will Come" discusses spiritual and physical salvation in words that could have been composed by Marley or Burning Spear: "Man a say man is doomed to die / Down in a Babylon is war and strife / Grief and terror and the throes of hate / This I know will soon abate / For I have seen the land of my Father in a vision … / Deliverance will come …"[3] "Concrete Castle King" is a commentary about Jamaica's class system and the island's social and economic inequality. Brown's tribute to Malcolm X captures the essence of the revolutionary nationalism of the post–Nation of Islam Malcolm. In addition to these three indictments of injustice, there are seven more satisfying recordings. Brown engages Rastafari concerns with "Repatriation" and "Jah Can Do It," touchingly illustrates a son involved in a tender comforting conversation with his mother as she endures troubled times in "Oh Mother," and crafts one of reggae's most sensitive romantic ballads with "Love Me Always."

In 1979, Joe Gibbs released a series of Dennis Brown songs on two albums *Joseph's Coat of Many Colours* and *Words of Wisdom*, the latter of which included the U.K. pop-chart hit "Money in My Pocket." By 1981, *Foul Play* appeared as Brown's initial effort for major American label A&M. The album took Brown into controversial crossover territory with the title track and the "Come on Baby" recording that were funky in a way that did not quite work. Fortunately, his core fan base and those unfamiliar with his satisfying vocal craft were treated to a hefty serving of undiluted roots tracks.

Brown reworked a fine rendition of his lovers' rock classic "If I Follow My Heart" for this album and infused "The World Is Troubled" and "I Need Your Love (Rasta Children)" with rebel attitude. A fire and brimstone spiritual message is conveyed by the smartly arranged "Existence of Jah," whose lyrics, if not Brown's voice, speak in threatening evangelical tones warning those who follow Satan rather than Jah that they will face the consequences. "If I Had the World," a love ballad with Brown's voice flowing through dense bass chords, singing words with a sour connotation so sweetly that a listener not paying keen attention could miss a crucial reference: "When I'm in misery / Girl it's just you that I see / You drive away the pains from me / Sometimes you're like cocaine baby."[4] Brown's comparison of the feeling he gets from the girl in the song to cocaine suggests a confirmation of the rumour that he had an addiction for that substance.

The second A&M album, 1982's *Love Has Found Its Way*, also led with a title track whose obvious objective was to crossover to a rhythm and blues/pop audience. Unlike previous attempts, "Love Has Found Its Way" was a success because Brown wrote an attractive melody brought to life by an emotional vocal performance, and because Val Douglas, a talented but often overlooked musician, effortlessly integrates reggae and rhythm and blues bass playing so smoothly it is difficult to tell where the reggae starts or where the rhythm and blues climaxes. The resulting rhythm does not crowd or overpower Brown's voice; it escorts his vocal through the tune's melody. This song is a good example of a seamless fusion of reggae and rhythm and blues in rhythmic texture and vocal styling. *Love Has Found Its Way* as an album is a particularly strong work, and possibly his best during the time with A&M. Brown's soulful vocal convinces on the insightful social commentary of "Handwriting on the Wall" and "Weep and Moan," while his voice tenderly illuminates lovers' rock tracks such as "I Couldn't Stand Losing You", "Why Baby Why," and his sensitive take on Burt Bacharach's "Any Day Now." "Get High on Your Love" is the only track attempting a funk crossover that does not quite connect.

The Prophet Rides Again, Brown's third and final effort for A&M, is a curious album. Half of the collection of songs on the album are forgettable pop or faux-funk disco-type workouts that did not work at the time of the album's release, and certainly do not stand the test of time. Even Brown's strong vocal performance on tracks like "Save a Little Love for Me" and "Wonders of the World" cannot save these recordings from themselves. Thankfully, the second half of the album is strictly reggae with the themes of three of the tracks dealing specifically with Brown's faith and his visit to Ethiopia. Like a number of high-profile roots reggae artists, including Freddie McGregor, Judy Mowatt, and Israel Vibration, Dennis Brown adopted the faith of Rastafari in the mid-'70s and became closely associated with the Twelve Tribes of Israel Rastafari organization. "The Prophet Rides Again" as the title track is a tribute to Vernon Carrington, the leader of the Twelve Tribes organization, who was known as Prophet Gad.

The story of Rastafari in Jamaica does not start with Twelve Tribes or Prophet Gad but in 1930 with the first Rasta, Leonard Howell. The '60s incarnation of Rastafari, however, was the most effective in bringing the movement's concerns to mainstream Jamaican society, and recruiting not just grassroots membership but also attracting middle-class intellectuals and personalities involved in the arts.

On April 21, 1966, Emperor Haile Selassie I of Ethiopia, the living Jah or god of Rastafari, arrived in Jamaica on a state visit. Mortimer Planno, possibly the most prominent Rasta leader of the day, was the first person to meet Selassie at Kingston's airport. Planno bounded up the portable steps placed at the side of the aircraft and greeted the Emperor as he emerged from inside the plane. The tarmac below was completely covered in an ocean of dreadlocks, individual Rastas whose awe burst out from the anticipation that held them captive when the Ethiopian state leader stepped into view. Selassie, denying he was God, came across humble, modest, and overwhelmed when confronted with the focused gaze of a multitude of dreadlocked disciples waiting to get a glimpse of their God.

Rastafari was empowered by what they perceived as the Emperor's connection to their movement. The publicity generated by the island's print and electronic media of the airport scene brought the entire nation of Jamaica face to face with the Rasta movement. Whether readers, listeners, and viewers loved, hated, tolerated, or admired Rastafari, they were forced to come to terms with a movement that had already become an integral component of the society and its psyche. Selassie's visit signalled the start of an era in which Rastafari could no longer be ignored.

Rastas exerted a greater influence on all classes in Jamaican society during the '60s and '70s through their contribution to Jamaican language, their African-inspired style of dress, their use of ganja, the lyrics and rhythms of popular Jamaican music, and their social activism. The diversity of a movement united by the acceptance of Haile Selassie's divinity, Marcus Garvey as prophet, and eventual repatriation to Africa meant that various other doctrines were subject to interpretation by different leaders.

In the '60s, Rasta leaders ranged from the strictly theological personalities of Prince Emmanuel and his Bobo Dread organization, to the more activist-oriented leaders such as Mortimer Planno and Ras Negus. By the '70s, the movement's diversity was in full bloom. The Twelve Tribes of Israel represented an organization that seemed primarily concerned with cultural affairs such as the staging of dances and concerts. Twelve Tribes had a significant middle-class membership with headquarters in a quiet uptown suburb of Jamaica's capital, located virtually across the road from Marley's Tuff Gong residence. Ras Historian's Rastafarian Movement Association continued the radical activist tradition of Rasta. Historian's group—with headquarters in a humble section of downtown Kingston on Church Street—was involved in grassroots organizing and support for the liberation movements in Southern Africa. The articulate Nyabinghi-order intellectual Jah Lloyd and his followers organized an international and very public binghi—a Rastafarian gathering of praise to Jah, discussion, and drumming—in downtown Kingston's National Heroes Park. The binghi itself was historic because Rasta gatherings of this kind were usually held in remote or obscure locations away from the public eye. When the permitted time in the park of several days elapsed, Jah Lloyd defied the authorities, overstayed his welcome, and burned down a tree planted by the queen of England in the process.

Civil discussions between Rasta leaders and organizations with different ideas about Rasta theology, Black liberation, and repatriation were the norm during '70s. There was even the formation of the Organization for Rasta Unity (ORU) to formally facilitate these kinds of discussions. In 1983, Masani Montague, a Toronto-based Jamaican-Canadian Rasta woman was the main organizer of a historic International Rastafari Conference in Jamaica at the University of the West Indies, in which most of the movement's Jamaican leaders and organizations participated. As a woman, Montague was not allowed to address the conference but her conception of Rastafari unity and her skills in making the conference happen remain historic.

Rastafari draws strength from its diversity. This diversity provides a balance in the movement in which some organizations may suffer setbacks, while others grow and progress. Many Rastas remain outside organized collectives but stand firm inside the movement. For example, neither Bunny Wailer nor the late Peter Tosh seemed to be publicly associated with any one group. Largely as a result of Bob Marley and other Rasta reggae musicians, Rastafari is now an international movement that has strongholds in various countries on a variety of continents.

Dennis Brown's album *The Prophet Rides Again* was released in the same year of the International Rastafari Conference. More important, the album tracks "Historical Places (Ethiopia)" and "Shashamane Living" spoke to Brown's first trip to the Rastafari promised land of Ethiopia and the special meaning of the visit. The words of "Historical Places" are like diary entries of Brown's experiences in Ethiopia. "Shashamane Living" alludes to the Jamaican Rastafari community of the town of Shashamane located in the southern part of Ethiopia. Despite the spark of the reggae recordings on *The Prophet Rides Again*, the album was a disappointment. Unfortunately, after Brown's departure from A&M, he was never able to secure another major label deal. Despite that setback, he remained the prince of reggae, second only to king Marley.

Brown's stature as a gifted reggae singer, vastly popular among reggae audiences in Jamaica and throughout the English-speaking Caribbean diaspora, continued to attract important producers to work with him. His collaboration with Sly and Robbie produced some of his outstanding work of the '80s and '90s. Sly Dunbar and Robbie Shakespeare remain not only Jamaica's most creative rhythm section but also reggae's innovative super-producers. As musicians, drummer Dunbar and bassist Shakespeare have worked on important albums of artists including folk-rock icon Bob Dylan, jazz pianist Herbie Hancock, Peter Tosh, Bunny Wailer, Grace Jones (Jamaica's alternative-pop diva of the '80s), and, more recently, No Doubt. As producers, Dunbar and Shakespeare have worked in the studio with Maxi Priest, Gregory Isaacs, the Tamlins, Black Uhuru, Ini Kamoze, Half Pint, Chaka Demus and Pliers, and some of Dennis Brown's best work of the '80s.

The great skill of these producers in the recording studio is to provide each artist with a distinct rhythmic quality. On Peter Tosh's *Equal Rights* album, for example, they furnish his music with carefully crafted, one-drop roots reggae that is mixed behind Tosh's vocal. For Black Uhuru's Grammy-winning album *Anthem*, Robbie supplies pleasingly supple yet domineering bass lines, while Sly's playing on electric drums sometimes produces syncopation with a mechanical robotic sensibility. The rhythm's position in the mix on *Anthem* is more prominent than on *Equal Rights*.

On their Dennis Brown productions, Sly and Robbie wisely make the decision to support and encourage Brown's velvet voice with vintage, early-'80s, roots dancehall rhythms that are mixed so that Brown's voice is clearly the star. Sly supplies Brown's single "Have You Ever" with a percussive popping sound that is mere relish to Robbie's slow-burning melodic bass, a suitable fit for Brown's choice to sing the tune's chorus in a higher voice than usual, saving his slightly echoed normal vocal for the song's verses.

The rhythmic feel of another Sly and Robbie–produced Brown single "Foundation" is fleshed out by an intense set of rub-a-dub bass notes interrupted by skittish drum rolls and haunting flute riff that appropriately decorates Brown's melodic rendering. Possibly Brown's most popular Sly and Robbie produced track is "Revolution," a rousing social commentary anthem about revolt against injustice and social depression, sung like a ballad that effortlessly negotiates a simmering rhythm.

During the '90s, Dennis Brown continued to record with an endless list of producers, including Mikey Bennett, who at the time was responsible for a number of significant recordings by international dancehall star Shabba Ranks. The Dennis Brown albums produced by Bennett came the closest to generating interest for Brown's music beyond the underground reggae scene in Caribbean diaspora cities of New York, Toronto, and London. Bennett once remarked that Dennis Brown was the best thing that happened to a reggae song. Brown's voice, however, is not the only significant voice in reggae.

Casual discussions about reggae singing between Jamaican reggae connoisseurs or analysts of the baby-boom generation usually involve, at some point in the conversation, each participant naming at least five of their favourite voices from the music's golden age of rocksteady and of roots reggae. While some enthusiasts restrict their concept of great reggae singing to smooth, "pure," rhythm and blues voice, the more enlightened observer will include singers with a rugged, husky, wailing tone. A short list of outstanding reggae voices that combines both the "pure" and the rugged—in addition to Delroy Wilson, Joseph Hill, and Dennis Brown—may include popular examples such as Winston "Burning Spear" Rodney, John Holt, Leroy Sibbles, and Frederick "Toots" Hibbert. While some enthusiasts may single out one individual as the best or the greatest singer, each creative reggae singer offers their own unique contribution to reggae culture.

Burning Spear's hollow emotional rasp sounds like the deep wail of a tenor sax, particularly when he dispatches those moaning scat improvisations. His voice sounds like an ancient cry channelling the spirits of African-Jamaican freedom fighters such as Nanny, Paul Bogle, and Marcus Garvey. His singing is weary— weary of having to continuously chant Afrocentricity and liberation. Burning Spear's voice does not have the range of other singers, but he does not need range because his singing has character and depth. As Rohan Preston suggests in his poem "Music," Burning Spear has a chasm in his voice; a chasm through which heroes of the African-Caribbean travel. When Burning Spear sings that Garvey is not appropriately remembered and honoured in his homeland on the tune "Old Marcus Garvey," there is a visceral sense of tragedy in his voice. When he pleads for the life of Rastafari in the live version of "The Lion," his wails and cries are so emotive that it sounds as if he is truly weeping. His a capella version of "Jah No Dead"—a song that challenges the idea of Emperor Haile Selassie's death in 1974—is delivered with such emotion, confidence, and sincerity that it is totally convincing in its emphatic statement that Selassie lives. Spear's classic "Marcus Garvey" converts a crucial element of Rasta theology into a reggae anthem by chanting about Garvey as a prophet through the clarity of his writing and his animated vocal tone. Burning Spear's distinctive voice as an integral aspect of roots reggae culture represents reggae singing that is rooted in the cadences of Rastafarian chants and nyabinghi hand drumming.

John Holt, on the other hand, has the kind of clean, warm, straightforward tenor—whose tone is rendered unique by a subtle quiver—that is most comfortable singing romantic ballads. As lead singer with harmony vocal trio the Paragons between 1966 and 1970, Holt established himself as one of the most popular and acclaimed singers of the rocksteady era. The Paragon's Jamaican hits such as "Happy Go Lucky Girl," "Memories by the Score," "On the Beach," "Wear You to the Ball," and "Tide is High"—impeccably produced by Duke Reid—situated Holt as a gifted singer who typified the Jamaicanized rhythm and blues approach of rocksteady vocalists whose lyrics focused on partying and romance.

Holt began his solo career in 1970, and immediately earned respect as a reggae vocalist with the fine collection of Coxsone-produced singles on the *Love I Can Feel* album. Every recording on the album was a ballad that worked a romantic theme. These ballads were taken to a higher creative level by Holt's skill in wrapping his attractive vocal around memorable melodies and by the production genius of Dodd, who was wise enough to support Holt's singing with rhythms sweating the kind of gyrate-your-waist rub-a-dub bass lines that made dancehall favourites out of the album tracks "Love I Can Feel," "Stranger in Love," "Make Up," and "My Heart Is Gone."

In 1974, John Holt's cool tenor ensured that the recording of his version of Kris Kristofferson's "Help Me Make It Through the Night" charted in the U.K. top ten. Strings sweetened the already smooth tone of Holt's vocal on that track, but this is what his record label Trojan thought they had to do in order to crossover to

Burning Spear at the Music Hall, Toronto, September 1982.
Photograph by Isobel Harry.

a pop audience. Trojan might have been right, but, from an artistic point of view, "Coxsone" Dodd and other producers proved that the best way to expose Holt's voice was through a more rootsy approach that can be heard on 1972's "Stick By Me," 1976's Sly and Robbie–produced "Up Park Camp," and 1987's "Police in Helicopter." Holt's enduring contribution is his smooth romantic ballad vocal combined with rootsy reggae beats—the definition of lovers' rock that some writers insist began in the U.K.

Leroy Sibbles' soft ethereal voice is a perfect vehicle for lovers' rock. As a lead singer for the Heptones during the rocksteady and early reggae eras, his sensuous tone enraptured popular roots ballads including "Why Did You Leave," "Love Don't Come Easy," "Baby," and "Fatty Fatty" like a Jamaican Smokey Robinson. The controversial "Fatty Fatty" was banned from radio at the time it was released in 1966 because of the non-explicit but vividly suggestive sexual overtures of the song's male protagonist toward the fat girl who was the object of his lust. As Colin Channer has eloquently described in his novel *Waiting in Vain*, a full-figured woman is usually more attractive to Jamaican men than their rail-thin counterparts. Banning "Fatty Fatty" consequently helped to make the record popular as it thrived underground through sound systems in dancehalls and jukeboxes in rum bars. It is entirely possible that Sibbles' sensual singing is what convinced the authorities to ban the song.

Although Sibbles' voice was closely associated with the Heptones' Jamaican hits such as "Fatty Fatty," their other classic recording "Party Time," and a definitive version of Phil Phillips' "Sea of Love," Sibbles' fine tone also engaged an equal number of social commentary songs. The Heptones' love ballads have attracted most of the attention, but Sibbles' performance on the Heptones' protest songs such as "Equal Rights," "We Gonna Fight," "Soul and Power," and "A Change is Gonna Come" were just as good. Sibbles' voice, though soft and ethereal, effectively conveyed the anti-discrimination humanitarian theme of "Equal Rights."

The Heptones seemed to carefully select American songs they chose to record as is evident in their versions of Curtis Mayfield's anti-racist diatribe "Choice of Colours" and Bob Dylan's "I Shall Be Released." Mayfield and Dylan are, of course, two of America's best songwriters of the '60s. It is not difficult to imagine Sibbles' voice working the melody of "Choice of Colours" since he and Mayfield have similar vocal tones. His interpretation of Dylan's song, however, is sublime—think Aaron Neville's take on Dylan's "With God on Our Side." Sibbles' exceptional soulful rendition of "I Shall Be Released" emotionally owns the song. Leroy Sibbles is the reggae singer with the lovers' rock voice that is equally capable of delivering soulful passionate social commentary.

The Maytals joined the Heptones and the Paragons as the third dominant vocal trio of the rocksteady era in Jamaica. The Maytals' lead voice, Frederick "Toots" Hibbert, is a very distinctive reggae voice because he incorporates Jamaican gospel, a Jamaican rural cadence, and American soul into his singing. At the dawn of their career, with ska recordings "Hallelujah" and "Six and Seven Books," the Maytals injected an undisguised vocal style into secular Jamaican music: the kind of Jamaican gospel singing usually heard from Church of God or Pentecostal congregations. These two recordings, as their titles suggest, are gospel songs set to a proto-ska beat.

The Maytals, though retaining the gospel influence in their work, moved into the secular domain during the rocksteady period. Some U.S. and U.K. music journalists have described Toots'

Peter Tosh at Convocation Hall, Toronto, March 1979.
Photograph by Isobel Harry.

voice as a blend of Wilson Pickett and Otis Redding. Following that logic, it would be more precise to say that his singing is a Jamaican blend of those two influential African-American soul singers. A Jamaican characterization of Toots' vocal approach would more accurately describe his voice as a smoky gravel tone soaked in the rich, rustic, rural cadence of the island's countryside. In terms of lyrics, music, and especially vocal phrasing and accentuation, Toots and the Maytals proudly and confidently represented a country-reggae sensibility through popular '60s recordings such as "Bam Bam" and "Scare Him," and 1970 releases "Monkey Man" and "Peeping Tom."

A number of Jamaican singers were born and raised outside of urban centres. Bob Marley and Burning Spear were born and spent their early years in the rural parish of St. Ann on Jamaica's north coast. Jimmy Cliff was born in the country town of Somerton in St. James—the parish where Montego Bay is located—where he lived as a young boy. Cliff, Marley, and Spear, though acknowledging their country roots, expressed their lyrics and music in an urban context. Although Spear's rustic chant has a salt-of-the-earth quality and his lyrics speak of living in the hills and the joys of nature, his framework is clearly urban in terms of his very urban Rasta-inspired phrasing, his use of sinister reggae beats and sophisticated horn harmonies. "Toots" Hibbert, originally from May Pen in Clarendon, wrote and performed "Sweet and Dandy," possibly the quintessential country-reggae song. It is a vivid depiction of a rural wedding that poetically presents various scenes just before the nuptials take place. The bride, Ettie, is crying in a room, her mama tells her to wipe away her tears. Johnson, the groom, appears nervous as his uncle encourages him to pull himself together. After the ceremony, the guests, dressed in white, party at the reception.

Toots, however, is a vocal chameleon. The Maytals' 1968 classic "54-46," a number assigned to Toots while he served a brief sentence in jail for alleged possession of ganja, is an urban gem. On this track, Toots' voice reflects an urban *rude-bwoy* rebel persona that negotiates the tune's defiant bass lines supporting his indignant claims that he is innocent. In a different vein on the 1988 *Toots in Memphis* album recorded at Ardent Studios in Memphis, Tennessee, Toots as a solo artist substantiates his vocal debt to Otis Redding. Sly, Robbie, Mikey "Mao" Chung, and Larry McDonald are joined by veteran Stax musicians—guitarist Teenie Hodges, keyboardist Jim Dickinson, and saxophonist Andrew Love on this session. Toots' interpretation of "I've Got Dreams to Remember" and "Hard to Handle" are remarkable in the way that he skillfully conjures the spirit and feel of Otis Redding's style without losing his own vocal identity. Frederick "Toots" Hibbert's voice, although soulful, defines the country, rural template of reggae singing.

A comprehensive assessment of reggae voices would require several books because there are so many talented vocalists. Jamaican singers such as Bunny Wailer, Freddie McGregor, Beres Hammond, Ken Boothe, Slim Smith, Gregory Isaacs, Pat Kelly, Brent Dowe, Alton Ellis, Justin Hines, Bob Marley, Peter Tosh, Michael Rose, Garnet Silk, Luciano, Judy Mowatt, Marcia Griffiths, Phyllis Dillon, Hortense Ellis, Doreen Schaeffer, Rita Marley, Millicent "Patsy" Todd, Norma Fraser, and Nadine Sutherland must be included in such an assessment. The U.K. voices of Maxi Priest, Steel Pulse lead singer David Hinds, plus Angus "Drummie Zeb" Gaye and Brinsley Forde of Aswad must also be considered. Even then, these names still reflect only a partial list.

Dennis Brown distinguished himself from several other gifted reggae singers in different ways. If his recorded output was often excellent, his concerts were quite often exhilarating. Several of his truly outstanding performances, including Reggae Sunsplash 1981 in Montego Bay and Kingston's Reggae Superjam 1983, often rivalled and sometimes exceeded his best studio work. At a typical Dennis Brown outdoor concert performance, his singing would pierce the night air high above the audience before he appeared on stage. He would then follow his voice out on to the stage revealing himself to the audience. Beaming a natural charisma and that trademark ray-of-sunshine smile, he would take complete control of the stage, a place he inhabited like a second layer of skin. He would skip, jump, and prance across the stage, his long dreadlocks dancing as he moved his head from side to side to the steady rock of a hit song's rapturous bass line. As he placed the cordless microphone to his lips and sang scat lines such as *wo-oh we-e-ell*, you better know, you *done know* it was going to be *wickid*, it was going to be *worries* at that night's concert.

Brown's catalogue of quality songs was so big and so varied that he could perform on stage for over two hours, which he did at a special charity concert for Twelve Tribes in the early '80s, without repeating a song and completely engaging the audience for the entire show. At the Reggae Superjam 1983 concert, Brown followed Beres Hammond and Steel Pulse, both headline-quality acts with charismatic audience appeal. Brown's performance that night inside the National Arena was so powerful that he received three genuine encores. He performed memorable concerts during the '80s at major venues outside of Jamaica such as New York's Madison Square Garden and Toronto's Roy Thompson Hall.

The influential nature of Dennis Brown's voice is another very important factor that sets him apart from most other outstanding reggae singers. His singing was so deeply charismatic that it imposed on the developing talent of reggae singers seeking an artistic identity and seduced those vocalists who may have been convinced that the Dennis Brown singing style was their key to success. Over the past thirty-five years, many of reggae's outstanding voices have come under the magical influence of his attractive style. Roman Stewart's 1975 recording *Natty Sings Hit Songs* is a clear example. Michael Rose sourced Dennis Brown's vocal flavour before he went on to develop his own unparalleled vocal attack as lead singer for Black Uhuru. From the first note that Frankie Paul sings on 1984's *Pass the Tusheng Peng* the listener is well aware that they are in Dennis Brown stylistic territory. Jamaican vocalist Luciano, one of the best reggae singers to emerge in the '90s, also has a voice forged in the Dennis Brown mould. And Canadian reggae singer Chester Miller sports a vocal that could be a virtual twin of Brown's voice.

Maxi Priest has never been shy about naming Brown as his main influence and inspiration. Priest eagerly admits he "used to mimic Dennis' voice" while listening to Brown's records such as *No Man Is an Island* or *Should I* from which he later modeled his own composition with the same name. In the days before he became a professional singer, Priest recalls that he met Brown through mutual friends, when the ace Jamaican vocalist visited London. Brown, Priest says, was supportive of his nascent career from the very start. Brown's voice had an enormous influence on Maxi Priest's singing style. Priest includes Bob Marley in the discussion to emphasize the specifics of his reggae influences: "I got the consciousness from Bob and (consulted the songs of) Dennis for the voice." No other reggae recording artist rivals Dennis Brown's impact on the singing style of reggae singers over a twenty-five-year period from the early years of roots reggae in the early '70s to the dancehall reggae of the mid-'90s.

Dennis Brown tragically passed away at the age of forty-two in 1999 from complications associated with the pneumonia he contracted. He nonetheless remains reggae's most influential voice.

Raggamuffin Rap

The Interconnections of Reggae and Hip-Hop

DJ Kool Herc, the chief architect of hip-hop, was born Clive Campbell in Kingston, Jamaica. At the age of twelve, in the winter of 1967, Campbell moved to Bronx, New York. The year he migrated to America, sound-system culture in Jamaica had a ubiquitous presence in Kingston's lower-class neighbourhoods. As a twelve-year-old preteen now living in the Bronx, Campbell already possessed a persistent reggae and sound-system consciousness having experienced the innovative music of Prince Buster, the Skatalites, Don Drummond, and dancehall deejay U-Roy.

At eighteen, Campbell attempted to recreate the Jamaican dancehall experience in the Bronx by spinning the latest Jamaican reggae records at neighbourhood parties, but his young African-American audience was not feeling the reggae beat and did not comprehend the Jamaican patois rhymes of sound-system MCs known as toasters.

As DJ Kool Herc, Campbell shifted to playing funk records, but his reggae background caused him to favour funk with heavy-weight bass lines and lively percussive drumming. Kool Herc's record selections were transmitted through hi-fi stereo equipment that spoke with the same awesome power and sonic quality of a roots Jamaican sound system.

The selector, as a deejay is called on a reggae sound system, though using one turntable—the norm during the '60s and '70s—was still capable of altering the arrangement of a tune spinning off a record on the turntable platter. The selector skillfully inflicted a completely different sound context on a roots reggae recording by manipulating the controls on the sound system's amplifier to briefly remove the bass on a tune, accentuate the singing of the song's vocalist, and highlight the harmony of trumpet, saxophone, and trombone. The selector would create tension in a live remix by bringing back the bass booming like a compact implosion. By the '70s, the selector had the ability to vary the sonic texture of the recording by creatively deploying reverb and echo chamber to repeat the sweetest elements of a vocal or horn solo and as a special sound effect that dramatized certain aspects of the recording with a live feel.

Kool Herc's approach to creating something fresh from pre-recorded funk on vinyl was different because he used two turntables. But his approach was similar in that he shared the same objective as the selector, which was to do a live remix of the record to heighten the entertainment of his audience. He extended the intoxicating rhythmic feel of percussive conga, bongo, or trap drums sizzling the break of records like Mandrill's "Fencewalk," the Incredible Bongo Band's "Apache," and the live version of James Brown's "Give It Up, Turn It Loose" by playing the same record on two turntables using a sound mixer to seamlessly prolong the percussive breakbeats. Herc pioneered the innovative use of two turntables and a sound mixer as active instruments that became more than passive facilitators, more than just pieces of electronic equipment that merely played what was recorded on vinyl. These electronic instruments were now used to rearrange pre-recorded music to suit the immediate needs of the disco and the dance floor. When DJ Kool Herc rocked a block party, dispatching African-American funk with the overwhelming sonic power of a reggae sound system, no other deejay dared to compete.

The birth of one aspect of hip-hop as the art of creating soundscapes through the delicate splicing and knitting together of pre-recorded music with two turntables clearly had reggae as its midwife and Kool Herc as its main creator. Unravelling the origins of rap is a little more complicated. African-American commentators correctly suggest that the antecedents of rap are found in jazz vocal scatting, playing the dozens (a form of repartee), the rhymes accompanying girls' rope-skipping games such as double dutch, and African-American radio jocks' bebop catchphrases of the '50s to name just a few sources. The controversial issue has been naming the originator of rap in the context of hip-hop's birth.

Important African-American analyst Nelson George—a writer usually conveying crucial insights on Black music in America—in his 1988 book *The Death of Rhythm and Blues*, and, particularly, in the 1980 essay "Rapping Deejays" in his anthology *Buppies, B-Boys, Baps, and Bohos*, not only identifies DJ Hollywood as a rap originator but privileges the seminal rapper as the sole originator. It is curious that neither DJ Kool Herc nor his MC Coke la Rock even rate a mention by George in either book. DJ Hollywood might have been a seminal force in rap, but as Afrika Bambaataa (another early hip-hop figure) tirelessly and insistently suggests, Herc

Jully Black and Kardinal Offishal at the Citytv studios, Toronto.
Photograph by Oscar Wai Loo.

and Coke la Rock were there at the very beginning and were probably more influential. In "Rapping Deejays," George acknowledges the earlier existence of the reggae deejay, but contends that
most of the early rappers were ignorant of Jamaican deejaying.
Kool Herc, however, actually attempted to use Jamaican deejaying
at his initial parties in the South Bronx. In a sense, he found his
way to hip-hop through reggae. His hip-hop sound system and his
use of American MCs were based on a Jamaican reggae model. In
his 1999 book *Hip Hop America*, George confesses that he once considered DJ Hollywood to be the first *rappin'* deejay but now realizes: "Coke la Rock, who pumped the crowds for Kool Herc, is
cited by some as a crucial creator of the style."[1]

If there has been equivocation about the roots of rap by certain
African-American analysts, many Jamaicans are absolutely
adamant that rap is a direct descendant of the island's toasting and
deejaying that predates the birth of hip-hop by more than ten
years. The evolution of Jamaican deejaying reveals a slightly different story. In the early '60s, the role of early Jamaican toasters
was to increase the level of excitement at a dance by using entertaining rhymes and verbal sound effects. Count Matchuki, a seminal Jamaican toaster, invigorated recordings played by "Coxsone"

Dodd's Downbeat sound system with his own Jamaican rhymes and catchphrases mixed with American jive talk sampled from the bebop jive of African American radio jocks such as Douglas "Jocko" Henderson.

A popular disc jockey hosting shows on Black radio stations in New York and Philadelphia, Henderson was influential to toasters including Matchuki and Lord Comic (another MC of the early Jamaican sound-system scene). A toaster such as Matchuki was not confined or restricted by an American sensibility; his creative ska scatting was very Jamaican in conception and execution. Henderson's influence can be found in Lord Comic's 1967 recording "The Great Wuga Wuga," a reworking of Henderson's phrase "great googa mooga." U-Roy's 1969 release *Your Ace from Space* takes its title from Henderson's on-air persona "the ace from space."

As toasting developed, it began to take on more of a Jamaican character with the arrival of King Stitt and the revolutionary stylistic approach of Ewart "U-Roy" Beckford. U-Roy introduced a distinctive singjay style phasing together singing with melodic talk that relied on an acute sense of timing to surf the rocksteady and early reggae beats over which he deejayed. This surfing of the beat is what Jamaicans refer to as "riding the rhythm." U-Roy, initially influenced by Matchuki, began his career in the era of early toasting as an MC for sound systems such as Doctor Dickie's Dynamic. When U-Roy joined King Tubby's Home Town Hi-Fi in the late '60s as MC and selector, sound-system culture, the sound of roots reggae, and the art of toasting were all transformed.

Electronics engineer Osbourne "King Tubby" Ruddock may not have invented dub but he remains the gifted innovator of dub, responsible for popularizing the art form during its initial period. As a creative sound artist, he applied the sound-system aesthetic to the recording studio by accentuating and de-emphasizing various aspects of an original recording to create a dub version or remix. King Tubby's front-and-centre positioning of the rhythm's pulsing drum-and-bass heartbeat is the essence of reggae dub soundscapes. Deconstructed snatches of vocals and horn phrases from the original recording—reconceived as aborted fractured dub riffs—were like lightning to the dub rhythm's thunder. Sometimes the rhythm is briefly absent from the mix, leaving maybe a piano, organ, or melodica groove or simply just a pregnant void of expectation indicating the ominous bass line's certain satisfying return.

Dub albums such as Augustus Pablo's *King Tubby Meets Rockers Uptown* and the Lee Perry–produced *Blackboard Jungle Dub* represent key recordings displaying Tubby's craft at the mixing board. Dub's lightning and thunder, its use of fractured sound, and its indulgence of reggae space as rhythmless pauses have inspired non-Jamaican analysts to describe dub as a kind of psychedelic reggae experience. The comparison is interesting and fairly accurate as an attempt to find a way to explain dub to those familiar with '60s psychedelic rock. But the idea that Rastas sat around listening to dub while sucking on big ganja spliffs the way that hippies dropped LSD while listening to Jimi Hendrix is not entirely correct. Dub originated as an innovation for the sound system, for the dancehall. Initially, dub remixes were created as recordings known as dub plates that were exclusive to a particular sound system. A dub plate could only be heard in the dancehall and was made available to the public as a regular recording if it became very popular and at the discretion of the producer. Dub plates were designed specifically for the heavyweight power pushed out by the sound system. The average living room stereo could never properly reproduce a dub plate's low-end sonic response.

King Tubby's initial dubs became the perfect vehicle for U-Roy, the resident deejay of King Tubby's Hi-Fi sound system. U-Roy's deejay approach moved beyond the catchy jive-talk phrases interjected over an original recording. U-Roy verbally riffed off lyrics sung by the vocalist engaging a dialogue with the singer during the moments on the dub when the singer's vocal was dropped out of the mix. Tubby's dub plates and U-Roy's dominant deejay style made King Tubby's Hi-Fi the island's number one sound system of the early roots reggae era.

U-Roy's deejay skills and his popularity in the dancehall eventually led to the initiation of a recording career in the late '60s. After U-Roy's initial studio efforts, Duke Reid, the outstanding record producer of the rocksteady era, invited U-Roy into his Treasure Isle Studios to record his deejay magic on to some of Treasure Isle's most popular rocksteady recordings. U-Roy's popularity reached a peak in 1970 when three Treasure Isle releases "Rule the Nation," "Wake the Town," and "Wear You to the Ball" transformed him from underground dancehall MC to mainstream acclaim with three recordings hitting the top five of the Jamaican charts. He was the first deejay to experience success as a viable recording artist. Today,

U-Roy is considered the godfather of all deejays, or, affectionately, Daddy Roy, whose style remained influential over a twenty-year period. There is no direct link between U-Roy and any of the early hip-hop MCs, although Kool Herc has named U-Roy as one of the main artists that formed his reggae consciousness.

In 1973, when Kool Herc deejayed his first parties in the Bronx, Big Youth was the dominant deejay in Jamaica and in diasporic communities. The influential Big Youth possessed a rugged chant-like flow that was the perfect foil for spacious roots reggae grooves on recordings such as "S-90 Skank" and "Screaming Target." As hip-hop gained popularity in the New York underground scene in 1978, Jamaican deejay style breached the mainstream for the first time when Althea and Donna's single "Uptown Top Ranking" hit the #1 spot on the U.K. charts. With their female take on Trinity's deejay recording "Three Piece Suit," Althea Forest and Donna Reid were the first deejay act to achieve international popularity. In many ways, much like Millie Small before them, Althea and Donna have been assessed as one-hit wonders and "Uptown Top Ranking" viewed as a novelty. While this song—using the classic reggae rhythm adapted from Alton Ellis' rocksteady tune "I'm Still in Love With You"—may not have been innovative, the tune's satisfying bass line and the infectious pop sensibilities of the duo's deejay vocals make it a decent recording. Deejays that captured the attention of hardcore fans in Jamaica when "Uptown Top Ranking" was a U.K. hit included Trinity, Ranking Trevor, Ringo, and General Echo.

General Echo is interesting because he was an influential figure in introducing risqué lyrics discussing sex and sex acts, which Jamaicans call *slackness*, into the dancehall dialogue as a legitimate theme during the 1979 to 1980 period. Up until that time, Big Youth's Rasta-inspired lyrics on "I Pray Thee" and Trinity's secular social-commentary tune "Three Piece Suit" were characteristic of the deejay scene. *Slackness* in Jamaican music did not start with General Echo or any other deejays of that era. Sex lyrics can be traced back to mento during the pre-ska days, but in the '60s, *slack* songs such as Jackie Opel's "Push Wood" and "Grinding," Lee Perry's "Dr. Dick," and the Wailers' "Pussy Galore" were recorded by prominent figures in the industry.

If these recordings were novelty tunes that did not attract much attention, Prince Buster's venture into *slackness* produced popular underground classics such as "Rough Rider" and, particularly, "Wreck a Pum Pum" (*poom poom* is Jamaican for vagina). These records were banned from being played on radio but could be heard in the dancehall, on jukeboxes, and at uptown parties. Prince Buster's appearance on sex records represented only one aspect of his multifaceted persona. He was responsible for being the first producer to take Count Ossie's drum ensemble into a recording studio, a move that resulted in the single "Oh Carolina." He was also associated with the Nation of Islam, the African-American organization for which Malcolm X had been the main spokesman and Muhammad Ali a key celebrity member.

Prince Buster projected himself as a progressive voice promoting peace and unity among certain youth in Kingston's ghettos. On his 1967 recording *Judge Dread*, he rebuked gang-affiliated *rude bwoys* for Black on Black violence and crimes. His 1968 album *Wreck a Pum Pum*, containing several of his tunes about sex, underlines his status as an important purveyor of *slackness*—a status that lives happily with his profile as a Black Power advocate, U.K. 2-Tone ska icon, and innovative recording artist and producer during the early days of the Jamaican music industry. The Heptones' "Fatty Fatty," another classic rocksteady, though not as explicit or raw as some of Prince Buster's efforts, was still considered *rude* enough to be banned by radio.

Women have also discussed their sexuality through music since the early days of rocksteady and reggae. The Rude Girls' response to Prince Buster's most popular *slack* record placed the woman as the subject of the sexual encounters in their tune "Wreck a Buddy" (*buddy* meaning penis). Nora Dean's "Barb Wire" and its allusions to her lover having barbwire in his underpants was very popular when it was released. Dean's career seemed to be defined by *slackness* as her other efforts "Mojo Girl" and her version of "Wreck a Buddy" signify.

In 1969, a Jamaican *slackness* recording even insinuated itself into the British charts. Max Romeo, better known for his later recordings such as "Macabee Version," "Let the Power Fall," and probably his most outstanding work of Rasta-inspired social commentary "War in a Babylon," sang about his nightly activities on "Wet Dream," which reached the top ten of the U.K. hit parade despite the fact it was banned by BBC radio. A decade later, dancehall deejays began the process of reintroducing sexual themes to reggae. Although not the only *slackness* deejay of his era, General Echo (who was shot and killed in Kingston in 1980) holds the distinction of being its most prominent voice at that time through his work on sound systems such as Gemini and his 1979 album *The Slackest LP*.

As *slackness* began to establish a presence in the reggae dancehall, hip-hop achieved its initial mainstream breakthrough when the Sugarhill Gang's "Rapper's Delight" climbed to #4 in the U.S. R&B charts. Sugarhill Gang were newcomers who did not emerge as performers from the underground hip-hop scene. In fact, they cribbed some of the rhymes of "Rapper's Delight" from established MCs such as Grandmaster Caz of the Cold Crush Brothers.

During the early '80s in London and New York, talented Caribbean diasporic deejays rocked microphones on diasporic sound systems and were distinct from Jamaican sound-system deejays. Sound-system culture existed in the diaspora since the '60s, but it was not until the '80s that a few of the high-profile sounds became the breeding ground for international reggae stars. In London, the vast majority of the deejay counterparts of British-Caribbean roots reggae artists such as Steel Pulse, Aswad, and Linton Kwesi Johnson chanted on the microphone of Saxon Studio International, a South London sound system. British-Caribbean reggae toasters such as Papa Levi, Tippa Irie, Macka B, Smiley Culture, and singer Maxi Priest—at one time or another during that period—nurtured their MC and singing skills on Saxon. Born in the mid-'70s, Saxon reached a peak as a nursery for emerging talent during the early '80s as these reggae deejays went on to stake their claim as successful recording artists in the U.K., Jamaica, and other regions of the diaspora. In addition to the international acclaim of Maxi Priest, Papa Levi's single "Mi God Mi King" went to #1 on the Jamaican charts, Tippa Irie's "Hello Darling" invaded the British pop charts, Smiley Culture's "Cockney Translation" received critical and popular acclaim in the U.K. and Jamaica, while his follow-up single "Police Officer" eased into the British top twenty.

In America, Caribbean diasporic reggae really came to life during the early '80s when the music started its transition away from roots reggae and shifted to dancehall as the dominant form. The initial stars of the New York diasporic dancehall environment moulded their talent as MCs on New York sound systems such as

Downbeat the Ruler and African Love. Downbeat (not to be confused with Coxsone's Jamaican sound system), in particular, was responsible, to some extent, for the early growth of Shinehead and Sister Carol. "Clashes" or competitions between sound systems were an integral aspect of the culture. A clash between two sounds from the same city was commonplace, but the practice of sound systems embarking on international tours to participate in an international sound clash took on new meaning in the '80s as diasporic deejays faced off against deejays from Jamaica and MCs from other regions of the diaspora.

In 1984, London's Saxon—featuring Maxi Priest and Papa Levi—clashed with New York's Downbeat—starring Shinehead—at downtown Toronto's Masonic Temple (later known as Concert Hall, now CTV studios). That night in Toronto signified a total diasporic experience involving three main centres of the Caribbean diaspora. Shinehead and Maxi Priest were the outstanding talents at that dance, each of them years away from international recognition. Shinehead, in particular, tore the place down with an exhilarating performance of "Billie Jean."

On December 28th of that same year at the Biltmore Ballroom in Brooklyn, New York, two sounds from Jamaica and one from New York clashed: Downbeat with Shinehead, another New York deejay Daddy Santa, and Eek-A-Mouse versus Gemini with Ringo and Sassafras, and Volcano with Papa Toyan and Lady Ann. Despite the presence of popular deejays from Jamaica such as Ringo, Sassafras, and Toyan, the unique vocal gymnastics of Jamaican MC Eek-A-Mouse and, especially, Shinehead—again working the immensely popular "Billie Jean"—were the high points of the dance.

While Shinehead was refining his schizophrenic rap-deejay persona during the first years of the '80s as MC on Downbeat, African Love, and at sound clashes, two of hip-hop's respected pioneer crews issued important recordings: "The Message" by Grandmaster Flash and the Furious Five and "Planet Rock" by Afrika Bambaataa and Soul Sonic Force. There is a significant Caribbean connection linking three of the most important seminal hip-hop deejays: Grandmaster Flash's heritage is in Barbados, Kool Herc is Jamaican, and one of Afrika Bambaataa's parents is from Jamaica, the other from Barbados. As a deejay, Bambaataa played an eclectic mix of music including calypso and Latin. Later in the '80s, he featured Sly and Robbie and Yellowman as guests on his recordings.

Yellowman, a Jamaican dancehall deejay, was a huge star on the island as a recording artist during the early '80s. As an albino, he endured a fair amount of humiliation and ridicule because of how he looked. But eventually his talent prevailed, and his distinctive skin colour was no longer an issue. Yellowman's vocal style developed in the U-Roy singjay tradition, although his voice had a deeper texture. He hit big in Jamaica with numerous tracks including "Mad Over Me," "Mr. Chin," and "Nobody Move, Nobody Get Hurt." His popularity extended to the Caribbean diaspora, especially New York City, and he consequently became the first reggae deejay to acquire a major label deal in America when he signed with CBS Records in 1983. Unfortunately, 1984's *King Yellowman*, the only Yellowman album released by CBS, received a mixed reception and his career did not quite make the leap into the international mainstream.

Yellowman reigned supreme as a deejay and recording artist in the reggae world during 1983 and 1984, as hip-hop continued its advance beyond the underground. Herbie Hancock's 1983 album *Future Shock* is probably the first example of hip-hop/jazz fusion that showcased Hancock's jazz piano and keyboards coaxed by funky electronic beats featuring DJ Grandmixer D.ST on turntables. "Rockit," the single from the album became a hit, but *Future Shock* also boasts a reggae connection—drummer Sly Dunbar guests on the decidedly funky track "Rough." In the same year, the documentary film *Wild Style* introduced a broad audience to hip-hop as a culture that offers art, dance, and music.

While hip-hop began its invasion of jazz and film, rap began to change and transform. Run-DMC's debut single, "Sucker MCs," and its flip side, "It's Like That," drove rap's evolution into a harder yet more fluid vocal flow underscored by an edgy rock sound that began to distance the new style from the way "old school" hip-hop sometimes used disco beats. By 1984, this new wave of hip-hop innovation gained a foothold through the birth of hip-hop record label Def Jam and its first single, LL Cool J's "I Need a Beat," and the release of Run-DMC's initial album, *Run-DMC*, which included tracks such as "Rock Box" sporting heavy-metal guitar riffs.

As hip-hop started the process of maturing in the first half of the '80s, New York–based Caribbean diasporic rap artists—in the tradition of Kool Herc—authored important contributions to hip-hop beginning in 1985. Barbados-born Doug E. Fresh, using his

Shinehead, 1988. Photograph by Ken Collins.

voice to create the sound of a drum-machine-driven hip-hop back-beat and other sound effects, popularized the vocalist as human beat box. Doug E. Fresh's Get Fresh crew included MC Ricky D, who later became Slick Rick. Born of Jamaican parents in South London, Slick Rick moved to New York at the age of eleven. He was influential in promoting the pimp persona through his lyrics. His 1989 album *The Great Adventures of Slick Rick* featured not only the track "Treat Her Like a Prostitute" but also "Hey Young World," a laid-back reggae recording.

While the Get Fresh Crew with Doug E. Fresh and MC Ricky D attracted attention in 1985 with "The Show" on one side of a single and "La-Di-Da-Di" on the other, reggae in Jamaica was trans-formed by the beat-box beat or "computer *riddim*" of Wayne Smith's "Under Mi Sleng Teng." This tune was produced by King Tubby's apprentice Lloyd "King Jammy" James and it radically transformed Jamaica's music industry. Musicians were already complaining about lost employment opportunities because of the ability of producers to create several versions of an existing recording without live instruments. They were in a worse situation now because even new tunes were being recorded without musicians. The fast-paced, energetic, dancehall reggae sound was often quite creative and eventually signalled the complete dominance of the deejay over singers for the first time in the music's history. If 1985 was the year of "Sleng Teng," then 1986 belonged to a deejay named Super Cat and his ubiquitous hit "Boops," which was about sugar daddy targets of so-called female gold diggers. At the same time that dancehall reggae began to exert an overwhelming presence in the popular music of Jamaica and the Caribbean diaspora, this new style of reggae also began its infiltration of hip-hop.

As "Boops" established itself as the dancehall anthem of choice in 1986, Boogie Down Productions (BDP), through DJ Scott la Rock and MC KRS-One, released a blazing reggae-influenced hip-hop single "The Bridge Is Over." KRS-One's animated dancehall deejay phrasing combines with his daring scatter-shot rap vocal while the tune's piano sound echoes the reggae bass line of Toots Hibbert's "54-46" as it skanks to a hard hip-hop backbeat. If Shinehead staked a claim for hip-hop in the reggae dancehall, then BDP represented the presence of reggae in the world of hip-hop. Earlier attempts by hip-hop artists at using reggae, other than Slick Rick, involved rap trio the Fat Boys whose recording "Hardcore Reggae" sounded more like a novelty track, and their obviously fake Jamaican accents did not assist their effort. "The Bridge Is Over" and BDP's 1987 single "9mm Goes Bang" work, in part, because of BDP's skill in uniting two rebel musics. Another factor may be that the late Scott la Rock was Jamaican, which qualifies BDP as a diasporic reggae hip-hop group.

Nineteen-eighty-seven was also the year that Shinehead's chameleon skills alternating rap and deejaying surfaced on a major label recording. Sly and Robbie's non-reggae Island album *Rhythm Killers* featured Shinehead as guest vocalist rapping a revision of Super Cat's lyrics on a straight-out funk version of "Boops" retitled "Boops (Here To Go)." On the title track, Shinehead spits patois rhymes over hype funk rhythms decorated with dissonant violin sounds.

The year after Shinehead's groundbreaking *Unity* album, Dwight "Heavy D" Myers—a Jamaican-born New York rap artist—included the reggae track "Mood for Love" on his chart-topping *Big Tyme* album. Heavy D's rap flow was capable of riding the rhythm of a hip-hop beat much like the delivery of a reggae deejay. In fact, Heavy D incorporated improvised vocal sounds like the "ba diddly diddly diddly deeee" scat he used in "We Got Our Own Thang" that was adapted from the creative scatting of innovative Jamaican MC Brigadier Jerry.

Brigadier was easily the most popular deejay of Jamaica's dancehall underground. His career began in the late '70s and reached an artistic peak during the early '80s. His underground fame in Jamaica and the Caribbean diaspora resulted from his reputation as possibly the most influential sound-system deejay of that time for Jah Love Muzik International. Jah Love—the resident sound system of the Twelve Tribes of Israel Rasta organization—was arguably the top sound system of the roots reggae or rub-a-dub era of sound systems during the early '80s.

Briggy's vocal approach, firmly in the vein of U-Roy, built on that framework to include a unique scat style that conveyed a sense of drumming, a kind percussive sound. He possessed the gift of witty freestyle rhymes of observation, social-commentary narrative, and, as a Twelve Tribes Rasta, his sincere preaching of praises to Jah. Brigadier Jerry was a deejay's deejay whose stylistic influence extended to many of his Jamaican contemporaries such as Charlie Chaplin, Josey Wales, and even Yellowman, in addition to Jamaican-Americans Heavy D and Shinehead.

During the height of his popularity, Brigadier did not venture into a full-scale career as a recording artist, and only a select few of the tunes he did commit to wax, such as "Jamaica Jamaica" and "Pain," came close to the skills he displayed as a deejay at a sound-system dance. Maybe he needed the right producer to guide his recording sessions, or maybe the studio was not his context.

Super Cat, a Brigadier Jerry protégé, relocated to New York in 1988 and later penned a major label deal with Sony, who released his 1992 *Don Dada* album. His deejay voice, though steeped in the influence of U-Roy, Brigadier Jerry, and Nicodemus, offered its own imposing, melodic, yet deadpan delivery. One of Super Cat's important legacies is the respect he earned in the hip-hop world and the role he played in connecting hip-hop and reggae. *Don Dada* has two tracks on which he shares the microphone with Heavy D. On these tunes—"Big and Ready" and "Them No Worry

We"—Heavy D unleashes an authentic deejay flow that proved he was just as skilled in reggae as he was in rap.

The year before *Don Dada* hit the streets, Heavy D's *Peaceful Journey* album underlined his status as a major rap star. *Peaceful Journey*'s success, in large part, was driven by the hit single "Now That We Found Love," a good hip-hop version of Third World's 1978 disco-reggae smash. Heavy D's appearance on *Don Dada* is significant because it is an early example of collaboration between two Caribbean diasporic artists.

Super Cat also collaborated with another Jamaican-American rap artist who was just getting started in the rap game but became one of rap's biggest superstars of the '90s. Before Christopher "Biggie Smalls" Wallace, the Notorious BIG, launched his debut solo recording in the spring of 1993, his voice graced a number of hot remixes such as Mary J. Blige's "Real Love" and "What's the 411" and a remix of Super Cat's "Dolly My Baby," which also presented Puff Daddy on possibly his first outing as a rapper. Biggie's accent displayed no characteristics of his Jamaican background, but his flow—the way he surfs the rhythm on "Dolly My Baby" and his future mega-hits—shares a direct kinship with the way in which skilled deejays ride a reggae *riddim*.

Shinehead, Super Cat, and female deejay Shelly Thunder were all New York–based Jamaican deejays signed to major labels. Shinehead's association with Elektra made him the first to sign since Yellowman. Shelly Thunder, a talented performer and recording artist with a proto-feminist viewpoint on tunes such as "Man Fi Get Kuff," "Walk Out a Mi House," and "Bwoy Nuh Come Back," saw her first Island Records release in 1989.

If Shinehead and Shelly Thunder as Jamaican residents of New York can be considered diasporic reggae artists whose craft developed and matured in America, then Shabba Ranks was the first Jamaica-based deejay of the digital dancehall age to break out of the reggae underground. Shabba Ranks did more than just breakthrough, he cracked the American mainstream in a way that neither Third World nor Bob Marley (when he was alive) or any other Jamaican reggae act had previously. Ranks' road to crossover success was carefully orchestrated. On his *Raw As Ever* debut, he combined computer-*riddim* reggae with the bouncy rhythm and blues cut "Housecall" that paired Ranks with Maxi Priest and the ominous hip-hop joint "The Jam" casting KRS-One's conversational flow as co-star to Shabba's gravelly bass boom. "Housecall" nestled in the top five of the R&B charts and "The Jam" reverberated the rap singles chart. In addition to its commercial success, "The Jam" signified an important juncture in the convergence of hip-hop and reggae. It was clearly not aimed at a pop audience but instead directed at hip-hop fans and listeners attuned to reggae-rap fusion.

As the face of reggae on American mainstream television, Shabba Ranks was considered the king of dancehall. His lyrics were completely immersed in dancehall's post–roots reggae obsession with sex, female body parts, "trailer-loads of girls," and sometimes romance. There has been a significant shift in thematic approach from the justice and equity sentiments that were dominant in '70s roots reggae to the language of sex and violence that has characterized dancehall through much of the '90s. There are many social, economic, political, and possibly artistic reasons for the transition but there are a few that are worth considering. This shift in the thematic focus of song lyrics, in some ways, reflected the shift from the socialist sensibility of the People's National Party (PNP) that governed Jamaica during the '70s to the conservative pro-capitalist climate engendered by the Jamaica Labour Party (JLP) that governed Jamaica during the '80s. This does not mean that these political parties necessarily succeeded or even attempted to steer culture in a particular direction, and it certainly does not mean that the PNP was beyond reproach. It did mean, however, that the socio-political environment each party nurtured may have been more conducive and receptive to certain kinds of song themes.

Another transition began in 1980 that can be related to the music's shift. It involved the replacement of the Rasta sage as the most influential figure in the ghetto communities of Kingston by the overarching presence of the drug "don." Laurie Gunst's book *Born Fi Dead* provides an incisive understanding of drug don culture in Jamaica, while "Rodney and the Cultural Politics of Rastafari and Rude Boy," a chapter in Rupert Lewis' excellent biography *Walter Rodney's Intellectual and Political Thought*, discusses the cultural and political leadership exercised by Rastas at the grassroots level in Kingston ghettos during the '60s. Throughout the '60s and '70s, Rastafarians as social activists plus the dissemination of Black Power, radical-left, and Marxist ideas had a significant impact not just on ghetto youth but also on young people from the middle-class as well. During the '70s, there was a variety of modest Marxist organizations including Trevor Munroe's Workers' Party of Jamaica (WPJ), Keith "Milo" Miles' Youth Forces for National Liberation (YFNL), Danny Barrett's Movement for Social and Political Consciousness (MSPC), and Chris Lawrence's Communist Party of Jamaica (CPJ), each of which had small pockets of influence.

Left politics in Jamaica began its dramatic decline in the early '80s, as did the tradition of radical activism in Rastafari. At the same time, cocaine began to seek supremacy over ganja as the island's main illicit drug of commerce if not consumption. The ghetto drug dons involved themselves in the international trade to the extent that they started to promote a "bling" lifestyle of conspicuous materialism and participate in turf wars in Jamaica and in the diaspora. This behaviour is reflected in the lyrics of *gun-talk* and macho *bad-man* posturing of deejays such as Super Cat on the *Don Dada* album and Cobra on the album *Bad Boy Talk* released the same year.

Sex lyrics in the dancehall are a hotly debated issue in Jamaica that is complicated by the fact that while some *slackness* tunes by male deejays are sexist or misogynist, it is incorrect to classify all of them that way. Female deejays' *slackness* performances expressing a sexuality that is empowering rather than demeaning to women also renders sweeping assessments of sex lyrics less than accurate.

Female deejay Lady Saw's explicit lyrics found in recordings such as "Stab Out the Meat" have come under harsh criticism. In her book *Sound Clash*, dancehall expert and Jamaican university professor Carolyn Cooper interprets Lady Saw's work as empowering female sexuality. Lady Saw is certainly an important dancehall talent in terms of deejay artistry and the skill with which her lyrics are crafted. Despite her characterization as a deejay completely immersed in sexual matters, her work includes conscious equity and justice tracks such as "What Is Slackness."

Shabba Ranks represented the *slackness* side of the sex / bad-boy talk equation of dancehall in the '90s. Ranks may not be the most erudite lyricist, but his talent and innovation lie in the flow of his deep voice and the way he lowered the pitch of deejaying to a gruff bassy standard, a practice which became influential to a new generation of deejays.

For a time, it seemed that only deejays discussing their sexual prowess could attract mainstream attention outside of Jamaica. Gifted lyricists such as progressive Jamaican deejays Tony Rebel

and Buju Banton (when he became Rasta), although they eventually signed to majors, were unable to achieve the notoriety of Ranks
or even someone like Mad Cobra whose "Flex" single was also a
major crossover hit. Tony Rebel's 1993 Sony release *Vibes of the Time*
and Buju Banton's 1995 *'Til Shiloh* were both very strong albums in
terms of artistry, but did not seem to be promoted or marketed in
the same way as the work of Mad Cobra or Shabba Ranks. Fuelled
by BDP, Shinehead, and the collaborations of Shabba Ranks and
Super Cat, the interconnections of hip-hop and reggae reached a
kind of critical mass during the late '80s and early '90s.

The late '80s and early '90s was also a period of thematic and
musical divergence in hip-hop. In thematic terms, there was the
Black-conscious rap of Public Enemy and KRS-One; the emerging
gangster ethos of NWA, Ice Cube, and Ice-T; and the politically
progressive messages of alternative rap artists such as A Tribe
Called Quest, Arrested Development, De La Soul, and Queen
Latifah. In musical terms, Public Enemy's production crew, the
Bomb Squad, created art out of sampling a multitude of previously recorded sounds, rhythms, and voices skillfully weaved into a
seamless quilt of swinging funky beats.

The beats heard on Public Enemy's classic albums *It Takes a
Nation of Millions to Hold Us Back* and *Fear of a Black Planet* provided
the group's outstanding poetic lyricist Chuck D with the appropriate musical context to deliver his rap vocal that combined the
authoritative quality of both Martin Luther King and Malcolm X. Dr.
Dre crafted his innovation in the West Coast G-Funk sound, while
Gang Starr, A Tribe Called Quest, Digable Planets, and The Roots
expressed a creative hip-hop/jazz fusion.

This period could easily be considered rap's golden age and
reggae was certainly an important aspect of hip-hop during that
time. All the major rap acts from that era worked reggae into their
music. On *Fear of a Black Planet*, "Reggie Jax" is Public Enemy's
interpretation of a reggae jam, while "Revolutionary Generation"
samples Musical Youth's "Pass the Dutchie." "Alwayz into
Somethin'," a track on NWA's 1991 album *Efil4zaggin*, includes
animated reggae deejaying, as does Arrested Development's
"People Everyday," and Ice Cube's "Wicked" (courtesy of
Trinidadian-born reggae deejay Don Jagwarr).

Queen Latifah, like KRS-One, loved seasoning her hip-hop
with reggae vibes. On her most successful album from that period,

1993's *Black Reign*, there are at least four reggae-influenced songs. On "Rough," a track with guest vocals by Heavy D, Treach, and KRS-One, Heavy D injects Jamaican flavour and KRS-One throws down some rugged deejaying while Latifah reacts to KRS-One's exciting flow in her best Jamaican accent with "gwaan" and "eeez up." On Latifah's feminist rap "U.N.I.T.Y.," the refrain sounds like the chorus to Desmond Dekker's rocksteady classic "Unity." The cool R&B tune "Weekend Love" wears an easy reggae groove as Tony Rebel deejays sensitive romantic interludes in duet with Queen Latifah's competent singing. Another track, "Winki's Theme," segues back and forth from a jazzy R&B ballad to a laid-back interpretation of a slow-burning reggae beat. The appearance of Busta Rhymes—another New Yorker of Jamaican heritage—on A Tribe Called Quest's classic track "Scenario" from their 1991 album *Low End Theory* provides a glimpse of crucial deejay-influenced rap talent about to make a major breakthrough.

The same year *Low End Theory* hit, another alternative hip-hop album *And Now the Legacy Begins* from Canadian rap group the Dream Warriors was released by Island Records. As Caribbean-Canadians, Capital Q and King Lou—the voices of the Dream Warriors—massage a portion of reggae seasoning into an album that was essentially an early example of hip-hop/jazz fusion. "My Definition of a Boombastic Jazz Style" is a track that hit big in Canada and the U.K. and was critically acclaimed in America. The track sampled Quincy Jones' 1967 instrumental "Soul Bossa Nova," a song that has an interesting history in Canada because it was the theme song to a very popular '70s game show on Canadian television called *Definition*. The Dream Warriors' salute to the game show's name is cleverly used to convey the jazz style of their brand of hip-hop. The introduction to the other popular *Legacy* track "Wash Your Face in My Sink" jocks a slick reggae syncopation that eases into jazz-flavoured hip-hop. "Ludi," a straight-ahead reggae tune, samples the classic rhythm of the Uniques' "My Conversation," while "U Could Get Arrested" is flecked with Jamaican-accented talk.

From the earliest moments of Canadian hip-hop's journey, diasporic Canadian rap artists have not been shy about promoting their Caribbean roots through their music. Before the Dream Warriors, Maestro Fresh Wes' 1989 single, the bangin' "Let Your Backbone Slide," established Canadian hip-hop as a legitimate force. But it was Maestro's second hit, 1991's "Conductin' Thangs," using a mean ska beat complete with horn riffs, that really gave his music a distinct feel. His heritage is Guyanese. Michi Mee, the other major player on the Toronto hip-hop scene at that time, is a Jamaican-Canadian. Michi Mee, as MC with DJ L.A. Luv, issued one album during the early '90s entitled *Jamaican Funk: Canadian Style* of which some tracks were actually recorded in Jamaica. The Dream Warriors, Michi Mee, and Maestro (as he is now known) proved that interesting hip-hop could be produced outside of America and demonstrated that Caribbean-Canadians of the hip-hop generation may choose to express reggae in a different way.

U.K. hip-hop also began to take its first steps in the late '80s, although the early history of U.K. diasporic rappers is intricately intertwined with American hip-hop history, starting with personalities such as Slick Rick and Young MC.

Born of Jamaican parents in London, Marvin "Young MC" Young relocated to Queens, New York with his family at a very young age. After completing high school, he went to the University of Southern California to study economics. On graduating, he began his career in hip-hop, first as a writer of Tone Loc's two huge hits "Wild Thing" and "Funky Cold Medina," then as Young MC rapping his own words on the Grammy-winning single "Bust a Move."

Unlike Slick Rick and Young MC, female diasporic rapper Simone "Monie Love" Johnson—also born in London, England—started in the rap game in the U.K. as a teenager in 1987 with a crew that included DJ Pogo. After embarking on a journey as a solo MC, Monie Love with DJ Pogo released a number of independent underground singles. In early 1989, their association with Cooltempo Records produced a U.K. top-forty hit "I Can Do This." That year, she moved to New York, and the following year her debut album, *Down to Earth*, included successful singles "Grandpa's Party," "Monie in the Middle," and "It's a Shame (My Sister)" that all charted in the U.K. Monie Love's profile was also enhanced by her contribution to Queen Latifah's initial hit, the female empowerment rap "Ladies First." Monie Love's distinction is that unlike most U.K. hip-hop acts, she was able to establish a profile in America.

Another U.K. rap group, the London Posse, broke ground as artists in true diasporic fashion by not being afraid to distinguish themselves as British through their cockney accents and by drawing on the reggae of their Caribbean roots. Their only album, *Gangster Chronicles*, surfaced on Island imprint Mango in 1990. London Posse is a group that was a pioneer of infusing Caribbean diasporic reggae into their brand of U.K. hip-hop.

By the mid-'90s, reggae had become an integral element of hip-hop's raw material for some of the most creative American innovators. Wu-Tang Clan member Method Man's 1994 album *Tical* contains two tracks, "What the Blood Clot" and "Bring the Pain," that both display a *rude-bwoy* reggae attitude and selective use of Jamaican patois. Outkast's hits "Elevators (Me and You)" and "SpottieOttieDopaliscious" both engage a creatively employed rhythmic sensibility of reggae dub. The Fugees, on their 1996 album *The Score*, cover Bob Marley's "No Woman No Cry" and include a mean Sly and Robbie reggae remix of "Fu-Gee-La." By the same token, Jamaican deejays signed to major labels were encouraged to include collaborations with rap artists on their albums. Rasta deejay Capleton's debut on Def Jam boasts a collaboration with Method Man. Bounty Killer's album *My Experience* offers a shopping list of hip-hop guests in the form of the Fugees, Busta Rhymes, Wu-Tang Clan's Raekwon, and Jeru Da Damaja. Fortunately, Bounty Killer's obvious talent shines through on the straight reggae tracks because some of the collaborations do not really work well. "Change Like the Weather"—the tune that co-stars Busta Rhymes—is one of the exceptions.

Busta Rhymes understands reggae and is also a good deejay. In that sense, he continues Heavy D's tradition of achieving mainstream acclaim and popularity as a gifted Jamaican-American rap artist who welcomes the opportunity to participate in interesting projects with reggae deejays and with reggae-inspired hip-hop recordings. Busta Rhymes' performance on the remix of Kardinal Offishal's "Ol' Time Killin'" is a special collaboration because it brings together two rap artists of Jamaican heritage immersed in an honest exploration of a reggae aesthetic in hip-hop. This has particular meaning because, in some ways, Kardinal is a direct descendant of Shinehead in the way that he alternates between reggae and hip-hop in the language he uses and the beats deployed in his music. Shinehead was not the only so-called raggamuffin rap artist during the early '90s. Don Jagwarr and Mad Lion both displayed talent in deejaying hardcore lyrics over fierce hip-hop beats. One factor that distinguishes the raggamuffin hip-hop of Shinehead, Kardinal, and MC Collizhun is the variety in the themes of their lyrics and their willingness to discuss progressive social-commentary issues as opposed to simply conveying *gun-talk*.

In 1998, dancehall reggae imposed itself on the mainstream hip-hop scene yet again. Beenie Man's "Who Am I," a single from *Many Moods of Moses*, an album released by Jamaican-American independent record company VP, broke into the Billboard hip-hop singles charts and peaked at #6. Unlike previous Jamaican hits, "Who Am I" represented authentic undiluted dancehall that did not attempt an obvious crossover to hip-hop or pop fans. On this track, Beenie Man's sometimes-impenetrable Jamaican language flows with skill and abandon, anchored by the melodic hook of phrases like "Sim simma / who got the keys to my Bimmer / Who am I? / The girls dem sugar."[2]

Since his initial breakthrough, Beenie Man signed to Virgin Records in 2000 and continued his successful run with the single "Girls Dem Sugar" from his Grammy-winning album *Art and Life*. The "Girls Dem Sugar" remix featuring R&B singer Mya and later collaborations with Guerilla Black and Haitian-American rapper Wyclef Jean underline Beenie Man's impact on hip-hop.

In the fall of 2002, when Sean Paul's *Dutty Rock* album was released by VP—possibly this era's equivalent of Chris Blackwell's Island Records—an interesting new dancehall story began to unfold. Sean Paul was dancehall's "man of the hour" throughout 2003 and much of 2004. The international recognition he has received includes the 2004 Grammy for Best Reggae Album for his *Dutty Rock* recording, Best New Artist–MTV Europe, Best Reggae Artist at the MOBO awards in the U.K., and a performance with Sting on the televised portion of the 2004 Grammy awards show.

Sean Paul has skills to match his success. His deejay flow does not favour the gruff, sandpaper vocal approach of Shabba Ranks and Capleton. His vocal style has more in common with the tradition of U-Roy, Brigadier Jerry, and Super Cat—deejays who express their lyrics by melodically chatting some phrases while they flat-out sing other phrases. On tracks such as "Gimmie the Light," "Like Glue," and "Punkie," that kind of singjay style is in full effect. Deejays and rappers live or die by the timbre of their voice and the way their lyrics flow. Sean Paul possesses a fluid yet rugged deejay vocal and unquestionable skill in how he flows. The undiluted roots bass line of "I'm Still in Love with You" not only recalls the roots reggae era but also suggests that Sean Paul wants to cross over without musical compromise. Although the lyrics of "Gimmie the Light"—the first single off the acclaimed *Dutty Rock* album—are laced with hip-hop slang, it does not compromise an album that is stubbornly Jamaican.

Sean Paul's words are not exactly poetry in the Bob Marley sense and are not really in the same ballpark as the lyrics of Buju Banton, Sizzla, or Damian "Junior Gong" Marley. As meditations about girls, weed, and having a good time, Sean Paul's lyrics work well partly because in his delivery there is something a little more militant lurking under the surface, something that reflects his determination to express a raw Jamaicanness. Sean Paul does not attempt to sound American even when he uses hip-hop slang.

Sean Paul broke into the mainstream as a Jamaican successor to Shaggy. Shaggy is the Jamaican–New Yorker as diasporic dancehall deejay who inherited Shabba's "crown" as the most commercially successful deejay throughout the '90s. Unlike Shabba and Sean Paul, Shaggy's crossover success has focused on a pop audience as opposed to hip-hop fans.

Sean Paul's mother lives in Toronto, so it comes as no surprise that he spends a lot of time there. Toronto has also contributed positively to his career. The music videos that played such an important role in vaulting him to international prominence were filmed in Toronto and directed by New York–based Caribbean-Canadian director Little X (now known as Mr. X). Even though Sean Paul is viewed as a Jamaican deejay, in some ways, because of his affiliation to Toronto, he has also assumed the persona of a Caribbean diasporic reggae artist. Sean Paul, through the quality of his partnership with diasporic reggae hip-hop artists, has raised the stakes of reggae/rap collaborations. His appearance on Kardinal Offishal's "Money Jane" is an excellent example of a tune where Kardinal's diasporic dancehall deejay style merged with his Canadian rap approach combines well with Sean Paul's Jamaican flow. Paul's appearance on this track is another indication of his connection to the Toronto scene. The *wickid* remix of Sean Paul's hit single "Gimmie the Light," which highlights Jamaican-American rapper Busta Rhymes' awesome deejay talk, offers something more creative and interesting than some of Paul's guest appearances on the tunes of other American rap artists because of the diasporic reggae–hip-hop sensibility Busta Rhymes brings to the collaboration.

In addition to the work of Kardinal, MC Collizhun, Sean Paul, and Busta Rhymes, there are some other creative examples of reggae's interconnections with hip-hop in these first five years of the new millennium. The Vancouver-based Canadian rap group the Rascalz are a good example of how the hip-hop of the Caribbean diaspora finds its voice through the use of reggae-inspired rap. On the Rascalz' 2000 album *Global Warning*, a reggae-MC style informs "Gunnfinga" and "Top of the World" features the unique reggae scatting of Jamaican singer Barrington Levy. Toronto's Trinidadian-Canadian alternative hip-hop artist K-OS on his 2004 album *Joyful Rebellion*, deploys a persistent roots-style reggae bass that tussles with guitars alternating delicious rock licks and atmospheric folk chords on the track "Crucial," whose lyrics wear a Bob Marley vibe. American hip-hop's continued fascination with reggae does not seem as if it will diminish any time soon. From the dancehall influences on the Black Eyed Peas' collection *Elephunk* to the undiluted roots reggae of Guerilla Black's *Compton*—on which Beenie Man dispatches *bad-bwoy* talk in duet with Guerilla Black's almost note-perfect channelling of Biggie Small's rap voice—rap and reggae remain firmly interconnected.

In 2001, Bob Marley's son Damian "Junior Gong" Marley matured into an outstanding lyricist on the solid set of recordings that constitute his second album *HalfWay Tree*—the album that included rap artist Treach from Naughty by Nature on "Educated Fools" and Drag-On's chilling rap performance on the remarkable "It Was Written."

In the U.K., a talented young man calling himself Roots Manuva creates dark sinister hip-hop beats from funky, dub-influenced, electronic soundscapes on his albums *Brand New Second Hand*, *Run Come Save Me*, *Dub Come Save Me*, and *Awfully Deep*. *Dub Come Save Me*, in some ways, is the new-millennium descendant of Aswad's early '80s masterpiece *New Chapter of Dub*. Roots Manuva's rap style is proud of its patchwork of cockney English and Jamaican patois phrases; his hip-hop is as creative as his name.

The focus of this chapter has been on the English-speaking Caribbean and its diaspora. However, reggae and dancehall have a pervasive influence in the Spanish- and French-speaking Caribbean and in Central and South America. Although this essay has restricted itself, the emergence of a new music called reggaeton must be considered, particularly because it seems poised to be the next reggae-influenced music to gain mainstream acceptance.

Reggaeton is a mixture of dancehall, hip-hop, and Latin rhythms. Its Puerto Rican origins, which seem to have roots in a Panamanian version of reggae, date back to the late '80s but gained popularity by the mid-'90s. As a Spanish-language music, reggaeton has established a prominent youth culture in several Latin American and Caribbean nations including Dominican Republic, Peru, Venezuela, Colombia, Mexico, Panama, and Nicaragua. Reggaeton's biggest names as of spring 2005 are Ivy Queen, Daddy Yankee, Don Chezina, and Tego Calderon, who is on the verge of a mainstream presence in America where reggaeton is already hugely popular among Latinos in cities including New York and Miami.

One of the most important accomplishments of thirty years of reggae's interaction with hip-hop is the innovative fusion found in the creative raggamuffin style of Shinehead and the inventive way reggae is expressed in the hip-hop of rappers such as Michi Mee, BDP, KRS-One, Queen Latifah, Dream Warriors, Mad Lion, Don Jagwarr, the Rascalz, Kardinal Offishall, Collizhun, the London Posse, Roots Manuva, and the reggaeton of Tego Calderon.

The Writing About Reggae Must Skank to an Authentic Rub-a-Dub Bass Line

The Insider Perspective

Over twenty years ago, Barry Gordon, a disc jockey hosting a reggae show on one of Jamaica's radio stations, used the platform of his show's broad popularity to comment on *Reggae International*, a new book about Jamaican popular music. In a colourful voice that set aside its Jamaican-patois identity in favour of "proper" English diction, Barry G mentioned that the book was written by a "foreigner," then smugly noted: "I wonder how many mistakes are in this one."

Reggae International is an anthology of thirty-five essays compiled by Americans Stephen Davis and Peter Simon. It is not accurate to say that the book is entirely the view of non-Jamaicans since respected Jamaican musicologist Garth White wrote two of the essays. The anthology was not a bad effort considering the standard of reggae books at the time. The book offers some interesting analyses of '70s roots reggae, and it attempts with some success to discuss the international impact of ska and reggae. It even includes a brief chapter that sketches an outline of women in reggae, a subject that has been ignored in much of the writing about Jamaica's music.

Barry G's statement, however, is true; *Reggae International* contains at least one significant error of fact: musician Tommy McCook is referenced as a keyboardist when in reality he was a tenor sax player and leader of the Skatalites—the premier Jamaican ska band of the '60s. Despite that mistake, *Reggae International* should not be totally condemned for a few errors of fact that could have resulted from erroneous research. Barry G's comment can also be interpreted as suggesting the more fundamental "mistakes" of context and perspective made by "foreign" writers as they observe Jamaican culture as outsiders. These kinds of mistakes are much more serious because they can have the effect of erasing or ignoring significant contributions of important artists and their role in the history of the music.

The case of ska trombonist Don Drummond is a good example. American Marley biographer Timothy White—whose work *Catch a Fire: The Life of Bob Marley* is one of the most celebrated reggae books—has a particular view of Drummond. Although White correctly describes him as a "gifted jazz trombonist" with an international reputation and a prominent profile in Jamaica, he does not place Drummond in the context of being the most important figure in Jamaica's ska era. He does not convey the significance of the sinister sense of dread and rebellion in Drummond's music that makes it a progenitor of roots reggae. White briefly mentions that Bob Marley relished collaborating with Don Drummond in "Coxsone" Dodd's recording studio, but does not recognize the collaborations as bringing together an innovative figure of Jamaican popular music and someone who, just a few years later, would become a major creative force in reggae. In terms of being music innovators and in terms of the power of their public personalities as cultural folk-heroes in Jamaica, Bob Marley was like the son of Drummond, the son that exceeded the achievements of the father.

American archivist Roger Steffens, considered a reggae expert, is the author of the title essay published in *Bob Marley: Spirit Dancer*, Bruce W. Talamon's book of Bob Marley photographs. Steffens finds time in his short essay to mention the Beatles, Bob Dylan, and James Brown and finds space to draw a one-sided sketch of the pivotal Jamaican producer Clement "Coxsone" Dodd. He cannot, however, spare any room to mention Don Drummond. Steffens' evaluation of Bob Marley, like Timothy White's, divorces Marley from the context of other innovative Jamaican artists. White and Steffens imply that Marley is the only important artist in reggae or Jamaican music as a whole. This perspective amounts to disrespect for Drummond and other significant figures of Jamaican music, and is not really a compliment to Bob Marley because an important aspect of Marley's greatness is that he was able to emerge and distinguish himself as outstanding in a rich tradition of very talented Jamaican musicians, singers, and songwriters. Marley's art was not nurtured in a vacuum.

To some extent, the early development of Marley's art was nurtured in the studio of "Coxsone" Dodd while recording the Wailers' ska singles together with the Skatalites band and Don Drummond. The "Running Away" track on the Wailers' 1978 *Kaya* album is a prime example of Drummond's influence on Marley's music. The horn section of the studio band for that recording session included trombonist Vin Gordon, whose haunting jazzy solo delivers the mournful melancholy quality that is at the heart of Drummond's playing. Marley was very much aware that Don D Junior is Gordon's nickname.

Catch a Fire, written by a high-profile rock journalist, and *Spirit Dancer*, which is, after all, only a brief essay authored by a noted Bob Marley fan and collector of all things related to Marley and reggae, can be seen as easy targets. This is because White and Steffens may not have intended to construct rigorous studies of reggae but, instead, popular biographies, if not hagiographies, of Bob Marley.

American academic and reggae enthusiast Norman Stolzoff's book *Wake the Town and Tell the People: Dancehall Culture in Jamaica* focuses on dancehall reggae. More than one-third of the book is dedicated to exploring the history of Jamaican music and its social and political implications during the pre–digital dancehall era. In this history section, Stolzoff also attempts to assess the origins of the current dancehall style by investigating the activity in popular-music dance venues during the ska era of the early '60s. In this context, he describes Drummond as a virtuoso and as one of ska's greatest horn players. These statements are fine, but the music of Drummond and the Skatalites was crucial to the sound systems (mobile discotheques) that blazed dances in lower-class neighbourhoods of Jamaica's capital of Kingston and in certain rural communities across the island during the '60s. The ghetto dancehall was an important avenue—maybe the most vital forum—for disseminating Drummond's musical innovations to a mass audience in Jamaica and diasporic participants at sound-system dances and nightclubs in the U.K. The dancehall was a key contributor to Drummond's status not just as a "great ska horn player" but also as an influential innovator and iconic figure in Jamaican music.

Through their writing, Timothy White, Roger Steffens, and Norman Stolzoff have all assisted in promoting reggae and Bob Marley to readers and students beyond the communities of Caribbean heritage in various parts of the world. These books present interesting information and insights revealing specific opinions about Jamaican music. They may play a positive role, but are not definitive or comprehensive by any stretch of the imagination. White, Steffens, and Stolzoff fit the description of "foreigners" that Barry G spoke about: these three American writers are outsiders in terms of their relationship to Jamaican culture. They are writers who rely mainly on second-hand information, either through discussion or previous research, and certain subtleties of context and perspective have therefore eluded them.

An insider, on the other hand, is a writer who has an intimate understanding of the social, political, and cultural conditions that gave birth to Jamaican popular music through actual experience with Jamaican culture. An insider is someone who has been a participant or witness to the unfolding history and development of the music. The insider perspective is a view that fuses the writer's lived experience with the music together with interviews, secondary sources, and other forms of research and analysis.

Jamaicans Garth White and Robin "Bongo Jerry" Small and Guyanese scholar Gordon Rohlehr, the seminal documentarians of Jamaican popular music, all wrote with an insider perspective during the '60s and early '70s. In the case of Small and G. White, they were an integral part of a loosely knit Jamaican arts scene of the '60s. Garth White as a writer-researcher specializing in Jamaican popular music is, in many ways, the definitive insider. He began collecting records, observing the music's gestation, developing associations with the Skatalites and friendships with reggae's future stars, including Bob Marley, at a time when these artists were just venturing into the island's embryonic music industry.

Garth White's writing on Jamaican music is comparable to the written discussions of bebop and free jazz by African-American writer Amiri Baraka in books such as *Blues People*. As an analyst and writer, G. White was not only a witness to the birth of ska, rocksteady, and reggae, he also had close connections to the creators of the music in the same way that Baraka was a witness to bebop and intimately connected to the creators of the jazz avant-garde and free jazz movements. White, like Baraka, understood that the evolution of Jamaican music was rooted in the journey of people who survived the dehumanization of slavery and continued to invent music culture to mirror their present-day efforts to contend with the residue of colonialism, the challenges of post-colonial change, and the negative effects of globalization.

Garth White—a '60s activist, Rastafari, and university graduate—is the author of the first essay to discuss Jamaican music as an important component of the island's culture of resistance and rebellion in relation to issues of race and class. The essay, "Rudie Oh Rudie," was initially published in 1966 and subsequently appeared in the September 1967 edition of *Caribbean Quarterly*, a journal produced by the staff of the University of the West Indies. G. White's writing on the early Jamaican popular-music forms of ska and rocksteady also appear in *Reggae International*.

The following insider assessment illustrates Garth White's keen understanding of the place the Skatalites and Don Drummond occupied in Jamaican culture during the '60s:

> ... the Skatalites came to represent the soul of a revitalized cultural movement among the Black poor (in Jamaica) ... the Skatalites became culture heroes ... Don became the musical conscience of the Jamaican people ... The slide trombone possessed a particularly Biblical ring in (Drummond's) hands ...[1]

These comments underscore the idea that Drummond and the Skatalites were seen as the musical anchor of Jamaica's nascent Black Power and radical arts movements of the '60s. When G. White mentions that Drummond's trombone playing possessed a Biblical ring, he is suggesting that the attraction to Drummond's playing was not simply due to his technique and musicianship but because of a spirituality conveyed in the tone of notes emerging from his trombone. The idea that his music became the conscience of the Jamaican people suggests that the underlying post-colonial Rastafarian message of Drummond's tunes coincided with the consciousness of Jamaicans searching for an identity independent of colonialism—the kind of identity represented in cultural terms by the creative impulse of ska and later reggae.

During the '60s, Robin "Bongo Jerry" Small—a Rastafari, activist, intellectual, and poet—introduced a new poetry that used Rasta-talk immersed in the rhythms of nyabinghi hand drums to discuss the cultural significance of Drummond and the ideas of Rastafari. Small is really the first dub poet. He is a seminal figure in the development of the various forms of reggae poetry that emerged in the '70s. His close connection to the '60s music scene in Jamaica is comparable to that of Garth White. Writing in May 1969, immediately after Drummond's death, Small eulogizes the following assessment of the iconic trombonist: "... by (19)59 they (the

Jamaican jazz men) had licensed and registered SKA or BONGO MUSIC in our name, the sufferers' name. And Don Drummond paid the registration fee. Don De Lion blew an iron that was black and blue, Peter Pan for lost Black man."[2]   Small's reference to Jamaican jazz men and bongo music alludes to the fact that Drummond's new musical language was crafted from jazz and the African retention inherent in the burru-inspired hand drumming of Rastafari.

A strict definition of bongo music specifically involves hand drumming, but in a more general sense it is the music created by lower-class African-Jamaicans, music yearning to make a connection with a repressed memory of Africa. Bongo music was denigrated and despised by the colonial-minded Eurocentric elements of the Jamaican upper-class elite. In his poetic tribute, Small identifies Drummond as a mythic figure—like Peter Pan or a Biblical Moses—who could lead his people out of Babylon through his music. His comments about Drummond's legacy can be interpreted to mean that Drummond registered ska or bongo music into the music history of Jamaica and, eventually, the world while paying the registration fee with his life. The views of Garth White and "Jerry" Small reflect their opinions as frontline observers when the Skatalites dominated the Jamaican music scene. They were analysts who shared a particular perspective about Drummond's place in the history of Jamaican music after his passing.

The idea of Drummond as a significant mythic and iconic figure in Jamaica's culture was also shared by a number of well-known Jamaican poets whose poems can be read as observations by insiders. In Mervyn Morris' "Valley Prince," the poet constructs a brief narrative that adopts Drummond's voice speaking his undisguised thoughts summarized in the following lines that conclude the poem: "... gimme back me trombone, man: is time to blow me mind."[3] Morris is obviously playing with an allusion to Drummond's mental state, but, more important, these lines of the poem can be read as a reference to Drummond speaking his mind—through his music—about the plight and suffering of poor African-Jamaicans like himself.

Anthony McNeill, in his poem "For the D," uses the inscription from Amiri Baraka's book *Black Music* to introduce his poem and therefore situates Don Drummond as a spirit as heavy as John Coltrane, which immediately positions Drummond as a brilliant

musician—an important icon of Jamaican music with a revolutionary spirit that opposes injustice. McNeill's poem describes
Drummond's trombone voice as a voice of the oppressed: "Don /
may I learn the shape of that hurt / which captured you nightly
into / dread city, discovering through / streets steep with the sufferer's beat."[4]

Gifted Jamaican poet Lorna Goodison (who now lives in
Toronto, Canada), in her poem "For Don Drummond," describes
Drummond's music using the following verse: "the Angel
Trombone / bell-mouthed sighs / and notes like petals rise / covering all a we."[5] Goodison's description of Drummond's instrument as an angel trombone suggests that it has a pure ethereal
quality. The reference to the instrument's sighing signifies
Drummond's trademark melancholy sound. Goodison's description of the notes he produced as petals conjure an image of soothing notes that massage the consciousness of those immersed in his
music. The poem is a word portrait of a great talent with a pervasive influence. "For Don Drummond" is also notable for its
humanization of Anita "Marguerita" Mahfood as a positive force
in Drummond's life who promised to protect him from his
demons. This characterization contrasts with Morris' poetic evaluation of Mahfood as the whore who exacerbated Drummond's
madness. Goodison's Marguerita is a complex three-dimensional
persona who sounds much more like the Marguerita encountered
in the recording "Woman A Come."

Gordon Rohlehr discusses the impact of Drummond's music
and iconography on the poetry of McNeill, Morris, and Small in a
historic essay titled "A Look at New Expressions in the Arts of the
Contemporary Caribbean" published in the journal *Caribbean
Quarterly* in 1971. Rohlehr's essay also provides an accurate assessment of Drummond's stature in the history of Jamaican music:

> The sensibility to which Drummond related was undoubt-
> edly Rastafarian. A major voice in the development of
> Jamaica Blues, he still dominates the city. One listens to the
> Abyssinians' "Satta Massa Gana" and hears Drummond's
> "Farther East"; one listens to the various experiments in the
> latest music from Kingston and hears Drummond's
> "Johnny Dark" and "Addis Ababa" ...[6]

264 — Klive Walker

Rohlehr clearly identifies Drummond as a major figure in Jamaican music and provides examples of his influence on reggae of the early '70s such as producer Herman Chin-Loy's instrumental "African Zulu," which samples the rhythm of "Johnny Dark." Rohlehr's choice of "Satta Massa Gana" as an example of Drummond's influence was insightful because that song has endured as a timeless roots reggae classic partly because the horn arrangements on the original recording of the song channelled Drummond's minor-key sensibility. Although Rohlehr writes before Third World recorded their version of "Addis Ababa"—renamed "Journey to Addis," the title of their 1978 album (which included the international hit "Now That We Found Love")—it is also a good example of how Drummond's music continued to energize reggae almost ten years after his passing.

Rohlehr's assessment of Drummond's contribution to the Black Power and Rastafari movements of '60s Jamaica is equally as insightful: "(Drummond's tunes) 'Marcus Junior,' 'Johnny Dark,' 'Reburial (of Marcus Garvey),' 'Man in the Street,' and 'Addis Ababa' were the forerunner to the upsurge of Black consciousness in the late '60s."[7] He also summarizes Drummond's iconic stature in Jamaican culture by indicating the perception of his mythic status: "Don Drummond achieved a kind of sainthood through his loneliness, the inner schizophrenic wound which he bore, his very crime in murdering an unfaithful woman, and the way that he expressed all of these tensions and made them sing in his music."[8] The idea that Drummond's murder of Anita Mahfood is a factor in the perception of his mythology is, to say the least, troubling, mainly because such a view introduces problems of male chauvinism and misogyny. This perception may also be out of step with the reality that Mahfood, in many ways, was Drummond's muse. Today, his iconography is focused on his genius in blowing innovative trombone notes that expressed his inner conflicts and the social conflicts of race and class that African-Jamaicans continue to experience.

Drummond's legacy is not confined to Jamaica. The international influence of Don Drummond and the Skatalites through the impact of ska in countries such as the U.S., the U.K., and Canada has been pervasive over more than thirty years since the essays and poems of the initial insider perspective were written. It is doubtful that the insider writing of Garth White, "Jerry" Small, and Gordon Rohlehr, from the vantage point of the early '70s, could have imagined that Drummond's legacy would have had powerful international implications thirty years into the future. These writers, and poets such as Goodison, McNeill, and Morris, however, all understood the importance of documenting the enormity of Drummond's presence in Jamaican culture—a presence that parallels Bob Marley's stature in the '70s and '80s. The importance of these writers' insider views should not be ignored by those involved in the research and documentation of any stage in the development of Jamaican music. Just as some analysts find parallels in the fashion, attitude, and initial mainstream rejection of bebop and hip-hop, these parallels exist with ska and post-1985 dancehall reggae.

It would be a mistake to confuse an insider perspective with a particular Jamaican or Caribbean perspective when reading a book about reggae. *Reggae Routes* by Jamaicans Kevin O'Brien Chang and Wayne Chen seems to indulge in a Jamaican version of an outsider perspective throughout most of the book. Its evaluation of Don Drummond repeats Timothy White's assessment of the celebrated trombonist when Chang and Chen offer the following unqualified statement: "Don Drummond ... the greatest instrumentalist Jamaica ever produced."[9] This evaluation is not necessarily a false claim, but Chang and Chen do not qualify it by explaining why Drummond was great. They do not share with the reader the elements that made him a great figure of the music. Is the assessment based on his popularity, his musicianship, his accomplishments as an innovator, or a combination of all these characteristics?

In discussing the Skatalites, Chang and Chen enthuse: "Skatalites had been together less than eighteen months, yet they created the best instrumentals in Jamaica's history."[10] A bold generalization that, without explanation, could be confusing to readers unfamiliar with the Skatalites but well aware of the innovative and creative instrumental work in the reggae dub genre by sound artists such as producers King Tubby and Lee Perry, and musicians such as Sly Dunbar and Robbie Shakespeare. The so-called Jamaican perspective of Chang and Chen is tainted with this kind of approach, which also suggests male chauvinism in the reggae industry is really the fault of women and that a bandleader named Byron Lee was more popular in Jamaica than Bob Marley and Dennis Brown.

It would also be incorrect to think that some outsider work cannot make valuable contributions to the research of reggae and Jamaican music. *Reggae: The Rough Guide*—a book with an outsider view by U.K. reggae enthusiasts Steve Barrow and Peter Dalton— also devises its own grand sentence for Drummond's excellence: "Drummond was a superb musician whose abilities were recognized by leading international jazz figures such as George Shearing, J. J. Johnson, and Sarah Vaughan."[11] Dalton and Barrow, however, venture beyond the obvious and attempt to dig a little deeper to tell their readers what was superb about Drummond: "(Drummond was) ... responsible for some of the most innovative work of the ska era."[12] They correctly point out that "(Drummond) anticipated later developments in Jamaican music including the Far East sound of Augustus Pablo ... "[13] *Reggae: The Rough Guide* is precise in the way it assesses Drummond and makes a number of attempts to break away from the old outsider framework by discussing the contributions of female artists and by identifying important innovators of reggae.

The difference in the way that insiders and outsiders view Don Drummond is very unsettling. It raises troubling questions for those in search of a more accurate historical evaluation of Jamaican music and its international implications. Questions such as: How many more innovative reggae artists have had their role in the music's history diluted or erased?

It is vital that the insider perspective of G. White, Small, and Rohlehr is resuscitated and adapted to the requirements of a new age by insiders in Jamaica, the Caribbean, and in the Caribbean diaspora of countries such as Canada, the U.S., and the U.K. Certain fiction writers and poets from the Caribbean diaspora are already documenting the music in creative and interesting ways through their verse and their stories. Colin Channer, a New York–based Jamaican-American novelist, has referenced reggae and its themes in many of his stories. In his novella *I'm Still Waiting*, Channer employs his insider knowledge of reggae to tell a story involving the professional and romantic interaction between Michael, a Jamaican-born Afro-Chinese record producer, and Patience, a biracial American singer. Channer's fictional character Michael is inserted into imaginary scenes of reggae history several times in the narrative. In one instance, Michael actually makes suggestions to Bob Marley about what his approach should be in attempting to record an update of the Wailers' 1965 ballad "I'm Still Waiting" while Marley ponders his affinity to Delroy Wilson's 1976 version of the song:

> That night in the mango tree, Michael was remembering now, he had spoken to Marley about redoing the song ... Marley ... said he liked the way Delroy approached it. And Michael told him that he should forget Delroy and approach it like a new song ... and Marley said his voice had lost its subtlety, that "I'm Still Waiting" was a supple song ...[14]

In the novel *Midnight Robbers*, Toronto resident Nalo Hopkinson, a Caribbean-Canadian science-fiction writer, inserts an insider sensibility into her speculative fabulist construction of worlds steeped in Caribbean folklore through sentences transported by rhythms of calypso and dub:

> New Half-Way Tree, it look a little bit like this Toussaint planet where I living ... But where Toussaint civilized, New Half-Way Tree does be rough. You know how a thing and the shadow of that thing could be in almost the same place together? You know the way a shadow is a dark version of the real thing, the dub side? Well, New Half-Way Tree is a dub version of Toussaint ...[15]

The reggae poems of Kwame Dawes and Lorna Goodison often sweat rub-a-dub rhythms while taking vivid snapshots of the music's history.

The non-fiction writers of Caribbean heritage that will take the investigation of the music's history to the next level—the way Bob Marley captured the international scene following the success of Eric Clapton's "I Shot The Sheriff"—have not yet arrived in a way that has seized widespread attention. However, a new wave of insider writing has begun to surface over the last decade. *Bob Marley: Lyrical Genius* by Kwame Dawes—author of the groundbreaking *Natural Mysticism: Towards a New Reggae Aesthetic*—takes an in-depth analytical look at Marley's songwriting. Herbie Miller, who managed Peter Tosh during the '70s and the Skatalites when they reunited in the '80s, is now lecturing a course on reggae at

New York's New School University. Miller's liner notes that appear in the re-release of the Wailers' *TrenchTown Days: Birth of a Legend* and the Skatalites' live album *Stretching Out* display his insider insight. He is working on a dissertation entitled "Syncopated Rhythms: Jazz and Caribbean Culture," which will include his incisive insider perspective on ska and Don Drummond. Carolyn Cooper, a professor of literary and cultural studies at the University of the West Indies (UWI) and author of *Noises in the Blood: Orality, Gender, and the "Vulgar" Body of Jamaican Popular Culture* and *Sound Clash: Jamaican Dancehall Culture at Large*, has laid a good foundation for insider work. Cooper is the founder of the Reggae Studies program at the UWI Mona campus in Jamaica where she has invited veteran roots reggae artists and old-school insiders to participate in various documenting and educational activities.

The existence of a more prominent insider perspective will provide a greater sense of balance in the writing about reggae; a balance that will hopefully lead to meaningful dialogue between varying perspectives and approaches to the study of the music, and, therefore, add more depth of analysis to the writing about reggae. As an insider work, the essays in this book attempt to validate the importance of an insider perspective.

Notes

Introduction

Recommended:

Abyssinians, "Satta Amassa Gana," on *Reggae Essentials — The Best of the Abyssinians.* Clinch, 2000, CD.

James Carnegie. 1970. "Notes on the History of Jazz and Its Role in Jamaica." *Jamaica Journal*, Vol. 4, #1.

Roger Steffens. 1992. "The Last Word on the Marley Box Set." *The Beat* (Los Angeles).

Klive Walker. 1992. "Marley on the Box." *Metro Word* (Toronto), November 8.

Roots Souljah

1. Bob Marley, "Top Rankin," Fifty Six Hope Road Music Ltd./Odnil Music Ltd./Blue Mountain Music Ltd. (PRS), 1979.
2. Bob Marley, "Africa Unite," Fifty Six Hope Road Music Ltd./Odnil Music Ltd./Blue Mountain Music Ltd. (PRS), 1979.
3. Bob Marley, "Zimbabwe," Fifty Six Hope Road Music Ltd./Odnil Music Ltd./Blue Mountain Music Ltd. (PRS), 1979.
4. Lecon Cogill/Carlton Barrett, "Them Belly Full," Fifty Six Hope Road Music Ltd./Odnil Music Ltd./Blue Mountain Music Ltd. (PRS), 1974.
5. Aston Barett/Hugh Peart, "Rebel Music," Fifty Six Hope Road Music Ltd./Odnil Music Ltd./Blue Mountain Music Ltd. (PRS), 1974.
6. Lecon Cogill/Carlton Barrett, "Talkin Blues," Fifty Six Hope Road Music Ltd./Odnil Music Ltd./Blue Mountain Music Ltd. (PRS), 1974.
7. Bob Marley, "Revolution," Fifty Six Hope Road Music Ltd./Odnil Music Ltd./Blue Mountain Music Ltd. (PRS), 1975.
8. Bob Marley, "Sun is Shining," Fifty Six Hope Road Music Ltd./Odnil Music Ltd./Blue Mountain Music Ltd. (PRS), 1975.
9. Bob Marley, "Running Away," Fifty Six Hope Road Music Ltd./Odnil Music Ltd./Blue Mountain Music Ltd. (PRS), 1977.
10. Bob Marley, "Waiting in Vain," Fifty Six Hope Road Music Ltd./Odnil Music Ltd./Blue Mountain Music Ltd. (PRS), 1977.
11. Bob Marley and the Wailers, "She's Gone," Fifty Six Hope Road

Music Ltd./Odnil Music Ltd./Blue Mountain Music Ltd. (PRS), 1972.

12. Klive Walker. "Ruff and Tuff: The Steppin' Razor Still Trods Through Creation."

13. *Rebel Music: The Bob Marley Story*, dir. Jeremy Marre, 89 minutes, Palm Pictures/Island Entertainment, 2000, DVD.

Other Sources:

Harry, Isobel, 1988. Interview by author. Toronto, 17 May.

Kwame Dawes. 2002. *Bob Marley—Lyrical Genius*. London: Sanctuary.

Francis, Alexander. 2005. Interview by author. Toronto, 7 February.

Recommended:

Classic Albums—Bob Marley and the Wailers: Catch a Fire, dir. Jeremy Marre, 60 minutes, Image Entertainment, 1999, DVD.

Rain a Fall, Dutty Tuff

1. Bob Marley, "Concrete Jungle," Fifty Six Hope Road Music Ltd./Odnil Music Ltd./Blue Mountain Music Ltd. (PRS), 1972.

2. Lecon Cogill/Carlton Barrett, "Talkin Blues," Fifty Six Hope Road Music Ltd./Odnil Music Ltd./Blue Mountain Music Ltd. (PRS), 1974.

3. Louise Bennett. 1966. Bans O' Killing. In *Jamaica Labrish: Jamaica Dialect Poems*. Kingston: Sangster's.

4. Rex Nettleford. 1966. Introduction to *Jamaica Labrish: Jamaica Dialect Poems*. Kingston: Sangster's.

5. Louise Bennett. 1966. Dutty Tough. In *Jamaica Labrish: Jamaica Dialect Poems*. Kingston: Sangster's.

6. Bob Marley, "Concrete Jungle," Fifty Six Hope Road Music Ltd./Odnil Music Ltd./Blue Mountain Music Ltd. (PRS), 1972.

7. Lecon Cogill/Carlton Barrett, "Them Belly Full," Fifty Six Hope Road Music Ltd./Odnil Music Ltd./Blue Mountain Music Ltd. (PRS), 1974.

8. Louise Bennett. 1966. Dutty Tough. In *Jamaica Labrish: Jamaica Dialect Poems*. Kingston: Sangster's.

9. Bob Marley, "Simmer Down" from *Songs of Freedom*, Island, 1993, CD.

10. Bob Marley, "Wake Up and Live," Fifty Six Hope Road Music Ltd./Odnil Music Ltd./Blue Mountain Music Ltd. (PRS), 1979.

11. Bongo Jerry. 1989. "Sooner or Later." *Voice Print*. Edited by Stewart Brown, Mervyn Morris and Gordon Rohlehr. London: Longman.

12. Michael Smith. 1989. I an I Alone. In *It a Come: Poems by Michael Smith*. San Francisco: City Lights Books.

13. Michael Smith. 1989. Me Cyaan Believe It. In *It a Come: Poems by Michael Smith*. San Francisco: City Lights Books.

Other Sources:

Edward Brathwaite. 1973. *The Arrivants—A New World Trilogy*. Oxford: Oxford University Press.

Jean Breeze. 1988. *Riddym Ravings and Other Poems*. London: Race Today Publications.

Kwame Dawes. 1999. *Natural Mysticism: Towards a New Reggae Aesthetic in Caribbean Writing*. Leeds: Peepal Tree.

Kwame Dawes. 1997. *Shook Foil: A Collection of Reggae Poems*. Leeds: Peepal Tree.

Lillian Allen. 1993. *Selected Poems of Lillian Allen—Women Do This Every Day*. Toronto: Women's Press.

Lorna Goodison. 2001. *Travelling Mercies*. Kingston: Ian Randle Publishers.

Louise Bennett. 1993. *Aunty Roachy She*. Kingston: Sangster's.

Reggae Sistas' Stories

1. Morris Levy and Johnny Roberts, "My Boy Lollipop," EMI Music Publishing, 1956.

2. Clement Dodd/Jackie Mittoo, "No No No," Jamrec/BMI, 1967.

3. Chen, Wayne and Kevin O'Brien Chang. 1998. *Reggae Routes*. Kingston: Ian Randle Publishers.

4. Barrow, Steve and Peter Dalton. 1997. Reggae—The Rough Guide. London: Rough Guides Ltd.

5. Garth White, "Behind the Scenes—From Sonia Pottinger to Trish Farrell," *The News* (Kingston), 13–16 August 1995.

6. Barrow, Steve and Peter Dalton. 1997. Reggae—The Rough Guide. London: Rough Guides Ltd.

7. Barrow, Steve and Peter Dalton. 1997. Reggae—The Rough Guide. London: Rough Guides Ltd.

8. Marcia Griffiths, "Steppin' Out of Babylon" from *Steppin'*, Sky Note/Shanachie, 1979, CD.

9. Carol Cooper. 1982. "Wrathful Madonna." *Reggae International*.

272 — Klive Walker

Edited by Stephen Davis and Peter Simon. New York: Rogner and Bernhard GMBH& Co.

10. Marcia Griffiths, "Peaceful Woman" from *Steppin'*, Sky Note/Shanachie, 1979, CD.

11. Bob Andy, "Let Them Say," Andisongs.

12. Bob Andy, "Check it Out," Andisongs.

13. Bob Andy, "Fires Burning," Andisongs.

14. Carol Cooper. 1982. "Wrathful Madonna." *Reggae International*. Edited by Stephen Davis and Peter Simon. New York: Rogner and Bernhard GMBH& Co.

15. Judy Mowatt, "Black Woman," Ashandan Music (ASCAP), 1979.

16. Judy Mowatt, "Black Woman," Ashandan Music (ASCAP), 1979.

17. Judy Mowatt, "Sisters' Chant," Ashandan Music (ASCAP), 1979.

18. Judy Mowatt, "Slave Queen," Ashandan Music (ASCAP), 1979.

19. Bob Marley, "Concrete Jungle," Fifty Six Hope Road Music Ltd./Odnil Music Ltd./Blue Mountain Music Ltd. (PRS), 1979.

20. Bob Marley, "Down in the Valley," Fifty Six Hope Road Music Ltd./Odnil Music Ltd./Blue Mountain Music Ltd. (PRS), 1979.

21. Bob Marley, "Down in the Valley," Fifty Six Hope Road Music Ltd./Odnil Music Ltd./Blue Mountain Music Ltd. (PRS), 1979.

22. "One Draw," Almo Music.

Other Sources:

Angela Y. Davis. 1999. *Blues Legacies and Black Feminism*. New York: First Vintage.

Timothy White. 1983. *Catch a Fire*. New York: Henry Holt and Co.

Various artists, *Holding Up Half the Sky—Women in Reggae: Roots Daughters*, Shanachie, 1996, CD.

Various artists, *Reggae Song Birds: 17 Great Tracks from the High Note Label*, High Note/Heartbeat, 1996, CD.

Gaylettes featuring Judy Mowatt, *We Shall Sing—Girl Group Rock Steady, Reggae and Soul 1967–73*, Demon/West Side, 2001, CD.

Blue Beat, Nyabinghi, Bebop

1. Levin, Robert. Liner notes to *Asia Minor*, by Dizzy Reece. New Jazz Records, 1962, CD.

2. Ian Carr. 1995. *Jazz—The Rough Guide*. London: Rough Guides Ltd.

3. Kevin Le Gendre, "Too Good to be Forgotten: Joe Harriott," *The Independent* (London), 13 November 1988.

Other Sources:
Garth White. 1977. Master Drummer. *Jamaica Journal* (August): 17.
Knibb, Lloyd. Interview by Carter Van Pelt. *Burru Style: An interview with Skatalites drummer Lloyd Knibb*. 23 March 1998 [cited 21 June 2005]. Available from http://incolor.inetnebr.com/cvanpelt/knibb.html; INTERNET.
Reckord, Verena. 1977. Rastafarian Music. *Jamaica Journal* (August): 3–13.

Eastern Standard Time
1. McCook, Tommy. 1984. Interview by David Rodigan. London. Available from http://www.georgwa.demon.co.uk/tommy_mccook.htm; INTERNET.
2. Small, Robin. "Bongo Jerry." 1970. *Requiem for Don Drummond*. Radio Jamaica and Redifusion.
3. McCook, Tommy. 1984. Interview by David Rodigan. London. Available from http://www.georgwa.demon.co.uk/tommy_mccook.htm; INTERNET.
4. Marguerita Mahfood, "Woman A Come," Jamrec Music, BMI from *Foundation Ska*, Heartbeat, 1997, CD.
5. Keyo, Brian. Liner notes to *Foundation Ska*, by Skatalites. Heartbeat, 1997, CD.
6. Miller, Herbie. Liner notes to *Stretching Out*, by Skatalites. ROIR, 1986, CD.
7. Monty Alexander. 1999. Fascinatin' Riddim. *Jazziz*. (July): 62.
8. Crosby, Gary. 2005. Interview by author. London, 16 December.

Other Sources:
Cynthia Wilmot, "The Ghosts of Kingston Harbour," *Jamaica Gleaner* (Kingston), 22 February 2004.
Helene Lee. 1999. *The First Rasta—Leonard Howell and the Rise of Rastafarianism*. Chicago: Lawrence Hill Books.
Reckord, Verena. 1977. Rastafarian Music. *Jamaica Journal* (August): 3–13.
Stephen Davis. 1983. *Bob Marley*. London: Panther Book/Granada.
Timothy White. 1983. *Catch a Fire*. New York: Henry Holt and Co.
Witmer, Robert. 1989. "A History of Kingston's Popular Music

Culture: Neo-Colonialism to Nationalism." *Jamaica Journal* (January).

Author Interviews:
Briscoe, Harold. 2004. Interview by author. Toronto, 26 November.
Miller, Herbie. 2005. Interview by author. New York, 5 October.
Mordecai, Pamela. 2005. Interview by author. Toronto, 20 October.
Taylor, Chris (formerly of One). 2004. Interview by author. Toronto, 26 November.

One-Drop Dubs the Maple Leaf

1. Lillian Allen. "I Fight Back" from *Revolutionary Tea Party*, Verse to Vinyl, 1986, CD.
2. Lillian Allen. "Rub a Dub Style Inna Regent Park" from *Revolutionary Tea Party*, Verse to Vinyl, 1986, CD.
3. Allen, Lillian. 1993. Interview by author. Toronto, 6 March.
4. Joseph, Clifton. "Caribana 84/ Smash Apartheid Dead!" from *Oral Transmissions*, independent, 1989, tape cassette.
5. Ainsley "Ato Seitu" Vaughn/Lloyd "Mohjah" Benn/Lillian Allen. "Acid Rain" Bucktu, 1980.
6. Vance Tynes/Terrence "Chico" Paul (now known as Xola). "Metro's No.1 Problem" Bucktu, 1980.
7. Liam Lacey, "Review of Compass," *The Globe and Mail (Toronto)*, [unknown date], October 1983.
8. Jason "Kardinal Offishall" Harrow and S. Pitt, "BaKardi Slang" from *Quest for Fire—Firestarter Vol.1*, MCA, 2001, CD.
9. Tristan "MC Collizhun" Graham, "Toe to Toe" from *Tough Dumplin' Foundation for Better Beats* by Nefarious, independent, 2000, CD.

Other Sources:
Adele Freeman, "Toronto reggae explodes despite security damper," *The Globe and Mail* (Toronto), 20 October 1980.
Alan Neister, "Parachute Club spreads its wings." *The Globe and Mail* (Toronto), 5 December 1984.
Harry, Isobel. 1983. Leroy Sibbles: Ranking with Bob Marley. *The Canadian Composer*, November, 10–12.
Harry, Isobel. 1980. Reggae Inna Canada. *The Canadian Composer*, June, 4–17.
Harry, Isobel and Lisa Steele. 1979. Immigration: Do you have

Canadian Experience? *Centrefold*, November, 24–28.

Jung, Daryl and James Marck, "Truth and Rights' reggae message." *Now* (Toronto), 8–14 July 1982.

Lacey, Liam. 1982. Review of *Metro's No.1 Problem*, by Truths and Rights. *The Globe and Mail* (Toronto), [section and date unavailable.] February.

Norman "Otis" Richmond. 1980. The Secret History of Black Music (in Canada). *Fuse*, December, 20–24.

Norman "Otis" Richmond, "Truths and Rights: Baddest band in the land!" *Contrast* (Toronto), 12 March 1982.

Paul Dorsey, "Sibbles discusses reggae's future," *Now* (Toronto), 1–7 October 1981.

Peter Goddard, "Truths and Rights Toronto's band of the year." *The Toronto Star*, 28 December 1983.

Peter Goddard, "What ever happened to rock anger?" *The Toronto Star*, 30 January 1982.

Author Interviews:
Allen, Lillian. 1988. Interview by author. Toronto, 5 July.
Allen, Lillian. 1992. Interview by author. Toronto, 4 April.
Harry, Isobel. 2000. Interview by author. Toronto, 24 February.
Joseph, Clifton. 2002. Interview by author. Toronto, 15 November.
Miller, Adrian "Sheriff". 2002. Interview by author. Toronto, 20 June.
Benn, Mohjah. 2002. Interview by author. Toronto, 29 September.
Seitu, Ato. 2000. Interview by author. Toronto, 19 October.
Williams, Quammie. 2001. Interview by author. Toronto, 10 January.

Dub Fire
1. Linton Kwesi Johnson, "Fite Dem Back" from *Linton Kwesi Johnson Reggae Greats*, Island/Mango CD, 1985, CD.
2. David Hinds, "Jah Pickney–R.A.R.," Songs of Polygram, Inc. (BMI).

Other Sources:
Aiken, Edmund Carl [of Shinehead]. 1989. Interview by author. Toronto, 30 March.
Forde, Brinsley [of Aswad]. 1985. Interview by Dermot Hussey. Radio. Inner Ear Radio Jamaica and Redifusion, 30 April.

Hinds, David [of Steel Pulse]. 1985. Interview by Dermot Hussey. Radio. Inner Ear Radio Jamaica and Redifusion, 5 March.

Lenny Kaye. 1982. "White Reggae." *Reggae International*. Edited by Stephen Davis and Peter Simon. New York: Rogner and Bernhard GMBH& Co.

Lloyd Bradley. 2000. *Bass Culture*. London: Viking.

Stephen Davis. 1983. *Bob Marley*. London: Panther Books/Granada.

Visions

1. Stan E. Smith. 1999. Dennis Brown. *Everybody's*, October.
2. Barrow, Steve and Peter Dalton. 1997. Reggae—The Rough Guide. London: Rough Guides Ltd.
3. Dennis Brown, "Deliverance Will Come" from *Visions*, Shanachie, 1988, CD.
4. Dennis Brown, "If I Had the World" from *The Complete A&M Years*, A&M, 2003, CD.

Other Sources:

Rohan Preston. 1998. "Music." *Wheel and Come Again An Anthology of Reggae Poetry*. Edited by Kwame Dawes. New Brunswick: Goose Lane.

Raggamuffin Rap

1. Nelson George. 1998. *Hip Hop America*. New York: Penguin.
2. Moses Davis [Beenie Man], "Who Am I" from *Many Moods of Moses*, VP, 1997, CD.

Other Sources:

Carolyn Cooper. 2004. *Sound Clash: Jamaican Dancehall Culture at Large*. New York: Palgrave McMillan.

David Toop. 1984. *The Rap Attack: African Jive to New York Hip Hop*. London: Pluto Press.

Jeff Chang. 2005. *Can't Stop, Won't Stop*. New York: St. Martin's Press.

Laurie Gunst. 1999. *Born Fi' Dead: A Journey Through the Jamaican Posse Underworld*. Edinburgh: Payback Press.

Rupert Charles Lewis. 1998. *Walter Rodney's Intellectual and Political Thought*. Jamaica/Detroit: The Press UWI/Wayne State University Press.

Author Interviews:
Cowie, Del. 2005 Interview by author. Toronto, 11 February.
Channer, Colin. 2005. Interview by author. Toronto, 15 January.
Davis, Nick. 2005. Interview by author. Toronto, 26 February.
Henry, Mark. 2005. Interview by author. Toronto, 12 January.
Prince, Fabian. 2005. Interview by author. Toronto, 9 January.
Vassell, Phil. 2005. Interview by author. Toronto, 19 January.

The Writing About Reggae Must Skank to an Authentic Rub-a-Dub Bass Line

1. Garth White. 1982. "Ska and Rock Steady." *Reggae International*. Edited by Stephen Davis and Peter Simon. New York: Rogner and Bernhard GMBH& Co.
2. Small, Robin "Bongo Jerry". 1969. Tribute to Don Drummond. (May 17) [page number(s) unavailable] *Abeng* (Kingston). Quoted in Gordon Rohlehr, 1971, "Some problems of assessment: A look at the new expressions in the arts of the Contemporary Caribbean." *Caribbean Quarterly*. (September–December): 100.
3. Mervyn Morris. 1998. "Valley Prince (For Don D)." *Wheel and Come Again An Anthology of Reggae Poetry*. Edited by Kwame Dawes. New Brunswick: Goose Lane.
4. Anthony McNeill. 1998. "For the D." *Wheel and Come Again An Anthology of Reggae Poetry*. Edited by Kwame Dawes. New Brunswick: Goose Lane.
5. Lorna Goodison. 1998. "For Don Drummond." *Wheel and Come Again An Anthology of Reggae Poetry*. Edited by Kwame Dawes. New Brunswick: Goose Lane.
6. Rohlehr, Gordon. 1971. Some problems of assessment: A look at the new expressions in the arts of the contemporary Caribbean. *Caribbean Quarterly* (September–December): 99-100.
7. Rohlehr, Gordon. 1971. Some problems of assessment: A look at the new expressions in the arts of the contemporary Caribbean. *Caribbean Quarterly* (September–December): 107.
8. Rohlehr, Gordon. 1971. Some problems of assessment: A look at the new expressions in the arts of the contemporary Caribbean. *Caribbean Quarterly* (September–December): 99.
9. Chen, Wayne and Kevin O'Brien Chang. 1998. *Reggae Routes*. Kingston: Ian Randle Publishers.
10. Chen, Wayne and Kevin O'Brien Chang. 1998. *Reggae Routes*.

Kingston: Ian Randle Publishers.

11 Barrow, Steve and Peter Dalton. 1997. Reggae—The Rough Guide. London: Rough Guides Ltd.

12. Barrow, Steve and Peter Dalton. 1997. Reggae—The Rough Guide. London: Rough Guides Ltd.

13. Barrow, Steve and Peter Dalton. 1997. Reggae—The Rough Guide. London: Rough Guides Ltd.

14. Channer, Colin. 2000. "I'm Still Waiting." *Got To Be Real—Four Original Love Stories*, by E. Lynn Harris, Eric Dickey, Marcus Major and Colin Channer. New York: New American Library.

15. Nalo Hopkinson. 2000. *Midnight Robber*. New York: Warner Books.

Other Sources:

Leroi Jones [Amiri Baraka]. 1963. *Blues People*. New York: Morrow Quill.

Index

Youssou N'Dour, 27

Zephaniah, Benjamin, 155
Zhina, Ahdri, 12, 155, 169

Acknowledgements

First and foremost, huge thanks to my wife, Michele; my daughter, Aisha; my sons, Kashka and Patrice; and my parents, Victor and Thelma, for their consistent support.

There are so many people I must *big up* for assistance in research, reading drafts, critical feedback, or simply for their love and encouragement:

Toronto

Lillian Allen, Isobel Harry, Clifton Joseph, Paul Kafele, Michael St. George, Nick Davis, Leslie Thompson, Mohjah, Alexander "Frano" Francis, Quammie Williams, Xola, Ato Seitu, Adrian "Sheriff" Miller, Tristan "MC Collizhun" Graham, Itah Sadu, Maureen Ford, Kareem Green, Ena Green, Del Cowie, Marcia Snape, Makeda Silvera, Oscar Wailoo, Winston Smith, Fabian Prince, Joel Reeves, Lisa Martin, Joe Chapman, Honor Ford Smith, Afua Cooper, Carolyn Jones, Phil Vassell, Jack Orbaum, Karen Orbaum, Mike Wise, Norman "Otis" Richmond, Harold Briscoe, Pam Mordecai, John Elliott, James Hayashi-Tenn, Chris Taylor, Luther Brown, Mark Henry, and Dennis Watson.

United States

Special thanks to Herbie Miller for his valuable insights and feedback. Special salute and props to Colin Channer for his generosity in sharing his knowledge of writing craft and reggae history. Kwame Dawes for all those enriching conversations. A big shout out to broadcaster Dermot Hussey, Paul Smith, my cousins Phillip Smart, Tony Wilmoth, Jennifer Wilmoth, Floyd Wilmoth, and Sharon Nangle.

London, U.K.

Gary Crosby; Janine Irons; my sisters, Maxine Edwards and Dionne Walker-Amponsah; George Amponsah; Roy Edwards; Carol Walker; my brothers, Shawn and Errol; and my cousin Junior Walker.

Jamaica

Garth White, Hilary Brown, Christopher Garel, Frank Thompson, Bunny McCook, Lorna Green, Carmen Tipling, Flo O'Connor, Jerry Small, and "Sammy" of Ministry of Finance, the first person to suggest that I write a book about reggae.

My gratitude to Dan Varrette and Mike O'Connor at Insomniac.

An extra special thank you to Isobel Harry for allowing her amazing photographs to grace the pages of *Dubwise*. Many of these photographs, including the images of Bob Marley and Peter Tosh, are being published for the first time in *Dubwise*.